MW00787723

Mines, Communities, and States

When do local communities benefit from natural resource extraction? In some regions of natural resource extraction, firms provide goods and services to local communities, but in others, protest may occur, leading to government regulatory or repressive intervention. *Mines, Communities, and States* explores these outcomes in Africa, where natural resource extraction is a particularly important source of revenue for states with otherwise limited capacity. Blending a mixture of methodological approaches, including formal modelling, structured case comparison, and quantitative geo-spatial empirical analysis, it argues that local populations are important actors in extractive regions because they have the potential to impose political and economic costs on the state as well as the extractive firm. Furthermore, the author argues that governments, in turn, must assess the economic benefits of extraction and the value of political support in the region and make a calculation about how to manage trade-offs that might arise between these alternatives.

Jessica Steinberg is Assistant Professor of International Studies, faculty affiliate of the Ostrom Workshop on Political Theory and Policy Analysis, and Adjunct Faculty in Political Science at Indiana University, Bloomington. She has conducted seven years of field work in Africa, in countries including the Democratic Republic of Congo, Mozambique, Senegal, Congo-Brazzaville, and Zambia. Her work has been published in the *Journal of Conflict Resolution, Political Geography, Journal of Theoretical Politics*, and *Perspectives on Politics*.

Mines, Communities, and States

The Local Politics of Natural Resource Extraction in Africa

JESSICA STEINBERG

Indiana University, Bloomington

CAMBRIDGE
UNIVERSITY PRESS

CAMBRIDGE
UNIVERSITY PRESS

University Printing House, Cambridge CB2 8BS, United Kingdom

One Liberty Plaza, 20th Floor, New York, NY 10006, USA

477 Williamstown Road, Port Melbourne, VIC 3207, Australia

314–321, 3rd Floor, Plot 3, Splendor Forum, Jasola District Centre,
New Delhi – 110025, India

79 Anson Road, #06–04/06, Singapore 079906

Cambridge University Press is part of the University of Cambridge.

It furthers the University's mission by disseminating knowledge in the pursuit of
education, learning, and research at the highest international levels of excellence.

www.cambridge.org
Information on this title: www.cambridge.org/9781108476935
DOI: 10.1017/9781108638173

First published 2019

Printed in the United Kingdom by TJ International Ltd, Padstow Cornwall

A catalogue record for this publication is available from the British Library.

ISBN 978-1-108-47693-5 Hardback

Dedicated to my family, near and far.

Contents

Figures

Tables

Acknowledgments

There are many minds that contributed in various ways to the development of this project and to whom I am grateful. First and foremost, I owe much of my intellectual trajectory to Anna Grzymala-Busse, from whom I learned discipline of thought, as well as intellectual honesty, flexibility, and insight. I am also indebted to Allan Stam for telling me first to think big and then to think small. Thanks to Scott Page, whose encouragement and guidance on the model and beyond have been invaluable. I am also grateful to Brian Min, whose capacity for clarification through reduction and whose demands of data have been immensely helpful, and Anne Pitcher, whose illumination of context and direction to many helpful people in the field made much of this work possible. Thanks to Bill Clark, who first sparked my interest in game theory (for better or worse), and to Pauline Jones Luong for her guidance, comments, and constructive critique. I am also grateful to Sinziana Dorobantu for her support in obtaining the mining dataset, Jim Morrow for his comments on earlier versions of the model, and Jenna Bednar for her support at the project's very earliest inception.

I am grateful for support from the Rackham International Research Award, University of Texas at Austin's Climate Change and Political Stability in Africa program, and Indiana University's International Studies Program. Thanks also to Padraic Kenney, Purnima Bose, Nick Cullather, and Lee Feinstein for supporting me as I worked to complete this book.

I also appreciate the many other colleagues that read portions of this project (some several times) over the last several years: Vincent

Arel-Bundock, Timm Betz, Trevor Johnston, Lisa Langdon Koch, Amy
Pond, Gary Uzonyi, and Matt Wells. More recently, I am particularly
grateful to Ben Smith and Ravi Bhavnani, as well as Federica Caru-
gati, Sarah Bauerle Danzman, Gardner Bovingdon, Keera Allendorf, Yan
Long, and Jen Brass. Thanks to Cyanne Loyle and members of the
Contentious Politics Workshop at Indiana University for their helpful
comments. And I benefited significantly from the anonymous reviewers
of this book who provided constructive and encouraging feedback.

While in the field, I relied on a great many individuals and organizations. In particular, I am grateful to Caritas, Worldvision, Human Rights
Watch, and the Carter Center. I am especially indebted to the residents
living in the mining communities in Mozambique, Zambia, and DRC,
for whom I hope the explanations provided in this book go some ways
to understanding the forces shaping their circumstances.

Thanks very much to A. J. Hegg, who accompanied me on a portion of the field work, easing the burdens of traveling as a woman and
enjoying the adventure, and to Chance Copeland for keeping me smiling
while writing early on. And to those who have supported me through
their close friendship, especially Bonnie Washick, Joshua Shipper, Alton
Worthington, and Julie Fosdick Gillingham, without whom this process
would have been a far less fruitful, engaging, and enjoyable enterprise.

Finally, thank you to the Steinberg clan: Ben, Amy, Jeffrey, and Court
for putting up with me as I navigated this project and for listening. To
my parents – for enduring and supporting my unrelenting questioning of
all manner of assumptions. And, I am grateful to Jon Eldon, with love,
for keeping me honest, aware, and compassionate in this and so many
other endeavors.

1

Introduction

Each year, approximately 10 million people are affected by large-scale development projects worldwide.[1] These projects include industrial mining projects arguably meant to bring both national and local development. For example, in 2009, more than 55 percent of the US$890 million in foreign direct investment to Mozambique went to the natural resource extractive sector, primarily to begin development of coal deposits in the northwest province, Tete. Soon after the discovery of these deposits, some of the largest recent discoveries in the world, international extractive firms bid on mining concessions in which to build open-pit coal mines. Two firms received adjacent coal concessions and began construction of the mine infrastructure – a massive endeavor requiring significant swaths of land. Both projects required the resettlement of thousands of people and created strains on resources required to sustain the livelihoods of the residents.

In January 2012, approximately 500 families relocated by one of the companies barricaded the rail line that delivers coal from the mine to the port of Beira on the eastern coast of Mozambique, halting exports and costing the firm over US$1 million in a few hours. The protesters asserted that the company had not fulfilled promises it had made to them to improve their living standards or adequately compensate them for their displacement. As a result of their displacement, the local population was not able to grow and sell staple crops and the compensatory housing and farmland did not meet the standards the firm promised to the residents.

[1] Cernea (2010).

1

However, in the neighboring coal concession, there was no such protest. This coal mine also displaced local residents from their homes, creating competition over access to agricultural land, and yet it was able to avoid the kind of mobilization that was occurring just next door. The railroad was not barricaded and the extraction of coal was able to begin, uninterrupted by local resistance.

Narratives relaying these kinds of outcomes are frequently in the media – albeit with a flair for the more dramatic outcomes of protest, violence, and displacement. In Madagascar, mining company Rio Tinto halted operations because protesters threatened the safety of the subsidiary's CEO, locking him in an office.[2] The government responded by teargassing and arresting protesters. In contrast, in response to the protests in Tete, Mozambique, the national government compelled the company to provide the promised compensation. These instances are not limited to Africa. In Peru, police shot at residents protesting the environmental effects of a copper mine project in the Andes.[3] In China, protesters near a manganese mine were beaten.[4]

Yet not all regions of natural resources appear in the media, which is drawn to report on instances of social mobilization or violent government response. Some of these regions do not see any observable resistance at all, which begs the question: Why do some regions of natural resource extraction experience protest and others do not? And what forces shape how governments respond to them?

Resistance and repression in regions of natural resource extraction are well-recognized phenomena, and they can threaten the potential value of resource extraction as well as the broader stability of the state. The fixed nature of natural resources ensures that extractive firms, local populations, and governments interact strategically in a defined territory. This interaction yields a variety of outcomes, including firm provision of goods and services to local communities, localized violent protest in response to resource extraction, and government regulatory or repressive intervention. This book explores the conditions under which these outcomes occur in Africa, where natural resource extraction is a particularly important source of revenue for states with otherwise limited capacity on average. It argues that local populations are important actors

---

[2] *Rio Tinto Threatens to Exit Madagascar after CEO Is Trapped by Protesters* (2013-01-11).

[3] *Peru Anti-Mining Protest Sees Deadly Clashes* (2015-9-29).

[4] Downey, Bonds, and Clark (2010).

in extractive regions because they have the potential to impose political costs on the state, and economic costs on the state and the extractive firm. Governments, in turn, must assess the economic benefits of extraction and the value of political support in the region and make a calculation about how to respond, managing trade-offs that might arise between these alternatives. The result of these calculations is a range of local outcomes in areas of natural resource extraction.

NATURAL RESOURCES IN AFRICA: TERRITORIALITY AND GLOBAL CAPITAL

Understanding variation in local outcomes around natural resources is of particular importance when the stakes are the highest: in developing countries where communities are likely to rely disproportionately on the natural environment for their livelihoods and where state capacity to provide basic services is limited. This is particularly true of many African countries, where the reach of the state may be minimal and agriculture remains a significant source of income. It should be noted here, however, that in spite of the lingering narrative that categorizing the entire continent as perpetually poor, the average overall output of countries in Africa in terms of gross domestic product (GDP) has increased since 1990. In part, this is due to investment by foreign companies, largely in the extractive industries. The stock of foreign direct investment (FDI) in Africa in 1990 was only 32 billion,[5] but by 2014, Africa received US$54 billion annually in FDI inflows (up from US$3.2 billion in flows in 1989). New extractive projects accounted for US$22 billion, and the extractive industry accounted for a total of 31% of all FDI inflows.[6] FDI inflows to the continent are still driven primarily by the extractive sector, even as manufacturing and services grow.

The distribution of the gains from FDI has, by all accounts, been uneven. It has been uneven across social and political strata, but it has also been uneven across space. Some countries have benefited more from this investment than others. These national differences in FDI are the result, in part, of international financial organizations and their evaluation of national level institutions, yielding patterns of distribution of foreign capital in a broad range of industries, including the extractives. Yet the costs and benefits of such extractive activities are often spatially

[5] UNCTAD Secretariat (1993).
[6] UNCTAD (2015).

distributed sub-nationally, in ways that do not merely reflect differences in sovereign boundaries. James Ferguson captures these uneven territorializations of capital, observing that "What is noteworthy is the extent to which this economic investment has been concentrated in secured enclaves, often with little or no economic benefit to the wider society. There are significant differences in the ways that such enclaves are secured, and the ways they are governed (or not) by the states that have nominal jurisdiction over them" (Ferguson (2005), p. 377).

One reason for this variation is that natural resource deposits are exogenously located. One cannot decide where copper, or gold, or coal is located – nature decides this. We should therefore expect some variation in the outcomes of their extraction, given heterogeneity in subnational context. It is important to note that many actors and decisions shape whether these resources are found and extracted, and thus political, social and economic factors must be taken into consideration in understanding that process. Countries must first locate natural resources, a costly problem requiring the mapping of the country's terrain where a country cannot be certain it will find sufficient resources to make up its cost – a sticky public goods problem that has led developing countries to rely on private companies for discovery. Once the resource is discovered, rights of extraction must be allocated and taxation and royalty schemes must be developed – also a thorny problem. Still, the geographical location of the resource is determined by nature, and it is the result of an historical timescale that dwarfs the human life span. Once natural resources are discovered, people are territorially stuck – they cannot pick up and move a copper deposit. As a consequence, the extraction of these resources must necessarily be, in Ferguson's words, territorial – defined and constrained in space by the somewhat random chance that natural resources reserves exist on or under a given piece of land or water.[7]

Nowhere are these economic enclaves more relevant than in Africa, which holds a significant portion of the world's existing natural resources. Africa has approximately 30 percent of the world's known reserves of non-renewable natural resources.[8] In 2013, the continent accounted for 63 percent of the world's cobalt production, 19 percent of the world's gold production, 55 percent of the world's diamonds, 11

---

[7] This is particularly true of the subsoil resources that this book is concerned with, such as metals, minerals, gems, coal, and oil, often called "point" resources, as opposed to "diffuse" resources, such as forests, fish, and water.

[8] *African Natural Resources Center* (n.d.).

percent of the world's copper production, 7 percent of the world's bauxite production, and 4 percent of the world's aluminum production. [9]

On average, countries in Africa are believed to have natural resource endowments that are larger than the global average. This conclusion rests on three factors. First, many point resources require significant capital for extraction, and countries that are perpetually lacking capital are unlikely to locate and extract resources at the rate of other, more capital-rich countries. In 2013, the estimated capital cost of the first phases of a copper project in Democratic Republic of Congo was nearly US$ 5 billion, and a coal project in Mozambique was estimated at US$ 3.3 billion. [10] Many African countries have traditionally been capital poor. As a consequence, resource reserves that require significant capital resources to extract have remained in the ground. Second, historical events shape the trajectory of resource extraction and consumption. Early discovery of natural resources, which are also likely to be resources that require less capital to discover and access (think oil discovery in Pennsylvania in the early nineteenth century in comparison to deep-sea mining off the coast of Vanuatu), means that a country with historically sufficient capital for extraction may have a much longer historical period of extraction and consumption, leading to fewer (finite) resources currently. And finally, evaluation of the amount of natural resources a country has is usually measured relative to other factors (industrial or human capital for instance). Relative to endowments in these areas, countries poor in capital and labor are seen to have much more in the way of natural resources. Furthermore, as Menaldo (2016) points out, countries poor in capital and relevant labor have limited choice but to focus on the extractive sector, even if they have to rely on foreign capital to do so.

While these characteristics can help explain the current abundance of natural resources in Africa, it is possible that Africa has even more than the 30 percent of the world's known reserves that is estimated. This is because *locating* natural resources constitutes a classic public goods problem; knowledge of the location of resource reserves is difficult to exclude people from once it is available, but costly to provide. This is why it is the government that often provides this service in wealthier countries (consider the United States Geological Survey). Conducting geological surveys that allow governments to know the potential location of valuable natural resources is an expensive endeavor. For example, it was only

---

[9] Yager et al. (2013).
[10] Yager et al. (2013).

in 2006 that one of the world's largest coal seams was discovered in the northwestern part of Mozambique. Globally, the rate of discovery has been declining, but Africa makes up an increasing percentage of new discoveries as large discoveries have shifted away from Canada, the USA, and Australia.[11] Countries with fewer capital resources are less likely to be able to do this themselves. As a consequence, the search and location task is often contracted to exploration and mining firms.

Given their role in locating and extracting natural resources, global extractive firms have become increasingly powerful actors. The importance of global capital is further heightened since so much of the world's resources are likely to be in countries with limited capital. It is therefore critical that we develop a strong understanding of how the distribution of costs and benefits from extraction is achieved, and under which conditions there are incentives for this distribution to yield locally peaceful outcomes.

THE PUZZLE

In some regions of natural resource extraction, local communities receive goods and services and the   environmental consequences of extraction are mitigated. Extractive companies often build schools and hospitals, roads and stadiums in and around the regions where they operate. Yet in other extractive regions, local populations receive few or no benefits from the resource extracted, and they often endure negative environmental externalities of extraction such as water contamination, noise pollution, increased cost of living, and increased competition over access to agricultural land. This often results in protests by these communities, occasionally leading to the destruction of property, barricading of roads, and threat to mining personnel. When these instances occur, governments are often compelled to respond, sometimes dispatching police forces to put down the protest, other times requiring that the firm rectify its behavior, and compensate the community members.

Of approximately 2,500 mines[12] in Africa in operation between 1990 and 2014, approximately one quarter of them saw some form of social conflict nearby (within 20 km). Social conflict[13] includes demonstrations,

---

[11] Schodde (n.d.).

[12] Mines collected from SNL Financial (formerly IntierraRMG) (2014) and joined to Social Conflict in Africa Dataset, Hendrix et al. (2012), by the author.

[13] While social mobilization may take place without protest, the form of social conflict of interest, social mobilization is indeed a necessary condition for protest. For the rest of

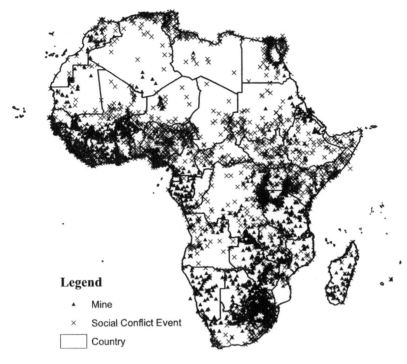

FIGURE 1.1: Map of mines and social conflict in Africa

riots, strikes, and low-level violence. While some countries certainly see more types and instances of social conflict than others, the likelihood of social conflict around mines varies significantly within a single country. Figure 1.1 is a map of the continent depicting mines and instances of social conflict. Among larger countries, approximately 43 percent of the 120 mines within the Democratic Republic of Congo saw social conflict, and in Nigeria, 59 percent. Within smaller countries, 37 percent of Liberian mines, and 32 percent of mines in Sierra Leone.

The likelihood of social conflict near a mine varies across nationalities of extractive firm as well. Of those mines with majority foreign equity, 25 percent saw some form of social conflict nearby. However, equity ownership is not a good predictor of variation in the likelihood of social conflict. Of the mines that saw conflict, approximately 31 percent of

the book, I use social mobilization, social conflict, and protest interchangeably to refer to an instance of collective action reflecting a shared claim among participants, who gather in a physical space to express that claim, often interrupting local economic activity.

these were Australian owned. In contrast, 5 percent of mines with conflict were Chinese owned. However, 31.4 percent of all of the mines are Australian owned, while approximately 2 percent of mines are Chinese owned. In other words, the fact that 31 percent of all mine-related conflict occurs near Australian-owned firms while only 3 percent of such conflict occurs near Chinese-owned firms is not a reflection of particularly problematic operations of Australian mines. Instead, it reflects that Australian firms own significantly more mines over this time period in Africa than Chinese firms do.

Of mines that saw conflict, 27 percent were South African owned, 20 percent were Australian owned, 14 percent had Canadian ownership, 11 percent were UK owned, and 3 percent were of Chinese ownership. However, as the table below demonstrates, the distribution of all mines by equity ownership is not significantly different from the distribution of mines with conflict by ownership. In other words, it does not appear that nationality of the firm makes some mines disproportionately likely to see conflict nearby. This is demonstrated in Figure 1.2.

Mineral type does not seem to explain which mines see social conflict either. Figure 1.3 demonstrates the distribution of mine commodity. Of those mines that saw social conflict, nearly 35 percent were gold mines, 20 percent were coal mines, and nearly 10 percent were copper

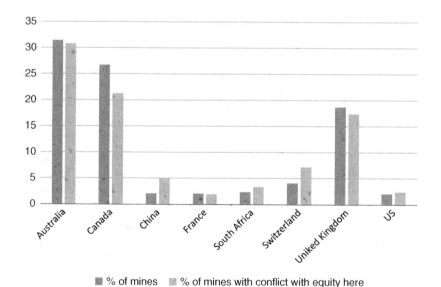

■ % of mines   ■ % of mines with conflict with equity here

FIGURE 1.2: Equity ownership and social conflict

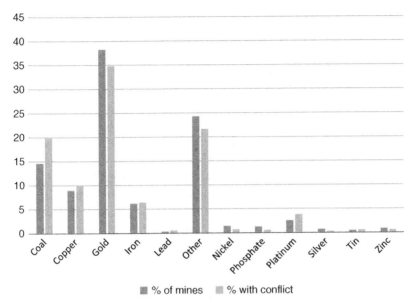

FIGURE 1.3: Commodity type and social conflict

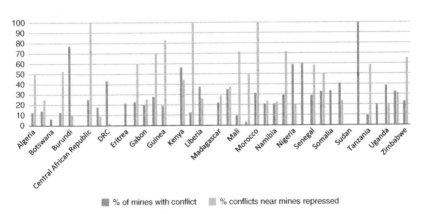

FIGURE 1.4: Repression near mines, by country

mines. This is roughly the distribution of these types of mines across the continent, suggesting that, on the surface, mineral type alone is not sufficient to explain why some mines see social conflict, while others do not.

How governments respond to these instances of social conflict varies significantly as well – countries repress social conflict at different rates. Figure 1.4 demonstrates the percentage of mines that saw conflict and percentage of conflicts that were repressed by country. To be sure, it is indeed the case that some countries repress social conflict near mines more often than others. Of the social conflicts that occurred in the vicinity of a mine, approximately 31 percent were repressed, with governments using coercive force, such as teargas, beatings, or killing participants in response to relatively low-intensity instances of social mobilization. Of those instances where repression was used, only 36 percent occurred in non-democratic countries and approximately 48 percent in democracies.[14] Even consolidated democracies respond to instances of social mobilization near mines with repression in some cases. However, within countries too, there is variation in whether the government represses a social conflict occurring near a mine. In Ghana, 70 percent of social conflicts near mines saw government repression, while in Mozambique and South Africa, this was approximately 24 percent.

Why Should We Care?

These numbers suggest variation in (a) whether social conflict occurs near mineral extraction, and (b) how the government responds to this conflict when it occurs. This variation does not correspond to national boundaries, firm nationality, or natural resource type. Why should we care about these regions, and why is it necessary to have a theory just about them? The obvious answer is that having a theory could guide policy makers and practitioners in trying to avoid some local version of the natural resource curse, where natural resources coincide with violent conflict and low socio-economic development.[15] Having a generalizable theory about these regions can help us understand if and when such a local curse is likely to emerge.

But natural resource extractive regions are interesting for another reason: these are areas where trade-offs between government access to revenue and political support are particularly acute. The fixed and somewhat random nature of natural resource deposits makes the asset particularly vulnerable to protest and local resistance. The costliness of potential resistance shapes the strategic incentives of the extractive

---

[14] Countries that scored a 0 or less on the Polity IV measure of democracy, democracies are those counties that score a 4 or above.

[15] Recent works by Arellano-Yanguas (2011), Arce (2014), Arce and Miller (2016), and Haslam and Ary Tanimoune (2016) have paved the way for a closer look at a local resource curse.

firm and the state, and compels the state to manage potential trade-offs between access to resource revenue and potential political consequences of resistance where natural resources and a politically relevant population occupy the same space. The outcomes in these regions reflect the strategic interaction among a firm, a government, and a local population. I refer to these outcomes as "governance outcomes" – which I describe in more detail in Chapter 2.

As a consequence, understanding the local politics of natural resource extraction in this way has implications for a broader question that has received little attention in the literature in comparative and world politics: how do non-state actors shape local outcomes related to stability and distribution? These local outcomes can shed light on a broader theoretical inquiry concerning localized goods provision such as infrastructure and welfare goods, and subnational variation in government presence across its sovereign territory. Economic and political trade-offs to state presence are likely to be particularly acute as the presence of natural resources fixes a location and forces a convergence of actors. As a result, these regions present governments with particular choices; that is, the government must assess the economic benefits of extraction and the value of political support in the region and make a calculation about how to manage trade-offs that might arise between these alternatives. As I will detail, the outcome of this calculation can result in the maintenance of regions of weak state presence, where the extractive firm, not the state, provides goods and services to an embedded, local population. Understanding extractive regions as strategic contexts in this way provides a lens for understanding subnational outcomes more broadly. They can help us to explore how and why regions of limited state presence might be sustained, with specific reference to regions of natural resource extraction where we might most expect states to maximize their presence, given the revenue potential.

POTENTIAL EXPLANATIONS

A theory of the local politics of natural resource extraction is needed both to guide policy and steer outcomes, as well as to account for the empirical puzzle described above. There is no single body of literature that addresses the research question at hand. Understanding the interactions that shape local outcomes in extractive regions requires drawing on multiple literatures. Specifically, it entails a discussion of potential explanations related to characteristics of the state and the firm, a burgeoning literature on non-state goods provision, and various iterations of the "natural resource curse." Each of these discussions provides relevant insights for understanding the variation in subnational outcomes, though each on its own is insufficient to explain such variation.

On State Capacity. One tempting framework for explaining the variation in these outcomes is that of state capacity: different levels of state capacity account for the different local outcomes of stability and distribution. Specifically, Herbst (2000) suggests that the way governments "broadcast power" (as Mann (1984) and then Herbst (2000) call it) is the result of relative differences in government resources, and that these resources are deployed at decreasing levels in concentric circles emanating from the country's seat of political power. This type of explanation has been a staple in state-centric approaches to understanding the way and extent to which government actors engage locally in goods provision, extraction, or regulation.[16] This literature has not directly or explicitly addressed the question of how the presence of large firms affects these local outcomes. Nonetheless, a state capacity framework would suggest that the effect of firms on local outcomes would vary with government strength: firm presence should have one effect on local outcomes in states of significant capacity, and another in states of limited capacity. However, as this study will demonstrate, these outcomes vary even within states of relatively low capacity, and across states with relatively similar resources. Consequently, this kind of observable variation necessitates local-level analysis, or at the very least, analysis that is not defined by national boundaries.

Scholars like Boone (2003) have certainly engaged in local-level analysis to understand how configurations of state power in rural regions depend, at least in part, on the relative bargaining power of local elites, as shaped by the social structures underpinning their authority and capacity. Building on Boone's work, this book focuses on the role of a non-state, local power broker: the firm. In the same way that states brokered deals with local elites in order to lessen the cost of state governance in these regions (often for the purpose of extraction), this study argues that firms operating in similarly peripheral environments engage in the task of

---

[16] Besley and Persson (2010), Scott (2004), Acemoglu (2005), and Goldsmith (2001) are a few.

building local support in order to lessen costs of their operation. However, this engagement does not occur in the absence of an authoritative state entirely, but in the state's "shadow of hierarchy."[17]

On Firms and Norms. The addition of the firm to an exploration of rural configurations of state power invites an alternative and equally tempting explanation for the puzzle at hand: the effect of firm presence on local outcomes depends on characteristics of, and constraints on, the firm (as opposed to the state). The observable outcome of this theoretical framework is that different firms are likely to affect local outcomes differently. It is certainly the case that firms have different cultural and management practices that shape their local engagement strategies.[18] The result should be that firms have strategies and practices that are distinct, but shared to some extent across operations held by a single firm.

Furthermore, the literature on localized firm investment also suggests that a shift in norms in the 1990s yielded a collective movement toward social spending in regions of foreign investment.[19] The transnational spread of norms regarding multinational firm conduct in host countries might be expected to affect the way firms behave.[20] The argument is that such norms have led to the emergence of standardized and accepted practices, which yield reputation costs for firms that are found to have violated them. Starting in the late 1980s, the practice of "corporate social responsibility" (CSR) emerged as a new norm advanced by international NGOs and international financial institutions. CSR is a set of quasi-voluntary behaviors funded through discretionary budget allocations by firms to support the procurement of a social license to operate – often known as "beyond compliance" with host country regulatory regimes.

The networks advancing and advocating for this new set of practices aimed to constrain international firm behavior in their regions of operation. The literature argues that there has been a degree of codification, and even standardization of firm practices that has begun to minimize the variance of firm behavior. As Pauline Jones notes, by the 1990s the terms of a model contract between resource firms and governments included not only the royalties and taxes, but also costs associated with providing

---

[17] Mayntz and Scharpf (1995).

[18] Waldman, Siegel, and Javidan (2006); Hart (1995).

[19] Dashwood (2012), Jones Luong (2014).

[20] Thauer (2014).

public goods and services to local communities.[21] A number of initiatives and codes of conduct have emerged to incentivize transparency in the mining sector and to coordinate and standardize the behavior of firms in and around their operations in host countries. For example, "Publish What You Pay," "Revenue Watch," and "Extractive Industry Transparency Initiative" are all aimed at ensuring transparency in mineral revenue payments between governments and firms. The United Nations Global Compact (a commitment by a network of business, labor, and non-governmental organizations to support a set of CSR principles drawn from existing international declarations, formed in 1999), and business's International Council on Mining and Metals (ICMM) Sustainable Development Charter (a code of conduct outlining management principles to be followed by the mining and metals industry) are some of the most prominent initiatives from this transnational norms cascade.

However, despite these well publicized efforts to signal the emergence, proliferation, and acceptance of these norms, evidence of their effectiveness is mixed. Dashwood (2007) found that norms were insufficient to explain the behavior of two Canadian mining firms, and furthermore, some have argued that such norms have worsened the well-being of communities living near resource extraction operations. There is diversity even within the sector regarding company CSR policies, and the degree of compliance with these norms varies. And the implementation of CSR policies varies with local contexts.[22] Norm cascades, particularly as they relate to CSR practices, are thus insufficient to explain variation in local extractive outcomes. Furthermore, while CSR is generally accepted as a voluntary investment by firms in the social welfare of the regions of operation, practitioners have come to conflate the required with the voluntary and goods provision by firms varies regardless of contractual obligation. The fluid and fuzzy definition of CSR undermines its usefulness as a frame for understanding the transfer firms promise to local populations.

Taken together, these two strands of literature suggest that firm behavior is likely to be a function of individual firm characteristics that are constrained by a cascade of international norms about their local behavior. Yet, as I will demonstrate, local engagement by the firm varies even among the projects of the same firm, suggesting that, while firm characteristics including organization or firm culture may indeed vary within

[21] Jones Luong (2014).
[22] Frynas (2005).

the international normative constraints, there is some part of the story that is still missing. Here too, consideration of local-level factors, as authors such as Brousseau and Fares (2000*b*) and Wolf, Deitelhoff, and Engert (2007) suggest, can provide a more fertile analysis for why a single firm might affect local   governance outcome differently at each site of operation.

On Non-State Goods Provision.   In addition to the literature on transnational norms of CSR as a driver of firm provision of social goods and services, the broader study of non-state goods provision has focused on the role of non-governmental organization in providing goods and services in regions where the state lacks the capacity to do so. Borzel et al. (2011) provides a collection of descriptions of how and when non-state goods provision occurs, particularly in regions where the state is absent. But much of the scholarship on non-state goods provision focuses on the provision of health care, potable water, and vocational training by NGOs whose primary purpose is the provision of these goods. As a consequence of the purported mission of most NGOs, discussions of the politics of non-state goods provision tend to focus on its *effects* on access to and quality of these goods and services, and on its effects on state legitimacy, and perceptions of the state by recipients of non-state goods provision.[23] In these studies the incentive for non-state goods provision is a given – NGOs aim to serve those populations unable to access such services, or who have access to those of substandard quality. For both outcomes of interest – improved access to goods and services or perceptions of state legitimacy – the results of these studies suggest that the effects of non-state goods provision depend on the historical and institutional context in which it is occurring. Furthermore, though studies are often at the national or transnational level, Brass (2016)'s discussion of the territoriality of NGOs suggests that the relevant level of analysis of historical and institutional contexts is local.

It is reasonable to assume these historical and contextual conditionalities extend to the effects of goods and service provision by private firms as well as NGOs. Since goods and services provision is not a given for private firms (natural resource firms or otherwise), a *politics* of goods and service provision by firms must include an explanation of the incentive to do so. Yet transnational norms of CSR are an insufficient source

[23] Brass (2016), Jones Luong (2014), Mcloughlin (2011), Batley and Mcloughlin (2010), Doyle and Patel (2008), and Bratton (1989).

of this incentive, as discussed above. The literature on non-state goods provision more broadly provides a useful starting point from which to consider incentives and local consequences of firm provision of goods.

On the "Curse" of Natural Resources. Thus far I have been concerned with an outcome in which natural resource extractive firms engage in the localized provision of goods and services around their sites of extraction, but this is only one of several outcomes occurring in regions of natural resource extraction that may also yield more violent outcomes. There is a prolific literature on the effects of natural resources on conflict, much of which relates natural resource rents to regime type and stability,[24] repression,[25] or civil war.[26] There are several mechanisms relating natural resources to instability that are commonly cited. First, the presence of natural resources can increase in the value of territory or government (resource as "prize" – this is particularly common with oil). Second, the availability of lootable resources[27] can fund rebel movements.[28] Third, natural resource wealth can decrease state capacity because they undermine the incentive to develop a strong, accountable, and bureaucratic state.[29]

There is, however, some debate as to whether the natural resource curse even exists – though the question has been more thoroughly considered in the natural resources and poor growth literature as opposed to the natural resources and conflict literature. Some have argued that the empirical results are flimsy or conflicting – with limited support depending on how relevant variables are measured,[30] or conditional on the type or characteristic of the resource or type of conflict.[31] A number of studies have been unable to identify a significant effect of natural resources on civil war onset.[32] Some argue that institutions, not natural resources, are to blame for poor outcomes relating to natural resource extraction.

[24] Smith (2004); Morrison (2009); Robinson, Torvik and Verdier (2006); Smith (2015).
[25] Clark (1997); Ross (2001*a*).
[26] Berdal and Malone (2000); Collier and Hoeffler (2005); Fearon (2005); Ross (2004*a*, 2006); Le Billon (2001*b*, *a*); Humphreys (2005); Soysa and Neumayer (2007).
[27] Those that are relatively easy to move and convert to cash.
[28] Ross (2001*a*); Humphreys (2005).
[29] Morrison (2009).
[30] Haber and Menaldo (2011); Brunnschweiler (2008).
[31] See Ross (2004*b*) and Ross (2004*a*) for reviews of the findings from an uptick in literature on this subject in the early 2000s.
[32] Including De Soysa and Neumayer (2007); Ross (2004*b*); Fearon and Laitin (2003); and Elbadawi and Sambanis (2002).

Menaldo (2016) and Jones Luong and Weinthal (2010) suggest that existing institutions shape whether natural resources are discovered and extracted, and thus the causal weight must be placed on institutional context, not on natural resources per se.

These studies tend to evaluate whether natural resources make civil war more likely, where the unit of analysis is the country or country year. More recent subnational studies have found results that suggest that the relationship between natural resources and conflict depends on the type of resource, type of conflict, and the scale of analysis.[33] However, even these studies often rely on national level characteristics (other than location of the resource and the conflict) to evaluate the relationship between conflict and natural resources, and focus on larger-scale civil wars.

The trajectory of research on the natural resource curse has led to several characteristics that make it unsuitable for explaining local-level, low-intensity conflict related to natural resource extraction. First, the existing body of work suggests that incentives of elites at the national level matter for the management and distribution of resource rents and that resource rents can, in turn, affect elite behavior, but it tells us little about how resource rents shape the way political elites interact with other actors at the geographic point of access to the resource. This is surprising since such interactions are likely to have significant consequences for the stability of elite access to these rents. As a result of this trend, political elites tend to be the primary actors in these studies, while the local populations are not often included as relevant actors, though these populations may become the source of regional unrest (as in the case of Nigeria in Watts (2004)).

Perhaps more importantly, this literature has been primarily concerned with organized forms of armed violence, as opposed to social mobilization and protest, forms of contentious politics that I am interested in here. The mechanism that scholars have proposed to explain more intense and organized forms of conflict may not apply to lower-intensity forms of local protest and resistance, and as Koubi et al. (2014) have noted, more research is needed. This is not to say that scholars have ignored how characteristics of the local extractive context affect natural resource–related instability. Watts (2004) and Le Billon (2001a) suggest the importance of the physical and social context of extraction for understanding variation in resource extraction outcomes in their respective

---

[33] Buhaug and Gates (2002); Lujala (2009); Buhaug and Rød (2006); Buhaug et al. (2011); Basedau and Pierskalla (2014); Asal et al. (2016); Cederman, Weidmann, and Gleditsch (2011); Weidmann and Ward (2010); Maystadt et al. (2014).

qualitative case studies of the Niger Delta and of Angola's Cabinda region. They introduce the extractive firm as an actor in the local land-scape, since in most resource-rich countries, the capital and technical investment for extraction is provided by a firm, making it a relevant and visible local actor. Reed (2009) indicates that the nature of oil enclaves in Angola protects the actual extraction of the resource and the corporate actors involved, but yields revenues that can be used to respond to local or broader discontent. These authors, along with Snyder and Bhavnani (2005), demonstrate that the context of resource extraction, including the engagement of local actors other than the state, is relevant for under-standing how natural resource extraction affects local instability. A more recent literature on localized resistance around natural resource extrac-tion has emerged.[34] This book builds on these works, to expand the regional diversity of cases (much of this work focuses on South America), and to build and test a unifying theory around localized natural resource extraction that links these contentious outcomes with distributive ones.

Where Does This Leave Us?. Variation in outcomes in extractive regions is thus particularly puzzling because it is observable within countries, and across countries of similar state capacity. Furthermore, it is observable across the operations of a single extractive firm. As a consequence, expla-nations that focus on state- or firm-level characteristics are insufficient for understanding when extractive projects lead to local resistance, and when the government represses this kind of protest. Explaining this varia-tion is thus a particularly messy endeavor, requiring subnational analysis that draws on multiple and cross-disciplinary literatures. The scholarship discussed above, along with additional extensive case studies,[35] suggests that actors such as firms and local communities interact with the state in and around extractive sites to realize preferences regarding the distribu-tion of the costs and benefits of extraction. Specifically, resistance toward natural resource–related development projects can emerge when local communities observe the potential benefits as well as costly consequences of extraction. Such resistance can be costly to all parties involved, lead-ing parties to attempt to reach an alternative solution. Firms promise compensation to secure a "social license to operate" in order to prevent

---

[34] Including Arce (2014); Arce and Miller (2016); Haslam and Ary Tanimoune (2016); Engels and Dietz (2017); Bebbington, Hinojosa, Bebbington, Burneo, and Warnaars (2008); and Bebbington, Humphreys, Bury, Lingan, Muñoz, and Scurrah (2008).

[35] Hilson (2002), Castro and Nielsen (2001), and Kapelus (2002).

such costly conflict. In fact, the idea that "corporate social responsibility" is a strategic behavior is explored by Baron (2001) and others[36] and cited explicitly by industry as a way of heading off potential costly protest. Given the costliness of the protest for governments receiving revenues from extraction, states too have an incentive to limit the likelihood of protest, if doing so is not more costly than the protest itself.

When framed this way, a rationalist approach appears appropriate for uncovering the logic resulting in localized conflict in regions of natural resource extraction. As Fearon (1995) describes, such explanations tend to fall into two categories: conflict resulting from the existence of private information or conflict resulting from commitment problems. Regions of natural resource extraction are often regions of limited state presence, especially at the time of firm investment and may be reasonably characterized as regions of limited information. The average distance between a mine and a political capital is 368 km, with only 141 mines (out of nearly 2500) existing within 50 km of the capital. The context is one of uncertainty derived from the existence of private information about the costliness of protest to the local population, and the costliness of government response to such resistance. A Pierskalla (2010) argues, formal models of protest and repression are somewhat limited, and variation in strategic context is limited. While such models typically consider two actors, and seek to understand the effect of repression on protest, this literature demonstrates that repression can carry political costs, in addition to the monetary costs modeled in other canonical models of larger-scale phenomena (such as Acemoglu and Robinson (2001)). I am interested precisely in when governments employ repression to protect access to revenue from natural resources, *given* that repression has political costs that might vary. The potential of costly resistance shapes the strategic incentives of the extractive firm and the state and compels the state to manage potential trade-offs between access to resource revenue and political consequences of resistance where natural resources and a politically relevant population occupy the same space.

THE ARGUMENT

I contend that regions of natural resource extraction constitute strategic contexts in which the interaction among extractive firms, local populations, and governments is compelled by the presence of the resource and territorialized by the concessionary allocation of extractive rights. The

---

[36] Khanna (2001), Khanna and Anton (2002).

fixed nature of natural resources ensures that extractive firms, local populations, and governments interact in a defined territory that is spatially limited by the fact that communities can uproot themselves only at a high cost, and firms cannot move natural resource deposits.

As a result, local populations are important actors in extractive regions because they have the potential to impose political costs on the state, and economic costs on the state and the extractive firm. Both firms and governments have economic interests in ensuring that natural resource extraction continues, and the government has the added burden of retaining sufficient political support to remain in power. Extractive regions, which may be far from the political center of a country, but which hold significant revenue potential, compel extractive firms to engage with local populations in order to secure access to the resource and continued extraction. Local residents may engage in instances of sabotage and protest in response to extractive externalities or exclusion from economic benefits, which can interrupt extractive operations, imposing significant monetary costs. It is this potentially costly interruption in the context of limited exit options that gives firms an incentive to provide some set of goods to the local community and to mitigate the externalities of extraction.

The monetary costs of interruption accrue to both the firm and the government, but the government may also face potential political costs, depending on how it responds. Should the local population engage in contentious behavior such as protest, government repression may carry with it costs to its support base and legitimacy, while a government decision to compel firms to secure approval by providing promised compensation, often in the form of collective goods and services, can increase its support in the region. Governments must assess the economic benefits of extraction and the value of political support in the region and make a calculation about how to respond, managing trade-offs that might arise between these alternatives. The result of these calculations is a range of local outcomes near natural resource extraction, including firm provision of goods and services to local communities, localized conflict in response to resource extraction, and government regulatory or repressive intervention. This book explores the conditions under which these outcomes occur in Africa, where natural resource extraction is a particularly important source of revenue for states with otherwise limited capacity on average.

Because local populations in extractive regions can impose political costs on the state, and economic costs on both the state and the extractive firm, governments must assess the economic benefits of extraction and the value of political support in the region and make a calculation about how to manage trade-offs that might arise. The local community is thus also an important actor in shaping how firms and governments behave in and around mining sites. Variance in the effect of firm presence on local outcomes cannot be explained without consideration of the support of the population at the local level. The local population residing in and around firm operations is an important actor, and its interactions with the firm and government are the crucial interactions on which an explanation of local outcomes must rely.

Introduction of the local population as an actor with agency and preferences justifies the consideration of regions of natural resource extraction as three-actor strategic contexts, where actors' decisions are conditional on a set of fixed parameters as well as the decisions of others. As a result, both the context and the actors' beliefs about each other matter in shaping different outcomes of interest. The local characteristics of the extractive environment, the revenue and political imperative of the state, and the firm's revenue demand shape whether firms engage in local goods provision, whether local populations engage in resistance, and whether the government represses this resistance. Ultimately, the actors' beliefs about each other are central for constraining their behavior and contextual parameters – such as resource interruptibility, environmental externalities, and costs of protest – matter by way of shaping the relevant cut points of these beliefs. The relevance of these beliefs is constrained by the costs of obtaining local support relative to the costs a local population can impose on firms and governments by protesting, and their political salience to the central government. These outcomes of localized firm investment, resistance by local populations, and government response are manifestations of a menu of governance strategies in a region where monetary and political resources create significant, territorialized trade-offs.

Contributions

This book makes four theoretical contributions. First, this study links local characteristics with those of the national government as well as the global firm to understand the local outcomes we observe. It does so in two ways. First, it takes seriously the role of geography and the environment in shaping local politics and preferences. The presence of natural resources and the geographic context in which they are extracted shapes the emergence and realization of preferences over local distributive outcomes. This is particularly important in regions where the modal economic activities and livelihoods are derived from the local, natural environment. In addition, in explicitly and systematically analyzing the role of a localized population who can constrain the extractive firm and the state, this study introduces a novel, multi-level framework for subnational analysis. The theoretical framework is multi-level in that the preferences and behaviors of the national government *and* of a local, spatially defined community (in addition to a private, spatially confined firm) matter for understanding outcomes of interest at the local level. It demonstrates that local trade-offs between revenue and political support can shape the incentives for governments and firms at the local level, thus exploring the local dimensions of the "resource curse" by emphasizing the agency of local populations. To be clear, this book is *not* about the ways in which local populations overcome obstacles to collective action in order to successfully mobilize, and thus I do not explore the ways in which local hierarchies of authority and heterogeneity facilitate or undermine the likelihood of mobilization and repression. It *is* about introducing the local population as a strategic actor, with its own set of preferences and beliefs. The strategies they employ can constrain and shape the behavior of the firm and the state. In taking seriously the geographic environment and the presence of a local community and adding them to an analysis that has traditionally occurred at the level of the national government and the transnational firm, I link the local with the national and transnational in order to provide a multi-level understanding of why we observe the local outcomes that we do.

Second, this book reorients the study of governance away from the state, by emphasizing the role of non-state actors, such as natural resource firms, while still recognizing that the state plays a crucial role in shaping local outcomes. Scholarship seems to cycle between "bringing the state back in" and then veering back away from the traditionally state-centric approach to governance.[37] In this book, I suggest that governance is the result of an interplay between state, non-state actors (such as firms), and a localized community. In regions of limited state presence, or in weak states more generally, it is commonly assumed that governments fail to provide goods and services or successfully maintain order because of a lack of capacity. I am suggesting here that governments with limited capacity still make strategic calculations about how they exercise power,

---

[37] Borzel et al. (2011), Soifer (2012).

and may rely on non-state actors as local focal points for governance. This is particularly important given the existence of competing and alternative sources of legitimacy in weak states, and the potential role of large, transnational firms in shaping local outcomes.

From a broader theoretical approach, this study builds on the literature about regions of limited state presence, by explicitly considering how and why regions of limited state presence might be sustained, with specific reference to regions of natural resource extraction where we might most expect states to maximize their presence, given the revenue potential.[38] Specifically, such regions reflect the outcome of a strategic interaction among a firm who may engage in the work of goods provision and even local governance, a government who may value the revenue provided by the firm more than any political support it might receive from engagement in the region, and an embedded local population with the potential to offer support to or impose costs on the firm or the state.

Third, I provide a unifying explanation of several phenomena that have, until now, been parts of multiple literatures. Works by Haslam and Ary Tanimoune (2016), Bebbington, Humphreys, Bury, Lingan, Muñoz, and Scurrah (2008), Bebbington, Hinojosa, Bebbington, Burneo, and Warnaars (2008), Bebbington (2010), Dietz and Engels (2017), and Arce (2014) explore when communities mobilize in areas of resource extraction, focusing on issues of environmental grievances and limited local institutions for the redistribution of benefits of natural resource extraction. Separately, there is a literature linking the use of government repression in resource-rich states. Much of this literature links natural resource rents with generally coercive states, though, as mentioned, scholars such as Downey, Bonds, and Clark (2010), Hönke (2009), and Maystadt et al. (2014) have considered the more-localized use of repression in and around natural resources. Furthermore, literatures on corporate social responsibility and on non-state goods provision describe normative cascades and state capacity shortfalls that result in goods and service provision by non-state actors, respectively. However, the theoretical frame here allows me to link the outcomes described separately in these literatures. I am able to explain incentives for goods provision by firms, mobilization by communities in extractive regions, and the use of government repression. In doing so, a single theoretical frame is able to unify all three of these outcomes – previously compartmentalized into disparate literatures.

---

[38] Levi (1989), Olson (1993), and Borzel et al. (2011) are only a few of the many scholars of this tradition.

Finally, this book contributes to a broader understanding of transaction costs in the context of natural resource extraction, primarily explored in the economics, business, and organization literatures. Transaction cost theory, advanced most famously by Ronald Coase and then Oliver Williamson, focuses on the economic transaction as the central unit of analysis, and it explores which functions should be carried out within the organizational form of the firm and which outside of it. Transaction costs have come to be thought of as friction inhibiting market exchange, and often include information and search costs, bargaining or decision costs, and enforcement costs. As Williamson (1985) suggested, any contracting problem can be usefully investigated in terms of transaction costs. In the context of natural resource extraction, the relevant transaction in the natural resource sector occurs between the firm and the government, and pertains to the exchange of the rights to extraction for taxation and royalties related to resource extraction.

Unclear, uncertain, weakly enforced, or overlapping property rights are one source of transaction costs, given that mineral extraction requires large areas of land that may be formally or informally occupied. Johnson (1972) suggests that customary property rights, a common institutional form of land rights across Africa, increase transaction costs. The local population is an invisible party to the initial transaction, with whom the firm makes a separate, implicit contract. Scholars of natural resource extraction have already come to acknowledge the navigation of access to land as a significant obstacle that firms face, but few have explicitly acknowledged it as a transaction cost in the context of natural resource extraction (except Christensen, Hartman, and Samii (n.d.)). Furthermore, as I will demonstrate, firms bargain over more than land access – they exchange public goods and services, jobs, and social investment to ensure continued production and avoid costly protest and interruption. As a result, this book elucidates and articulates a set of previously unidentified transaction costs to firms in the natural resource extractive context, particularly where the state is weak and property rights are poorly specified or enforced.

SCOPE

While the empirical chapters of this book will confine their evidentiary base to the African continent, the question that drives this book does not necessarily connote a limited scope of application. After all, economically powerful transnational actors such as firms do not confine their activities to a single country or continent, and subnational variation in outcomes is not limited to African states. In fact, many of the scholars' ideas on which I regularly rely were generated through field work and case analysis of South America[39] and Southeast Asia[40] – as well as Africa.[41] However, I limit the scope of this book to the study of non-renewable, point, natural resource extraction on the continent of Africa between 1990 and 2014 for several reasons.

First, the post-1990s' context in Africa is a time in which, following the end of the Cold War, many African countries had shed a socialist political rhetoric and economic structure, and, for better or worse, implemented the tenets of the Washington Consensus. Notably, not all African countries followed in the socialist wake of the Soviet Union up until the 1990s; there were many that continued to denounce Soviet economic practices and loudly supported those of its counterpart, the United States. Furthermore, the Washington Consensus was not implemented equally, evenly, or with similar comprehensiveness across African countries, nor were its consequences uniform across the continent. And yet, the end of the Cold War brought to fruition a wave of democratization across Africa, with dominant, single-party regimes giving way to multi-party systems (some more consolidated than others). This wave of political change, accompanied by the privatization of many state-owned enterprises, resulted in an increase from US$15.3 million in 1989 to US$6.87 billion of foreign direct investment by the year 2000. Much of this was driven by the extractives industry.[42] As a consequence of liberalization and privatization, transnational mineral exploration and extraction companies began bidding for mineral concessions, and investing in the development of large-scale projects that would allow them to recuperate the costs of exploration. By the time the 1990s began, approximately 75 percent of foreign direct investment in Africa was in the extractive industry.

Second, existing literature on resistance and mobilization around natural resources focuses primarily on Latin America, with some exceptions. Arce (2014) and Haslam and Ary Tanimoune (2016) in particular quantitatively evaluate the likelihood of collective protest and resistance around mining sites. Many more qualitative studies evaluate similar phenomena (Bebbington, 2010; Bebbington, Hinojosa, Bebbington, Burneo, and

---

[39] Soifer (2012), O'Donnell (1993).
[40] Scott (2009).
[41] Hönke (2009), Watts (2004), Herbst (2000), and Boone (2003).
[42] *Global Value Chains: Investment and Trade for Development* (2007).

Warnaars, 2008; Bebbington, Humphreys, Bury, Lingan, Muñoz, and Scurrah, 2008; Bury, 2005, 2007) in Latin America. This regional focus also characterizes the limited number of studies exploring the distributive outcomes around mining.[43] By focusing on Africa, this book provides a useful collection of cases to compare to the existing scholarship on Latin America. The (at least minimally similar) historical trajectory of the majority of countries on the African continent suggests that they can be grouped together in an analysis separate from the Latin American context. Furthermore, given the historically limited state capacity of many African countries, they provide a useful (if imperfect) benchmark for evaluating the local politics of natural resource extraction in weak states. Future work should endeavor to compare how these local politics play out across these disparate geographic contexts.

In addition to limiting the spatial and temporal scope of the project to Africa after 1990, there is good reason to limit the scope of natural resource types as well. In general, typologies and classifications of natural resources are conceptualized in order to fit the substance and methodology of the study at hand, and the resource curse literature has proposed and operationalized several classifications. For this exploration, I am concerned primarily with non-renewable, point resources. This includes resources such as gold, copper, silver, iron, phosphate, and coal. These resources are all of potentially high value, the price of which is globally determined. Additionally, the resources all require the allocation of significant concessions – large swaths of land for mineral exploration, mine construction, ore processing, and waste disposal. The concession borders are clearly (though perhaps not uncontroversially) delineated, and they constitute territories of operation for the firm. I also limit my analysis to large-scale mining, as opposed to artisanal mining. While these two types of activities may indeed occur in the same space, artisanal mining does not necessarily imply or require the presence of a large firm – and it is the consequence of the presence of the firm for governance outcomes that ultimately interests me.

METHODOLOGICAL APPROACH

This study capitalizes on a mixed methods approach. I rely on multiple methodological tools in order to first develop and then test my theoretical

---

[43] Amengual (2018).

claims. In particular, I employ formal modeling, structured comparative case analysis, and statistical analysis of geospatial data.

I rely on formal modeling in order to develop a clear, logically consistent theory. I present a stylized, simplified representation of the interactions of multiple actors, in a defined spatial context. Given the assumptions and stylizations, it is necessary to consider why one needs to develop a formal model, instead of laying out a set of hypotheses or a set of logical presumptions and hypothesized causal mechanisms. Formal modeling, and more specifically game theoretic modeling in which the consequences of individual decisions depend on the decisions of others, provides several specific benefits for the study at hand. First, understanding the effect of non-state actors on local outcomes requires the inclusion of multiple actors (including resource firms, local communities, and state actors), and the result of their strategic interaction is not necessarily apparent at the outset. Defining these actors and their preferences, and specifying the rules of their interaction so as to best represent their incentives can allow for a precise elucidation of the logic that results in different outcomes, and consequently, generate precise hypotheses. In doing so, I posit a set of strategic interactions among natural resource firms, government actors, and local communities that we can map onto observed outcomes.

Second, the reduction of political economic outcomes into stylized representations of these actors, their preferences, and the surrounding contextual parameters can allow us to define and posit the relevant values of these variables. Modeling in this way can allow us to identify when certain parameters matter for making particular outcomes more or less likely, and at what relative values they have the greatest effect.

Finally, limited data presents a significant challenge for evaluating the effect of non-state actors on local outcomes in natural resource regions. The puzzle requires, as noted, consideration of multiple levels of analysis, and while national-level data is available for most countries (if somewhat unreliable for many African nations), data at the local level is not freely available, and the task of gathering such data across the continent remains prohibitively onerous. The exercise of formal modeling can provide a useful aid in positing causal mechanisms when the intermediate steps may be difficult to observe or measure systematically.

But to what extent does this formal model capture the variance predicted, if we zoom in to a few case studies that exhibit this variance? Relying on interviews, and primary and secondary document collection,

I explore the applicability of the model to four regions of natural resource extraction in central and eastern Africa. First, I compare two coal concessions leased by different companies in Mozambique in order to elucidate how the strategic logic underpinning the model explains variation of governance outcomes within Mozambique. I then compare governance outcomes in copper concessions leased by the same firms in Zambia and Democratic Republic of Congo (DRC).

The structured comparative case analysis of resource concessions serves two specific purposes. First, this research design, specifically a within-country comparison and a within-firm comparison, ensures that the variance I am interested in cannot be explained solely by state-level or firm-level characteristics. Consequently, I reduce the likelihood that competing explanations of firm- or state-level characteristics are the primary driver of these local outcomes, and instead lend support to the claim that a strategic interaction, shaped by the local context, can better account for the variance observed. Second, the comparative case analysis provides an opportunity to evaluate the internal validity of the posited mechanisms. While the case selection strategy limits the threat of competing theories that rely on state-level or firm-level characteristics, the posited causal linkages require critical evaluation of the qualitative evidence to further limit the possibility that other explanations can better account for the outcomes observed.

Finally, to evaluate the external validity of the causal mechanisms posited by the model, and the causal mechanisms traced in the comparative case analysis, I rely on statistical analysis of spatial data. I employ a geospatial dataset of mining-related social conflict across the continent of Africa between 1990 and 2014 to test a subset of the hypotheses generated by the model and unpacked in the comparative case study. Specifically, I evaluate two separate empirical outcomes: the likelihood of social conflict near a mine, and the likelihood that such an instance of social conflict is repressed. In order to test my theoretical argument, I evaluate the effects of local and national factors derived from the formal model on these outcomes.

The mixed methods approach I employ provides several benefits for advancing and supporting theoretical claims. The combination of a formal model with multi-level parameters, a structured comparative case analysis, and a continent-wide statistical analysis allow me to link micro- and macro-level phenomenon. Specifically, while the formal model and structured case analysis elucidate the mechanisms by which different outcomes emerge, the continent-wide statistical analysis allows me to test more generally the relationship between parameters and outcomes. As a result, the traditional trade-off between generalizability and contextual accuracy is mitigated, at least in part. Furthermore, the theory itself includes characteristics of local actors as well as national ones, linking local outcomes with both local and national characteristics, allowing for a multi-level understanding of the drivers of local outcomes.

KEY FINDINGS

The theory argues that the local characteristics of the extractive environment, the revenue and political imperative of the state, and the firm's revenue demand shape whether firms engage in local goods provision, whether local populations engage in resistance, and whether the government represses this resistance. Ultimately, the formal model conveys two central results: (1) the actors' beliefs about each other are central for constraining their behavior and (2) parameters such as resource interruptibility, environmental externalities, and costs of protest matter by way of shaping the relevant cut points of these beliefs. The methodological approach laid out above allows me to test the internal validity as well as the generalizability of the theory.

In the structured case analysis of coal concessions in Mozambique, and copper concessions in Zambia and Democratic Republic of Congo, I find support for the mechanisms and processes proposed by the formal model. Relying on field work (including interviews and archival work) I demonstrate that the firm, local population, and government interact in the sequential manner proposed by my theory, and I rule out competing explanations that rely on primarily state- or firm-specific characteristics for understanding local outcomes. Specifically, I demonstrate how pursuing local support drives firm and government behavior when the costs of doing so are not too great. These costs are determined by firm beliefs about the likelihood of protest, the actual monetary cost to the firm and government of protest, and the perceived cost of securing support from the local population. However, for the firm, the government response to a protest shapes the firm's cost of failing to secure local support. For the government, whether and how it responds is dependent on the trade-off between the potential political costs and benefits from repression or regulatory enforcement.

When these mechanisms are generalized to the continent of Africa, I find moderate support for the specific hypotheses that emerge from the formal model. Specifically, in deciding whether to protest, communities weigh their relative effectiveness in terms of their ability to interrupt a commodity to market. I find that the more interruptible mineral extraction is, the greater the likelihood of social conflict near a mine. Additionally, in deciding whether to live up to promises made to the local population of compensation and benefits, firms weigh the cost of providing them to communities against the potential cost of community mobilization. I find that as the cost of the promised transfer to the local population increases, firms are less likely to provide it and consequently, protest near the mine becomes more likely. Furthermore, because an increase in the government's take of natural resource rents decreases firms' resources and willingness to provide the promised transfer, as the government's take increases, the likelihood of protest near a mine increases.

When social conflict does occur in close proximity to a mine, my theory suggests that governments weigh the potential political cost of repressing a social mobilization when deciding if or how to respond. Yet governments rely on repression to protect a mine whose productivity may be threatened by social mobilization. As the political relevance of the local population increases, repression of a nearby conflict becomes less likely. Since the benefit of repression increases with the value of the mine, as the value of the mine increases, repression of a nearby conflict event becomes more likely.

ROADMAP

The book proceeds as follows. In the next chapter, I outline a theory of the logic of governance in regions of natural resource extraction. This chapter provides the conceptual foundation and analytical framework for the rest of the book. It introduces the firm, local community, and government's preferences, beliefs, and interactions, and explains how these interactions yield different governance outcomes in regions of natural resource extraction. In Chapter 3, I detail this strategic interaction in a formal game theoretic model, which underpins the theory discussed in Chapter 2. In the model, I specify the relevant actors, preferences, actions, and payoffs that generate different outcomes, and yield testable hypotheses. Given the subnational and within-firm variation observed, naming the actors and preferences, the relevant parameters, and the order of play allows for the identification of the central dynamics that might yield variation. The solution specifies the conditions under which the firm will provide promised transfers to a local population, the conditions under which resistance will occur, and how the government will respond. Broadly, the model examines a scenario in which a non-state actor has incentives to engage in goods provision, and in which the state may have an incentive to compel it to do so. It outlines the logic underpinning the incentives for goods provision in regions in which non-state actors are a relevant, resource-endowed actor that can shape the way governments manage trade-offs in the extraction of political support and revenue.

Chapter 4 begins Part II, in which I provide two structured case comparisons. I study coal extraction in Mozambique and copper extraction in Zambia and DRC in order to evaluate the internal validity of the model proposed in Chapter 3, and to elucidate the causal mechanisms detailed therein. I consider how the stylized model plays out on the ground, identifying the actors and tracing their beliefs that result in the outcomes that characterize four extractive sites in Mozambique, Zambia, and DRC. Specifically, I describe how in some of these regions governments monitor and regulate extractive firm behavior, ensuring that they engage in goods provision and mitigate adverse consequences, while in others they respond to local discontent with repressive campaigns. Chapter 4 introduces the research design of the comparative structured cases that follow in Chapters 5 and 6. The case analyses present a plausible account of the formation and implications of the beliefs actors have about each other, which are central to understanding the conflict and regulatory outcomes predicted by the formal model. Drawing on interviews, firm documents and reports, and participatory observation, I assess the effect of firm presence on governance outcomes in two comparative contexts: within the same country, and among concessions of the same firm. Chapter 7 provides an overview of the implications of the structured case comparisons.

Chapter 8 introduces Part III, in which I turn to the generalizability of the theory developed in Part I. I test hypotheses indicated by the model and detailed in the case study with geospatial data of mines, conflict, and repression in Africa. I evaluate the factors that systematically contribute to the subnational and within-firm variation in protest and repression around extractive sites. In Chapters 9 and 10, I use a quantitative dataset to test several hypotheses that emerge from the model, lending support for the veracity of its characterization of the local logic. While similar studies have considered the importance of the presence of natural resources for larger phenomena such as civil wars and failed growth at the national level, I use a dataset that includes the location of mineral extraction projects and individual social conflict events to consider the local outcomes of resource extraction. These chapters provide support for the generalizability of the dynamics suggested by the formal model and case analysis across extractive regions in Africa.

Finally, in Chapter 11, I offer some concluding thoughts on the implications of the study for further research and policy. The appendices provides formal proofs of the model presented in Chapter 3 and robustness checks for the quantitative empirical analysis in Chapters 9 and 10.

PART I

THE LOCAL POLITICS OF NATURAL RESOURCE EXTRACTION: A THEORY

2

A Logic of Governance

In the introduction I observed that some mines face local resistance in the form of social conflict and others do not, and that among those that face resistance only some of these are repressed by the government. These different outcomes do not correspond to any one country or any one firm. Variation observed within a single country suggests that reliance on national-level characteristics, and hence analysis at the level of the nation-state, cannot account for variation of these outcomes within states. Variation across a single firm's operations suggests that firm characteristics are insufficient to explain variation, and further suggests that local-level analysis is required to understand variation in the role of the firm in local governance outcomes. As a consequence, explanations that focus on state- or firm-level characteristics are insufficient for understanding when extractive projects yield local development outcomes in the form of goods and service provision, and when they lead to localized conflict.

Given that characteristics of the government, the firm, or of the resource are insufficient to explain these outcomes around natural resource extraction, it is necessary to look at how these actors interact to evaluate the conditions under which these interactions yield different outcomes. A theory of the logic of governance in regions of natural resource extraction needs to specify the actors, preferences, and mechanisms by which local outcomes emerge. I am concerned here with providing an account of the incentives and interactions among a set of actors in a defined, subnational space. Local governance outcomes in extractive regions are the result of both firm and government behavior, and reliance on local support is relevant for understanding the incentives of both actors. Questions about when social mobilization around mining occurs, when firms provide promised benefits, and how governments respond if mobilization does in fact occur cannot be answered in isolation from each other – the answer to one relies on the answer to the others.

In this chapter, I build a theory that both elucidates mechanisms at the local level and ties the local context to national-level structural characteristics and extractive firms to explain local governance outcomes in natural resource extractive regions. I will specify the beliefs, preferences, and order of interactions of the firm, local community, and government that yield different outcomes. Because the theory suggests a strategic interaction, outcomes rely on each actor's response to each other. However, the order of interactions and the information available to each actor help identify the structural parameters and beliefs that matter for the likelihood that a particular outcome occurs. The specific values and cut points at which these parameters matter will be derived in the formal model in the next chapter.

I argue that regions of natural resource extraction constitute strategic contexts in which the interaction among extractive firms, local populations, and governments is compelled by the presence of the resource and territorialized by the concessionary allocation of extractive rights. Because local populations in extractive regions can impose political costs on the state, and economic costs on both the state and the extractive firm, governments must assess the economic benefits of extraction and the value of political support in the region and make a calculation about how to manage trade-offs that might arise between these alternatives. These local interactions between extractive firms, governments, and locally embedded populations yield spatial variation in governance outcomes including goods and services provision by a firm, localized conflict including protest and repression, and government regulatory intervention.

I consider a governance outcome to be an observable, behavioral outcome resulting from the interactions between the local community, firm, and government, within a formal set of entrenched rule-making arrangements. A governance outcome is a spatially confined local equilibrium of behavior. Because of the spatial constraint, this outcome is not divorced from geography, but instead remarries political economic equilibrium outcomes with geographic context: spaces of extraction. The outcomes of interest include political (dis)order and the localized provision of goods and services.

The interaction between a government and a resource firm has been explored in economics in an attempt to understand bargaining between a sovereign government and a private enterprise, often to evaluate the applicability of the obsolescing bargain theory first described by Vernon (1971). This relationship is important, in that it highlights the leverage that each of these actors has in the context of natural resource extraction: governments can leverage the fixed costs that firms invest for the development of a mine, while firms can leverage their technical expertise and capital required for extraction, as well as any private information they possess about the value of the mineral in the ground. This well-trodden discussion of firm–government contract negotiation is a useful departure point, because while it is a classic conundrum for understanding foreign direct investment, it is of particular relevance for natural resource extractive firms, where the significant sunk costs of investment combine with limited exit options to make it particularly difficult for firms to easily relocate, compelling their interaction with both the government and an embedded local population.

Regions of natural resource extraction present a unique microcosm for understanding local governance outcomes because they are regions where trade-offs between revenue and political support are likely to be particularly acute. The presence of natural resources fixes a location and forces a convergence of actors, from which there are limited exit options, ensuring territorial implication. Extractive firms in these regions often engage in the provision of goods and services such as clinics, schools, infrastructure, and employment opportunities. Notably, many of these kinds of provision are part of what is traditionally captured by the notion of a modern, bureaucratic, and welfare-providing state.

In the next section, I lay out the relevant actors, their characteristics, and the drivers of their preferences. I then specify the way these preferences shape how actors interact to yield different governance outcomes.

THE ACTORS

Extractive Firms

Privatization of state-owned enterprises accompanied structural adjustment in Africa in the late 1980s and throughout the early 1990s. While many countries retained regulations requiring at least partial domestic ownership of mining companies, this liberalization increased foreign investment in the extractive sector. The chronology of firm investment in the extractive sector in most African states (which continue to retain explicit ownership of all sub-soil resources, even once leased out to transnational firms) is relatively similar. The process may be divided into several phases: the exploration and feasibility phase in which firms assess the availability and quality of mineral resources and obtain permits for extractive rights, the development phase in which the mine is constructed, the operational phase in which production is under way, and mine closure.

Much has been made of the challenges that governments and natural resource firms face in reaching a fair and durable agreement with governments, especially in the early phases of exploration and feasibility. Governments face the challenge of asymmetric information (firms have greater technical knowledge, allowing for better estimation of the value of the resource in the ground). Firms face time inconsistency problems in making contracts with sovereign governments who, theoretically, may renege at any time. However, an increased reliance on auctions for the allocation of mineral concessions has mitigated some of these challenges.

There is some variation in the process of obtaining a mining concession, but in general, the government issues a call for firms to purchase exploratory permits, and the winning firm sends geologists and engineers to assess the presence, grade, and value of the total reserves of the resource. There is significant uncertainty in assessing sub-surface resources.[1] Following this exploration, firms develop feasibility plans for the extraction of the resource and bid for the rights to extract the mineral from a predefined concession. Often, those with prospecting or exploration licenses are granted priority in receiving development and extraction licenses. In many cases, junior firms conduct the exploration, while senior, larger firms with more significant capital reserves can bid on the contract to develop the concession after purchasing the exploration license from the junior firm. Alternatively, junior or senior firms may bid on exploration and extractive rights in the same auction process, as was the case in Mozambique's Moatize concession (explored in Chapter 5). Once a firm's bid for rights to development and extraction is accepted by the government, the firm assesses the local social and environmental effects of its planned operations through the development of an Environmental Impact Assessment (EIA), often required before mining can begin.

The transnational spread of EIAs, as well as broader, voluntary investment in socially and environmentally responsible practices resulted from

---

[1] Sources of this uncertainty include number, grade, and exact location of deposits, mineral and metal prices, mining methods and costs, and timing.

the emergence of a set of norms and guidelines for the conduct of private foreign and transnational firms in host countries. In Jones Luong (2014), Jones and others trace the emergence of these norms, which have been codified by the World Bank and other international financial institutions.[2] These guidelines pertain to the conduct of firms with respect to the rights of local populations in their region of operation, including management of resettlement of local populations and the adverse effects of firm operations on these populations. EIAs are conducted by independent contractors who survey the potential environmental and social effects of the firm's planned operations. EIAs are contractual agreements that must be approved by a government ministry of environment or mines in order for the firm to proceed with mine development and operation. If the concession encloses an existing local population, the firm may also contract out the development of a Resettlement Action Plan (RAP), which details the assets and occupations of individuals that will be directly affected through resettlement as a result of the mine's construction.

While EIAs and RAPs are contractual documents specifying the costs of managing the local environmental and social effects of mining operations and related firm responsibilities, and thus carry the full weight of government enforcement, firms are also expected to invest voluntarily in local economic development in the regions in which they operate. Discretionary spending regularly falls under the title of CSR, and firms report these investments in their annual financial and sustainability reports. The belief that extractive firms need to invest locally to obtain a "social license to operate" is prominent across most extractive firms, and this incentive is well understood even by those outside of the industry. One mining executive indicated that he and colleagues from other firms "developed some approach to social responsibility, because [they] know that unless [they] help that local population, [they] are never going to improve [their] own production rates."[3] These investments can include construction and staffing of schools and medical clinics, sports clubs and venues, educational outreach, and scholarship provision.

While CSR is discretionary spending in comparison to the spending stipulated and required by the EIA and RAP, it is often impossible for local populations to differentiate between CSR and the local transfers stipulated by the contractual EIA/RAP. Local communities are often

---

[2] International Finance Corporation, World Bank Group (2012); International Finance Corporation, World Bank Group (2002); World Bank Group (2009).

[3] Aravat (2012); Svendlund Private Interview (2012).

uninformed about the difference between rules shaping these kinds of investments, and there is significant overlap between the goods and services that the EIA/RAP requires as compensation and those that firms choose to engage in that constitute CSR. Firms often make promises about the potential benefits and local effects of the mining project to the local communities in what are called "stakeholder meetings." Stakeholder meetings are meant to include local leadership and members of the community as part of a consultation process, following the norms of "participatory development" and free, prior, and informed consent (FPIC). While these norms have become ubiquitous across transnational firms with significant operational footprints, the existing variance in governance outcomes across operations held by a single firm suggests that they are not the sole driver of firm incentives. During the stakeholder meetings, firm employees, often part of a community liaison office, discuss the local and national effects of the mine, and firms–community liaisons convey compensation and benefits that the community should expect to receive. The meetings serve as an opportunity for firms to convey information about what the community should expect from them over the course of mining operations.

However, local populations are often largely unaware of the extent to which these promises are backed by the contractual agreement of the EIA/RAP or whether they are a part of voluntary CSR. As a result, community members often find it difficult to differentiate between the two practices. Furthermore, many firms see the stipulation and superficial fulfillment of these assessments and plans merely as "box ticking" exercises.[4] In addition to the provisions stipulated in the international guidelines and the resource extraction contract with the government, firms also make extra-contractual decisions about the existence and size of transfers to the local population. As a result, the total package that extractive firms offer varies, and it varies independently of stipulations for social and environmental spending in the contract.

In addition to variability in the firm's social and environmental spending, the firm must consider site specific variation in the fixed, marginal, labor, and capital costs, as well as the technological transfer possibilities, which are shaped by the national and subnational context in which firms decide to invest. The nature of the deposit, for example, can shape the cost per weight of unit extracted, as well as the infrastructure required for

---

[4] Davies Private Interview (2012).

extraction, shaping both the marginal and fixed costs respectively. Labor costs are likely to be shaped both by the history of mining in the region (and thus availability of skilled workers), and by government policy on local content. For example, Zambia has a "hire local" policy, requiring that mining firms hire workers from populations living in the province. Though these costs vary significantly, they are factored into the decision to invest in the project in the first place (at least to the extent that they are known). The interaction I am concerned with is that which occurs after the firm has already decided to invest – thus the firm has already evaluated the investment as "bankable" – i.e., profitable given its cost structure. Importantly, by the time the firm gets to the EIA stage, these other known and measurable costs have been factored in to the firm's decision to invest.

However, in spite of this variation in cost structure across project sites, there is a shared characteristic of the investment context for many mining companies in Africa. In general, though certainly not without exception, the environment is one of high transaction costs. One source of these transaction costs is the constellation and level of enforcement of property rights over land. As I will detail further in the next section, property rights on the continent are often overlapping, with customary and formal land tenure systems often applied to the same parcels of land. In addition, enforcement of either type of property rights institution varies. Customary rights holders rely on local chiefs or customary authorities to delineate and enforce property rights, while those with formal titles often rely on a relatively weak state for enforcement. This creates both informational search costs for the firm since it may allocate resources to understand the local property rights system, as well as bargaining and decision-making costs since the firm may bargain with local chiefs and communities for access to land.[5] Subsoil and land rights are held by the state (by and large across the continent), and thus the government is the relevant party to the contract. However, the often limited reach of the government where mineral extraction occurs means that firms are tasked with negotiating access to land with local actors, regardless of the formal property rights regime that is in place. Thus, firms are often left to make implicit contracts with the local population, about which

---

[5] Christensen, Hartman, and Samii (n.d.) focus on the difference between internationally "legible," private, individual property rights (yielding low transaction costs) and internationally "illegible," customary community rights (resulting in higher transaction costs) as differential drivers of investment.

the government is only concerned when the violation of this contract threatens to undermine the formal contract between the government and the firm. As a consequence, in addition to the fixed and marginal costs of production, firms are also faced with a high transaction cost environment in which they incur costs to securing a sort of unofficial property right to the land required for mining. While these transaction costs most certainly vary across mining projects, they are not known at the outset, and may be thought of as the ultimate cost of buying off the population (or what will be called the cost of the transfer, $\chi(T)$, in the next chapter).

Local Residents and Livelihoods

The random distribution of natural resource deposits and the somewhat less random distribution of mines for their extraction ensures a level of heterogeneity across local mining communities. Identifying generalizable characteristics and preferences of communities that live around mining sites is therefore difficult, and would require significant subnational data that is not available. Forms and degrees of social cohesion that might shape the capacity to mobilize is likely to vary dramatically across space (and time for that matter), and the structure of local formal and informal institutions is shaped by the many variations of history. I therefore limit my description of local mining communities to the ways in which the mine boundaries might intersect or interfere with livelihoods and expectations of local residents. However, it is the case that sites of extraction tend to occur in areas with lower population density – the vast majority of mining sites have fewer than 300 people per km^2. Some extractive sites occur near or in a city, but this is less common because of the land requirements for large-scale industrial mining.

Communities living in and around mining sites vary in asset ownership and livelihoods derivation. Because extractive sites tend to occur in regions of lower population density and because other forms of investment, such as manufacturing, have been, on average, limited relative to extractive foreign direct investment (FDI) in Africa, much of the population in these areas continues to rely on more rural forms of livelihood derivation. These include a mixture of subsistence and cash-based activities including small holder farming, harvesting of timber and non-timber products from forests, fishing, and the processing and sale of other natural resources. Those livelihoods that rely less on the natural environment include local service provision and small business or shop owners.

When natural resource concessions are awarded to firms, they may overlap with existing villages, or land formally or informally claimed by local residents. Property rights vary significantly across the continent in formality, and fluidity, and they often overlap with the formal land title of the mineral concession. It has been estimated that close to 75 percent of the land in sub-Saharan Africa is held under some form of customary land tenure.[6] The variance here is significant, however (90 percent of land in Mozambique, 78 percent of land in Ghana, and 10 to 13 percent of land in South Africa), and the degree to which individuals have formal land titling corresponds in part to the degree of urbanization, as formal titling is more common in urban regions. Attempts to clarify and formalize property rights advanced in several countries (Burkina Faso, Niger, South Africa, Mozambique, Ethiopia, Ghana, Kenya, Rwanda, and Uganda).[7] However, as Joireman (2008) notes, the effective implementation of these laws in regions far from the political center is difficult across much of the continent. In fact, traditional authorities still control access to land and land tenure in much of rural Africa, especially since the 1990s, a period that saw a reduction in central government led attempts to formalize rural land titles, and a greater role for local actors.[8] Thus, it is often the case that communities living in and around mines are rural, and have informal institutions securing access to land often based on local, traditional authorities. The absence of formal property rights regimes, or the overlapping of customary and formal property rights regimes affect whether there are legal avenues for claim making by local populations, potentially lessening the need for protest.

The geographically fixed nature of natural resources makes local populations likely to make claims to the resource or revenues from its extraction, a phenomenon dubbed "local resource nationalism" by some.[9] While property rights regimes affect whether there are legal avenues for claim making by local populations, it is reasonable that residents feel greater entitlement to the resource over which they live, even if they have no formal claim to it, than they might feel toward other types of FDI. This is particularly true if residents are adversely affected by its extraction.

[6] Augustinus (2003).
[7] Joireman (2008).
[8] Bruce and Knox (2009).
[9] Aravat (2012).

Thus, as a result of claims to ownership of the benefits of resource extraction, or as a result of the negative externalities of extraction, local residents develop strong expectations about how extractive firms should behave. In addition, expectations of benefits from natural resource extraction also result from socialist histories across much of Africa. State ownership of natural resource extractive firms, which was common before the 1990s, often meant that governments provided cradle-to-grave welfare benefits for workers, and built towns in and around mining sites. Because of government involvement, communities developed strong expectations about the social and economic benefits that mining might yield. And firms are often present and visible to local communities even in the early stages of mining, including the exploration and feasibility stages, making them the target of these expectations.

The Government

Much has been written about the nature of the state in Africa.[10] While the spatial distribution of the state is often taken for granted, in part as a result of national level indicators that constitute the bulk of comparative measurement, most scholars (and travelers, for that matter) recognize that the reach of the state is in fact uneven. Nowhere is it more uneven than in the post-colonial "weak states" of Africa. Arguably, the fundamental challenge of the sovereign state is how to extract resources while retaining authority.

On the Revenue Imperative across Africa. The revenue imperative is central for all sovereign states: the capacity to extract wealth is necessary for the funding of the state apparatus. It is so fundamental as to be considered a measure of the degree of state-ness. As Herbst (2000) wrote, "there is no better measure of a state's reach than its ability to collect taxes" (p. 113). Yet, across the African continent, the collection of taxes from non-trade sectors of the economy is notably low. As van de Walle (2001) writes, "Some African states cannot even claim to fully control the territory over which they declare sovereignty. Tax and tariff collection is weak, laws are unevenly applied, superiors exert little authority on subordinates and the entire administration is weakened by non-developmental concerns such as patronage and rent seeking" (van de Walle 2001, p. 55).

---

[10] Herbst (2000), Mamdani (1996), Englebert (2002), Boone (2003), Reno (1997), and Bates (2005), to name a few.

Historical reliance on non-tax revenue and low economic integration have undermined the incentive to extend the state's extractive capacity far outside of the political center. As has been detailed by Herbst (2000), a legacy of colonial regimes was that the capacity to collect income taxes was limited – African countries continued to rely on non-tax, or easily taxable revenue. Because of low population densities, and informal, non-European forms of property rights, colonial administrations relied on taxing trade. As a consequence, leaders have been under "very little pressure to expand their taxation systems in particular so that the state would have a physical presence throughout the country. Indeed there was often no immediate imperative to improve tax collection in the hinterlands or to do the necessary work so that those outside of the capital could be bound to the state through symbolic politics" (Herbst 2000, p. 134).

One indicator of physical presence of the state is the access to hinter regions through the paving of roads. Across the continent, approximately 53 percent of roads are unpaved, and less than half of Africa's rural population has access to an all-season road.[11] Access to much of the territory within African states has been limited for some time, impeding the development of rural regions of the country and limiting state access. As of 1988, only 52 percent of the paved roads in Africa were rated as being in "good" condition, while 25 percent were in fair, and 23 percent were in poor condition. Of unpaved roads, only 29 percent were rated as good, 32 percent fair, and 39 percent poor. By 2004, approximately 41 percent of the roads in Africa were still considered in poor condition.[12] By 2008, there were approximately 204 km of road per 1,000 km of land.[13] This continues to increase, but Africa still remains far below the rest of the world.

Consequently, economic integration over the physical space of sovereign territory in Africa has been, on average, limited. Low spatial economic integration of the country has undermined economic development in the hinterlands, and increased the cost of extracting taxes. Even by the late 1990s, nearly 40 years after the majority of African countries became independent, most relied much more on non-tax revenue and taxes on international trade and transactions than did developing countries in other regions of the world. This continues to be true, even after widespread (if now stalled) implementation of structural adjustment

[11] *African Natural Resources Center* (n.d.).
[12] Program (2006).
[13] World Bank (2009); Yepes, Pierce, and Foster (2009).

programs in the late 1980s and early 1990s. Across the continent, average tax revenue as a percentage of gross domestic product (GDP) has remained between 15 and 18 percent of GDP since 1990.[14]

Instead, many African governments have tended to rely on non-tax revenue, including natural resource rents. In 1990, minerals accounted for more than 50 percent of foreign exchange earnings in at least 12 African countries.[15] Grants and other non-tax revenue, as a percentage of total government revenue, has increased from 18.6 percent in 1990 to 25.1 percent in 2014 (peaking at 30 percent in 2010), while taxes on international trade have decreased from an average of 25.6 percent in 1990 to 14.3 percent in 2014. Average total natural resource rents as a percentage of GDP have remained at approximately 13 percent in that same time frame.

Actual revenues from natural resources at the country level are difficult to measure, as most African governments do not report total revenues collected from natural resources. Between 2000 and 2004, of the 20 countries with the largest percentage of export revenue from minerals or metals, nine were African countries. Leading the way were Guinea (at 89.8 percent), Botswana (87.2 percent), and Zambia (61.5 percent).[16] Royalty rates on minerals in Africa tend to range from 0 to 12 percent, but this does not include the significant fees and taxes that governments also collect. As many scholars have pointed out, the historical thinness of the African state has been perpetuated by over reliance on non-tax revenue.

Retaining Authority: On the Nature of Political Support in Africa. The nature of state building and the importance of popular support for leaders across Africa is of course contextual, but at its core, not unique. Bureaucratic capacity to carry out state functions over space (what Mann (1984) would call "infrastructural power"), is low on average. However, leaders still rely, to varying degrees, on political support from citizens in order to retain authority and so rely on alternative ways of building and retaining political support. At least up until 1990, neo-patrimonialism, a form of regime in which the executive relies on personal patronage to maintain authority, as opposed to ideology or rule of law, was the

---

[14] *World Development Indicators | Data* (n.d.).

[15] Morgan and Staff (2000).

[16] *Transnational Corporations, Extractive Industries and Development* (2007).

dominant regime type across the continent.[17] As Bratton and van de Walle note, "The essence of neo-patrimonialism is the award by public officials of personal favors, both within the state (notably public sector jobs), and in society (for instance, licenses, contracts, and projects). In return for material rewards, clients mobilize political support and refer all decisions upward as a mark of deference to patrons" (Bratton and van de Walle 1994, p. 458). They argue that neopatrimonialism is the "core feature" of politics in Africa.

In the post-colonial period, and in the absence of a uniform and well funded bureaucracy, political leaders developed various strategies to mobilize and extract political support outside of geographic political centers. Various forms of devolution to local elites, such as chiefs, reflected attempts by African governments to consolidate support in more rural areas. In post-independence Cote d'Ivoire, Boone (1998) notes that there were "few official sites, positions, or organizations in the rural areas that offered local people direct access to state resources" (Boone 1998, p. 11). In contrast, the new government of Ghana sought to create a more visible network of state institutions at the local level. The ruling CPP party worked through these outposts to gain support for the government by distributing benefits. Similarly, Senegal's Senghor attempted to extend state agencies into the most profitable groundnut basins in rural regions, though in this case, the Senegalese government did so through existing networks of local and traditional authorities. Notably, in these cases the relevant regions tended to be the most economically valuable, given their production of groundnut. In Mozambique, while economic penetration of newly private enterprises has been uneven, the Frelimo party has sought opportunities to increase political legitimacy and to create support for its policy agenda.[18] These cases demonstrate that the degree and nature of the extension of the state took different forms in the immediate aftermath of decolonization, where leaders have often relied on local chiefs or other intermediaries to secure support for their tenure.

By the 1990s, a sort of neo-patrimonial democracy became common. Between 1990 and 1993, a majority of African countries held competitive elections, either at the presidential or parliamentary level. While this did not erase neo-patrimonial tendencies, it brought the procedural nature of multi-party democracy to the fore. More importantly, it

---

[17] Bratton and van de Walle (1994).
[18] Pitcher (1996).

created a stronger impetus to build political support for the regime across a broader coalition, economically, politically and geographically.

The local state, however, did not become uniformly or observably distributed over space. Municipal offices constitute outposts of the state, but on average, they rely fundamentally on the center for resources. Where decentralization has occurred, it has been informal and incomplete.[19] To be sure, manifestations of the local state vary, and party politics and ethnic identities shape the extent to which the interests of the local outposts of the state align perfectly with the center. However, limited formal decentralization (resulting in limited resources and autonomy) and the limited broadcasting of the state over space described by Herbst, suggest that where there are localized physical manifestations of the state, capacity is limited, especially in the face of local hierarchies of power that may exist outside of the state.[20]

It is necessary to pause here to acknowledge that differentiating between efforts toward building political support and efforts towards building state legitimacy presents a significant empirical and theoretical challenge. Regime interest in political support is often more immediate than the consolidation of the state through building long-term legitimacy in a sparsely populated region far from the seat of power. In particular, strategies of state engagement in a region are likely to reflect the immediate demands of political support for the continued survival of a leader or the importance of the revenue potential from the region. However, in regions of historically limited state presence, building political support in order to contribute to the government's support base may be a tool for building legitimacy in the state as a local actor, regardless of the party or leader in power. Thus regions of limited state presence, often far from the political capital, are likely to be regions wherein populations are skeptical of the state, and thus the consequences of government response to firm behavior and local resistance are likely to have longer-term effects. To be sure, there are exceptions, but my aim is not to assess the relationship between short-term political support building and longer-term legitimacy building, but only to make explicit the assumption that, in regions of limited state presence, strategies of achieving these two goals are unlikely to be observably or significantly different.

In sum, given weak capacities to raise taxes, an enduring reliance on non-tax revenue, governments are likely to give particular strategic

---

[19] Ribot (2002b).
[20] Boone (1998).

importance to revenues from natural resources. However, given limited state presence in the hinterlands, but a need to secure political support for leaders to remain in power, states have incentives to look for low-cost ways to build and maintain support.

MECHANISMS AND A LOGIC OF GOVERNANCE

In this section, I detail how these actors interact to yield different local governance outcomes. Broadly speaking, the conventional wisdom in political science is that natural resources are a "free" source of revenue for the government: the cost of obtaining the rents from their extraction is the economic cost of extracting them. In comparison to tax revenue, which can distort productive incentives and requires an implicit or explicit contract with taxpayers about the use of such revenue, revenues derived from natural resources do not come with obligations, nor do they impose a significant bargaining cost for obtaining them. This is the foundational assumption behind much of the literature about the resource curse, which compares natural resource revenue to foreign aid and other forms of non-tax revenue.[21]

Yet, there are often barriers that make it costly for states to access rents from natural resource extraction. Some of these derive from the local context of extraction. Snyder and Bhavnani (2005) point out, for instance, that the accrual of natural resource revenue to the state is contingent on the mode of extraction: industrially extracted minerals create larger tax handles than artisanal mining. Yet, the stability of access to these revenues is shaped by the local context even across industrially mine extractive sites. Natural resource extraction creates the potential for costly (if localized) conflict. Ultimately, natural resource rents are not "free," and the costs of obtaining them are shaped by variation in specific characteristics of the extractive context, including the presence of an embedded population.

In the following paragraphs I detail the mechanisms driving outcomes in extractive regions, or *how* actors' preferences and behaviors lead to different outcomes. They may be summarized in the following way. Though extractive regions are often far from the political center of a country, they hold significant revenue potential for both an extractive firm and the state, both of which aim to ensure continued profits from resource extraction. Instances of protest and resistance, which local

[21] Morrison (2009).

residents might engage if they are negatively affected by extractive externalities or excluded from economic benefits, can interrupt production.
As a result, firms may offer some transfer, often in the form of collective
goods and services, to the local population to secure local support and
prevent costly protest. But the monetary costs of interruptions in production accrue to both the firm and the government, and so the state
also experiences monetary costs should the firm fail to secure the support of the local population. Unlike the firm, however, the government
faces potential political costs to protest, depending on how it responds.
Government repression may carry with it costs to its political support
base, while protecting revenues by immediately allowing production to
continue. A government decision to compel firms to secure approval by
providing compensation, can increase the government's support in the
region, though it may be economically costly.

On Social Mobilization

Because of the high expectations held by local populations about the
potential benefits of mining, when the negative externalities of mining affect the livelihoods of local communities, communities that can
overcome barriers to collective action may engage in forms of social
mobilization such as protests or riots. However, whether social mobilization occurs depends on a multitude of factors. I focus on three here.
First, the fundamental barriers to collective action have been detailed by
a broad literature,[22] and include heterogeneity and size of the group,
as well as degree of organization, information, and networks that allow
individuals to respond not only to an individual signal about the likelihood that participation is warranted, but also to observe a signal from
their peers. Thus, the distribution of radical sentiment grievances among
the potentially mobilized population is likely to affect whether mobilization occurs. In and around mines, heterogeneity of the effects of the
mine on individual asset ownership and livelihoods is another relevant
heterogeneity.

Second, expectations about the likelihood that such mobilization will
be effective in changing firm behavior matter in understanding when
and whether it will occur. Characteristics of the local mining context
that shape the vulnerability of extraction to interruption can affect

---

[22] Marwell and Oliver (1993), Lohmann (1994), Ostrom (2014), Olson (2009), and
  Lichbach (1994).

the likelihood that social mobilization will be effective. Specifically, the infrastructure for natural resource extraction presents a target at which local populations can direct resistance efforts. It both lowers barriers to collective action because it presents a focal point, and it can increase the ease of imposing costs on the firm and government. Several cases highlighted by Downey et al. (2010) demonstrate that protesters make use of the mining infrastructure to interrupt extraction. In China in 2005, residents blockaded the entrance to a manganese mine to protest contamination of the water supply. In Brazil in 1998, local residents blockaded the road to a development parcel near a newly developed iron ore and manganese extractive site. In these cases, the natural resource constituted significant revenue potential for a government in a region with limited infrastructure for extracting it. Interrupting production by targeting infrastructure is a low effort way to impose significant costs on firms, which might lead to concessions. As such, protest becomes more likely effort required to impose sufficient costs to extract concessions from the firm and government makes social mobilization more likely.

Finally, the decision to engage in protest is contingent on the expected costs to community members of doing so. In particular, expectations about the government's response to protest shape individual decisions about whether to participate. James Scott's (1987) discussion of peasant resistance in the context of significant power asymmetries demonstrates that the peasants' beliefs about the probability and severity of retaliation can shape their decision to engage in resistance, making the state's potential reaction a relevant factor in the local population's decision to protest. For example, the forced eviction of the Dayaks in Indonesia for the development of a gold mine was accompanied by repressive tactics meant to convince the villagers of the consequences, should they protest.[23] Communities that expect the government will use excessive force in response to an incident or episode of protest are less likely to engage in this type of behavior.

One can also view the local population's decision to mobilize in the following light. Because of the quasi-rent nature of natural resource extraction, surplus of extraction accrues to the firm, resulting in a struggle over access to this surplus. If the government was an accountable representative of the local community with sufficient capacity for redistribution, than this struggle might have occurred between the firm and

[23] Downey, Bonds, and Clark (2010).

the government. However, communities in these extractive regions may not be able to rely on governments to act in their interest given the revenue imperative and limited capacity. Thus communities who bear some portion of the costs of extraction may mobilize to extract their share of the surplus from the firm so as to be compensated for the localized costs of extraction. Given a weak system of property rights and variation in government accountability to local communities, local communities may perceive protest as the only way to extract concessions and protect livelihoods.

On Firm Provision of Goods

Firms recognize this potential for costly resistance near their operations, but the locational rigidity of natural resources and the magnitude of initial costs limits a firm's investment choices and exit options. As noted earlier, the distribution of mineral, metal, and energy resources is, for the most part, random. The construction of an industrial mine can cost over US$1 billion.[24] Sunk costs deter relocation, which is further exacerbated by limited geographic distribution of the resource. Consequently, regions of extraction regularly compel interaction with a local population, leading firms to incur costs to mitigate the consequences of extraction and act as a local redistributer. Bennett (2002) and Gunningham, Kagan, and Thornton (2004) provide evidence that these efforts vary, discovering that "some companies took a strategic approach, such as 'buying off' the local community's objections . . . by offering to supply it with better-quality drinking water" (Gunningham, Kagan, and Thornton 2004, p. 326). In these cases, the firm incurs the costs of providing goods to the local population in order to avoid future, larger costs of protest. As work by Brousseau and Farès (2000a) and Wolf, Deitelhoff, and Engert (2007) indicates, specific local conditions shape the costs of this kind of firm behavior in a given region and thus, whether firms engage in this kind of behavior.

For firms, one might naturally suggest that local support is important for firms because international norms create reputation costs for poor behavior. Since the 1990s, most large-scale firms have a community liaison or office of community affairs in order to develop and maintain a relationship with community members, in part as a response to the norms cascade. However, reliance on international norms for

---

[24] *Transnational Corporations, Extractive Industries and Development* (2007).

constraining and shaping firm behavior requires that their local behavior and its consequences are internationally observable, or that there is an avenue for conveying information to international actors with sanctioning capacity. Furthermore, it assumes that firms care specifically about international reputation costs. While firms often have entire teams of personnel devoted to monitoring shifts in stock prices that might reflect this priority, the operational offices at the project sites are arguably concerned more with immediate threats to their operations (and the way these threats are expected to be dealt with by the state). These are the phenomena that may grow large enough to signal potentially sanctioning actors of poor firm behavior, but present a more immediate threat to firm production and personnel. The manifestation of this concern is conveyed through the frequent mention and discussion by firm community liaisons of the concept of "a social license to operate" obtained through "building local legitimacy" in and around the firm's site of operation. The development of such an abstract license for most firms means a very concrete and material set of processes and tasks including holding local meetings, providing social goods and services, and mitigating any adverse environmental consequences of their operations.

Providing collective goods to local residents as a way to secure support and prevent costly resistance is likely to be less expensive than identifying individuals who are likely to engage in sabotage, and providing private goods to them over the course of the mine's life. The average duration of a mine is approximately 30 years, making the provision of collective goods and the mitigation of environmental consequences less costly in the long run than identifying individuals that are particularly unhappy and more importantly, who may multiply over time, and providing individual private goods to an increasing number of individuals. It also has the added benefit of mitigating the response by local residents to accidents or firm behaviors that unintentionally harm local communities. To be sure, we do observe the provision of private goods to local leaders at earlier points in the exploration process, where local chiefs often serve as immediate gatekeepers to land for prospecting activity. But the continued provision of a set of compensatory goods to the local population is likely to contribute to a durable acceptance of firm operations over the course of a mining project. Building local support is an explicit form of risk management for firms, as Hönke (2009) notes. Furthermore, Henisz, Dorobantu, and Nartey (2014) indicate that stakeholder satisfaction yields increases in firm financial outcomes, lending additional support to the idea that firms see costs to failing to obtain support from local denizens.

The costs associated with this failure can be significant. In a study of 50 company–community conflicts, Franks et al. (2014) found that the most frequent costs identified were those resulting from lost productivity due to delay. They found that companies can suffer as much as US$20 million per week in net present value. It was estimated that during the initial exploration phase, each day of delay costs firms approximately US$10,000 and during advance exploration, US$50,000 per day. These costs vary with the size of the mine and the volume and value of the mineral extracted. In a report by Davis and Franks (2014), the authors found that nearly half of the cases of company and community conflict involved a blockade, and approximately 33 percent resulted in damage to property, injuries, or even fatalities. These costs result from delayed production, and are likely to accrue even at the earlier stages of mining (during the exploration, feasibility, and construction phases). Costs also included added labor costs, as mining staff time diverted their attention to mitigating the conflict. Clearly, the operational risk to the firm of successful social mobilization can be significant.

In addition to these more recent measurements of costs associated with "community–company" conflict, historical events have shaped how firms have come to associate costs with the failure to obtain local support. Our collective understanding of the governance outcomes around natural resource extractive sites is the result of the generally violent outcomes that are publicly reported (Bougainville, Niger Delta, etc.). In many of these cases, governments are assumed to have rentier motivations, and firms act as a sort of "spaceship extractor," which arrives to extract a resource with minimal local engagement. While the historical record of local governance outcomes is littered with cases of the dog that didn't bark (firms did not engage locally or their engagement led to non-violent outcomes that did not attract the attention of scholars or the media), this skewed record has shaped the belief that failing to obtain legitimacy at the local level for firms has the potential to carry significant costs.

But if this is the case, why would all firms not engage in a strategy of local support-building through the provision of a combination of goods and services, in and around each and every one of their operations? Indeed firms vary in the extent to which they do so. One reason is that the costs of this support differ in each operational context. For instance, some local populations are more reliant on the natural environment for livelihoods, and thus ensuring they are not adversely affected by firm presence may be more costly than in other contexts. Firms must weigh the long-term value of local support against the cost of obtaining it. Recall that RAPs and EIAs specify the formally and legally required compensation by the firm for the local consequences of extraction. These documents present some baseline estimation of the costs of compensation. However, promises to local community members over the course of consultations often include some combination of these requirements as well as voluntary commitments by the firm, and frequently it is not clear to community members which of these they are legally entitled to, and which are voluntary commitments.

In sum, there is some literature that links corporate social performance with the overall financial performance of a firm,[25] but more limited discussion of local discontent at operational sites, which is of particular concern for mining firms and may drive behavior. Local support shapes firm strategies of local engagement, since loss of local support can result in local discontent, thus threatening the firm's existing and future production. Mining infrastructure is a fixed, sunk cost, and often requires low effort to significantly affect firm operations by interrupting production. Barricading a railroad may only require a relatively small number of people to stop resource extraction or production for several days incentivizing the firm to incur costs to keep communities from doing so.

In addition to the locally determined cost of the transfer, whether firms have an incentive to live up to these promises, particularly in regions of weak state presence, depends on two other factors. First, local firm behavior depends on the likelihood that the affected local population will actually engage in behavior, such as protest or sabotage, that imposes costs on the firm and the anticipated size of the costs associated with interrupted production. Second, it depends on how firms anticipate the government might respond if social mobilization does occur. Neither of these can be evaluated in isolation from existing and historical state engagement in the region.

On Government Repression and Enforcement

Local configurations of the state are important for understanding why, even in the absence of firm efforts to build local support through the provision of a combination of public and private compensatory goods and mitigation of environmental consequences, local residents may still

---

[25] Griffin and Mahon (1997); McWilliams and Siegel (2000); and Orlitzky, Schmidt, and Rynes (2003) are a few.

decide not to engage in resistance against the firm. Observably, the uninterrupted operations of a firm may be the outcome of local support or just a failure to protest on the part of the local population (a sort of mere acquiescence). Local communities may decide not to protest either because the firm has obtained local support for their operations, or because the local population's fear of government response to resistance deters them from doing so. This latter outcome is the result of local acquiescence, as opposed to actual acceptance or legitimacy of the firm's activities. Thus the local governance outcomes I am concerned with cannot only be explained through analysis of the interactions of the firm and local population, but must also include the existing and historical role of the state in the region. Local communities who expect repression may be less likely to engage in resistance.

When local communities do mobilize, the costs of protest accrue not only to the firm through delays and interruption in production, but also to the government. Royalties are tied to production volume and are thus also significantly affected by interruptions in production. Even delays in the commencement of production yield costs for the government. While the government may receive some use taxes and fees based on fixed inputs such as land and licensing, it loses access to otherwise available revenue from production. As a consequence, the occurrence of social mobilization provides the impetus for state engagement in the region, given its economic interest in continued production.

In response to local resistance, the government has a menu of responses from which to choose, each of which depends on the revenue imperative and the leader's reliance on political support in the region in order to stay in power. On one hand, the government may decide to compel the firm to honor its commitments in the event of protest.[26] In this "regulatory outcome," the government exercises the power of regulatory enforcement to side with the local population. Doing so is likely to increase political support in the region. As Brass (2016) demonstrates, the non-state provision of goods and services can improve perceptions of the state.

However, it is also the case that such enforcement may come with a cost to the government, which may be framed either in terms of future

---

[26] This builds on the idea put forth by authors such as Mayntz and Scharpf (1995), Scharpf (1997), and Héritier and Lehmkuhl (2008) that the state casts a shadow of hierarchy that can incentivize firm behavior, and the threat of state intervention can make voluntary commitments more binding.

investment or in terms of corruption. First, government enforcement of firm commitments signals a willingness to side with the local population, which may signal to future investors a hostile business environment. As a consequence, governments worry about deterring future investment by supporting local demands that effectively impose greater costs on the firm. Second, a common form of corruption in resource-dependent countries (and indeed the impetus for large-scale transparency initiatives such as the Extractive Industry Transparency Initiative) is the provision of side payments by firms to government officials. Exercising regulatory force ensures that governments forgo these side payments. While the actual amount of revenue foregone by compelling firms to provide local benefits is difficult to measure given the clandestine nature of side payments, the expectation of forgoing this revenue, particularly in the context of the strong revenue imperative, may be sufficient to drive government behavior.

On the other hand, given the monetary costs that arise from interruption of mining operations, governments may decide to respond to social mobilization with repression. Governments may rely on the use of force to quell protests, even those that are not violent, in order to ensure continued production. This amounts to effectively siding with the firm. Downey et al. (2010) provide some evidence of this, finding that governments are likely to use repressive tactics particularly to "support capital accumulation" related to resource extraction. They find that repression occurred against local populations protesting around industrial mining sites of major minerals in South Africa, Mongolia, Malaysia, China, Brazil, Tibet, Sierra Leone, Indonesia, and Papua New Guinea in the last 15 years, with forced removal of local populations in countries such as South Africa, Brazil, Sierra Leone, and Kenya. They conclude that "developing nation governments may . . . use all means necessary to protect resource extraction activities so as to meet their debt obligations, ensure continued foreign investment, and minimize conflict with more powerful nations and institutions."[27]

However, inherent in the repression and escalation literature that explores the potential deterrent or escalatory effects of repression on protest[28] is the assumption that there are potential political costs to repression (this is one explanation for renewed mobilization after repression has occurred). Thus, protest by the local population can

---

[27] Downey, Bonds, and Clark (2010), p. 424.
[28] Rasler (1996), Davenport (2007), Pierskalla (2010).

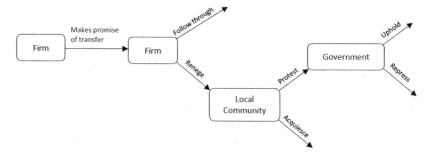

FIGURE 2.1: Sequence of interactions

result in political costs (in addition to monetary costs) on the state, particularly if the state represses such protest. However, these costs depend on the extent to which the government relies on the political support of the local population in the extractive region to retain power.

On Sequencing and Information

The preceding sections indicate the possibility of four governance outcomes: (a) the firm follows through and provides its promised transfer, (b) the firm reneges but the local population does not successfully mobilize, (c) the local population successfully mobilizes and the government responds coercively, and (d) the local population successfully mobilizes and the government enforces the firm's promise. These outcomes are the result of a particular order of interactions between the firm, community, and government, which is depicted in Figure 2.1. The firm promises a transfer to the community, often through stakeholder meetings. It may decide not to follow through on its promise, at which point the community may express its discontent by mobilizing, imposing monetary costs on the firm and government. If it successfully mobilizes, the government may intervene, either to support the firm by repressing the community, or to support the community by compelling the firm to uphold its promise.

Rational explanations of conflict tell us that, since conflict is costly, it should occur only when there are information asymmetries that lead to bargaining breakdown, or when there are commitment problems that give one party or the other an incentive to renege on an agreement. In other words, in a world in which firms know whether local populations are likely to engage in costly mobilization, they would take this into account and ensure that they provide a transfer when the community will protest, and renege when it will not. However, the collective action cost to communities of social mobilization is not known to the firm, or the government for that matter. As a result, firms and governments must make decisions about how to behave in the context of uncertainty over whether the community will successfully overcome its collective action costs to protesting. While firms and governments have some expectations over whether this is the case often the result of country-level reports that detail aggregate levels of conflict in the country, they must act based on their expectation about whether social mobilization will occur or not.

However, the local population suffers from limited information as well. If local residents knew exactly when their government was likely to use violence in response to protest, they would likely engage in protest only when the government will not repress. Whether the government represses or not is a function of its calculation about the relative enforcement costs realized in foregone revenue, and the political costliness of responding to protest with coercive force. However, local communities are unlikely to be aware of the exact nature of this calculation. In particular, while they are certainly likely to recognize their own value to the leader in terms of geographically concentrated political support, they are unlikely to have knowledge of the amount of revenue the government foregoes if it sides with them. These two sources of uncertainty – whether the local population will protest, and whether the government will repress – ensure that social conflict will occur at least some of the time.

Summarizing the Structural Conditions and Beliefs that Matter

Above, I have specified the relevant actors, their beliefs and behaviors, and the order of interactions of the firm, community, and government that lead to different outcomes. Given the order of interactions, and the information available to each actor, which factors actually shape the likelihood of different outcomes? Because the theory above suggests a strategic interaction, outcomes rely on each actor's response to the other. However, we can clarify the structural parameters and beliefs that matter for the likelihood that a particular outcome occurs. The specific values and cut points at which these parameters matter will be derived in the formal model in the next chapter. This section summarizes which aspects of the context and interaction shape the likelihood of each outcome, and I provide and test formal hypotheses in Chapters 9 and 10.

Because social mobilization may interrupt or halt mining operations, mobilization that affects a particularly valuable mine is likely to be especially costly. As the revenue derived from extraction increases, the government may be more tempted to use repression to protect a particularly valuable mine threatened by social mobilization. If a particular mine is an especially large contributor to the government's overall natural resource revenue portfolio, or to the government's revenue overall, it may be more inclined to use repression to ensure that production continues. Increased value of a particular mine should increase the likelihood of a repressive outcome if the community protests, as the interruption of more lucrative mining operation will yield greater costs. Perhaps more accurately, the state may be more willing to endure any political costs incurred by repression, if the **value of the mine** is particularly and relatively high.

This decision by the government is made while weighing the potential political cost of repression. In other words, the **political cost of repression** in the short term could outweigh the monetary value of the mine. This is particularly true if the government sees itself as especially vulnerable. A government that loses power will not be able to access the revenue extracted from a mine, and thus the first-order priority is to remain in power. As a consequence, if the local population near the mine is a pivotal constituency for a leader whose tenure is uncertain, the leader may be less willing to deploy coercive resources, deciding instead to ensure that the firm provides the promised transfer. The government will choose to uphold the community's interest, at the expense of the firm and at the expense of its own economic benefit, if it believes doing so will earn it political support, or at least acquiescence when leadership is vulnerable.

This decision is also affected by the **cost to the government of enforcing** the firm's promise. If the government believes it will forgo sufficient future mining investment or side payments from firms, it may be less willing to enforce the firm's promise. A government relying heavily on side payments from firms will perceive enforcement as more costly, as side payments often allow firms to skirt or avoid expenses such as promised social provisions. A government worried about attracting future mining investment may worry that failing to repress a protest suggests that the government is unwilling or incapable of protecting the firm's assets.

As discussed earlier, the local population's decision to mobilize (given the firm's failure to live up to its promise) depends on the **effort required to interrupt extraction**, the **belief about the likelihood of a repressive** response from the government, and its **capacity to overcome the collective action problem**. The effort required to impose sufficient costs on the firm and government through interrupting mineral production is shaped, at least in part, by the infrastructure for extraction and transport. The less effort is needed to interrupt the extraction or transport of mineral ore to processing plants or to market, the more likely communities are to mobilize. This might be called the "interruptibility" of the resource, and may be shaped by the transportation infrastructure, or the spatial layout of infrastructure for extraction. In addition, because a repressive response from the government makes mobilization more costly, the perception that repression is likely may deter the local population from protesting. Finally, inherent characteristics of the local population, such as asset or grievance heterogeneity, may determine whether it has a low or high capacity to overcome the barriers to collective action.

The factors that shape the firm's likelihood of providing promised benefits to the local population include the **government's take** of mining revenue, the **cost of providing the transfer**, and the **belief about the likelihood of interruption** of production resulting from protest. The government's take of the mining revenue and the cost of providing the transfer shape the firm's monetary costs of living up to its promise. Extractive regions in countries where the government's take from natural resource extraction is large (relative to other countries) are likely to see more repression (as explained earlier) *and* more protest. An increased government take places additional financial burden on firms, decreasing the firms available resources for the promised transfer. It may also undermine the firm's interest in providing such a transfer, preferring that the government use its increased stake to provide local benefits. In addition, if the cost of providing the transfer is too high, the firm is less likely to provide the promised transfer. One implication of this is that it is not only the environmental degradation resulting from mining that may result in a lower likelihood that the firm follows through, but that those communities who occupy particularly valuable land (well irrigated and fertile) and are displaced by mining will be more costly to compensate. Thus, comparatively better-off rural communities are actually *more* likely to mobilize, since firms will be less likely to follow through. The **value of the mine** indirectly affects the likelihood that the firm provides the promised transfer, since it determines the cost to the firm if the community mobilizes and successfully interrupts mining operations.

ALTERNATIVE THEORETICAL CLAIMS

In this section, I address alternative specifications of the interactions listed above, given that social conflict around mining has been explored by other scholars. In particular, Arce and Miller (2016) build on the analysis of Bebbington, Humphreys, Bury, Lingan, Muñoz, and Scurrah (2008) of extractive resources and mobilization in Peru, who argue that those likely to participate in mining-related protest are those whose livelihoods are likely to be threatened by mining activities. Arce and Miller differentiate between a "rights"-based motivation and a "service"-based protest. In the former, local residents express grievances relying on the frame of "environmental vulnerability." Local residents thus are more likely to protest if there are particularly large negative environmental externalities of mining. In contrast, a "service"-based protest results from distributive conflict similar to what Arellano-Yanguas (2011) describes, whereby conflict results over the local distribution of mineral revenue by formally decentralized units. The differentiation of these mechanisms suggests they are independent, and it is the result of parsing the actors into pairs: firms and communities on the one hand, and governments and communities on the other.

However, if these local outcomes are conceived of as the result of the interaction among all three actors, as described in my theory, it begins to make more sense to consider these two mechanisms along a single dimension. Much of the distributive conflict emerges as a result of what local communities believe they are entitled to, in part resulting from what they are promised by community liaisons working for the extractive firm. The calculation and promised allocation of benefits from mining companies to local residents are related to the expected local consequences of extraction (displacement for example) as well as the expected revenue generated by the mine, so separating environmental vulnerability from distributive conflict is an artificial division.

This is not to say that the local institutional context, in particular formal decentralization is irrelevant. As framed by Arellano-Yanguas (2011) and Arce and Miller (2016), distributive conflict requires a formal mechanism of downward distribution from the central government to local districts or provinces. Institutionalization and implementation of these practices in the Latin American context is much more advanced than it is in the African context.[29] For those African countries that do have formal

---

[29] While at least 10 African countries have implemented revenue decentralization since 1990, downward revenue sharing is limited; see Ribot (2002b).

mechanisms for the distribution of a percentage of extractive revenues to mining regions, the implementation of this policy is often limited for several reasons. First, corruption levels in Africa are according to business indicators and industry transparency measures, on average, higher than those in Latin America. Local governments may claim they did not receive the promised revenue. Second, local institutional capacity in Africa is notoriously low – even if rents are distributed at the stipulated rate, the amount of personnel and infrastructure for the implementation of local service and works projects that might serve as visible indicators of resource rent redistribution in regions far from the economic or political capital is limited. Finally, it is often the case that formal decentralization is a reflection of the central government exerting more control (not less), since formal decentralization is an attempt to formally constrain local actors, as described by Ribot (2002a).

More importantly, the firm can act as a local distributor, not unlike Baron's (2001) model of private politics. In the context of weak states and large extractive firms, it is firms that are the relevant actor, and thus distributive conflict that is traditionally described as deriving from formal state institutions becomes inseparable from rights-driven protests that are more directly tied to mining activity. Thus, even in the presence of formal institutions of decentralization (which supposedly provide local government with access to mining revenue, while ensuring autonomy), a weak central government is unlikely to have the will or capacity to devolve resources and influence to local government officials.

One might argue that these two types of government response to social mobilization around mining (enforce or repress) are somewhat coarse, and it is certainly the case that governments might use some combination of these two strategies, or might do nothing at all in response to protest. Yet distilling the government response into these two discrete responses provides the clearest reflection of how government preferences might play out on the ground. In his analysis of government and corporate response to protest around the Niger Delta, Frynas (2001) identifies these strategies as well. It should be noted that he also identifies a third type of government response: the reliance on a public relations campaign to quell discontent. I omit this strategy here because, as Frynas describes it, it is a strategy that appears aimed at lessening the reputation costs of protest, and not a direct response to protesters on the ground.

Furthermore, one might argue that the government (or the firm, for that matter) has the option to buy off individual protesters. This might happen at one of two different points in the course of the interaction.

First, the government could buy off individual *potential* protesters. However, given the fundamental fact of incomplete information, identifying which members of the local community might potentially protest would be prohibitively costly. Firms could focus on individual local chiefs, but this presumes that the firm trusts that local leaders have sufficient influence so as to control whether costly mobilization occurs. If the firm believes the chief is a credible mobilizer, then the firm may attempt to buy him off. However, a rational chief would continuously extract payments from the firm, but, to curry favor with his own community, would suggest the firm is not following through, leading to mobilization anyway. Second, the government could co-opt individual members of the protest after the protest has begun. This would not necessarily limit costly damage and interruption to operations, and the government would still face the trade-off between siding with the firm and siding with the community.

CONCLUSION

In this chapter, I have outlined the relevant concepts and theoretical thrust of my argument. Regions of natural resource extraction constitute strategic contexts in which the interaction among extractive firms, local populations, and governments is compelled by the presence of the resource and territorialized by the concessionary allocation of extractive rights. Variance in the effect of firm presence on local governance outcomes cannot be explained without consideration of the support of the population at the local level. The local population residing in and around firm operations is an important actor, and its interactions with the firm and government are crucial for a more comprehensive explanation of local governance outcomes. Both the government and the extractive firm, to varying degrees, require local support to continue to operate. However, while the procurement of support from local communities may help to maximize firm revenue, the goal of revenue accumulation for the government may in fact be in tension with the goal of obtaining political support at the local level.

More generally, the theory outlines conditions under which a nonstate actor, in this case an extractive firm, has incentives to engage in the provision of goods and services in a defined region. It also outlines how a government can benefit from ensuring that the firm does so. The infrastructure required for extraction and the locational rigidity of the asset make the firm vulnerable to protest by local populations living in the region. The government recognizes this, and though it may lose out on revenue it collects from the firm in the event of protest, it has the added calculation of the effect of protest on its political support base. Under the assumption that the government has limited and finite resources, it can take advantage of firm presence in these areas since it can be less costly for the government to compel the firm to provide goods and services than to incur the costs of protest should they not be provided. The government can thus leverage the potential costs of protest to the firm in order to garner regional support resulting from goods provision in the region. A government's capacity to do so depends on the relative costs (monetary and political) of protest to and each actor's beliefs about each other.

In the next chapter, I refine this theory with the development of a formal model that disciplines the actors, their interactions, and their preferences to better specify when we are likely to observe each outcome. The model and its analysis are motivated by the post-1990s context described above, in which firms under pressure from international institutions and the norms they perpetuate make explicit promises regarding the provision of some compensation or benefits.

3

Model: A (More) Formal Logic

In the last chapter I provided a theoretical argument about governance in regions of natural resource extraction. I described the relevant actors and their preferences, and detailed how their interactions yielded different governance outcomes. In this chapter I formalize the logic underlying the theoretical argument with a game theoretic model.

A formal model is a precise and logically consistent specification of the actors, preferences, and possible actions of each of the actors that yields the conditions under which the outcomes of interest occur. Rules of logic and mathematics allow for the identification and evaluation of the outcomes that occur in equilibrium. While all models of the real world are wrong in some way (by way of being reductions of more-complex phenomena), formal models serve several useful purposes, three of which I focus on here.

First, formal models can allow a particular phenomenon or interaction to be broken down into its component parts. A formal model allows the articulation of answers to the following questions: Which actors matter for the outcomes of interest? For the firm, government and local community, what would each actor like to have happen? What kinds of actions are available to these actors in order to achieve these goals, and in what order do they occur? And which actors have information about others' preferences and actions at what point in the interaction? Articulating answers to these questions can compel precision and transparency in our assumptions. This is particularly important for phenomena that have been under-theorized, and thus lack a clear foundation of the relevant actors and environment in which any theory should be situated. Significant qualitative and case-based scholarship of local conflict near mines, particularly in South America,[1] and more quantitative evaluation of the empirical regularities of protest around mining sites have provided a foundation and justification for focus on these regions and their politics. However, a general theory that explains the broad range of outcomes that includes not only protest, but also firm concession and government repression is not yet available. The outcomes in these regions remain under-theorized, and so naming the parts, including defining the relevant actors, their preferences, and the order and nature of the actions they may take is therefore a particularly useful endeavor.

Second, a formal model allows us to identify relevant constraints on these actors. Under what conditions are actors able to realize their preferences? For example, when is the government able to avoid protest and maximize the revenue it captures from the mine? When are governments more likely to rely on coercion in response to a protest? When do communities receive a local transfer from the extractive firms and when do firms fail to provide these transfers? Evaluating the conditions under which each outcome occurs in equilibrium provides insight into which parameters matter in shaping how actors realize their preferred outcomes.

Finally, a formal model can provide for a clear statement of relevant cut points of the parameters that shape the likelihood of each equilibrium outcome. For instance, *how much* does the value of the mine matter relative to the tax rate in affecting the likelihood of repression? At what point is it too costly for communities to protest? A formal model allows for the identification of relative values of each of these parameters. This is perhaps the most common justification for the development or use of a formal model in political science, as it allows for the derivation of clear, often testable hypotheses.

Ferejohn and Satz (1995) argue that to make a sufficiently useful theoretical contribution, a formal model relying on a rational choice approach must do at least one of the following things: (a) it must help to identify a new problem that requires explanation, often thereby shifting the research agenda of what needs to be explained, or (b) it must provide a unifying explanation for what are otherwise apparently unrelated phenomenon. I submit, if brazenly, that the model in this chapter does both of these things.

First it identifies or, more accurately, reframes an existing problem in the literature: it suggests that understanding extractive firm behavior requires acknowledging the relevance of a locally embedded,

---

[1] Arce (2014), Arellano-Yanguas (2011).

geographically defined population. It conveys that understanding the local politics of natural resource extraction is (at least) a three-actor problem: firm-state,[2] state-population, or firm-population,[3] interactions are insufficient for understanding local outcomes. New theories need to incorporate all three of these actors to understand the variation in outcomes of resistance, repression, and goods provision around natural resources. Furthermore, it suggests a broader question that has received little attention in the literature in comparative and world politics: how do non-state actors affect governance outcomes at the subnational level? Specifically, how can we think about the ways that firm presence might affect local outcomes of protest, repression, and goods provision? Understanding extractive regions as strategic contexts in this way not only explains the range of outcomes observed across extractive contexts demonstrating the need to consider (at least) three relevant actors in the local space, but it provides a lens for understanding subnational governance outcomes more broadly.

Second, this model provides a unifying explanation of several phenomenon that have heretofore been parts of several different literatures. There is a growing literature on mobilization around extractivism, which relies on both qualitative and quantitative methodological approaches to understand when communities mobilize in areas of resource extraction. These studies tend to focus on issues of environmental grievances and limited local institutions for the redistribution of benefits of natural resource extraction. Separately, there is a literature linking the use of government repression in resource-rich states. Much of this literature links natural resource rents with generally coercive states, though, as mentioned, scholars such as Downey, Bonds, and Clark (2010), Hönke (2009), and Maystadt et al. (2014) have considered the more localized use of repression in and around natural resources. Furthermore, literatures on corporate social responsibility and on non-state goods provision describe normative cascades and state capacity shortfalls that result in goods and service provision by non-state actors, respectively. However, the formal model here allows me to link all of the outcomes described separately in these literatures. I am able to explain incentives for goods provision by firms, mobilization by communities in extractive regions, and the use of government repression. In doing so, a single mechanistic process is able to unify all three of these outcomes – previously compartmentalized into disparate literatures.

[2] Vernon (1971)
[3] Baron (2001)

The construction of this formal model was an iterative process in which I traversed repeatedly between the field and the modeling board. Though my observations in the field suggested the importance of context as shaped by space and place, there were similarities that seemed to be shared across the cases I encountered. Mining brought with it great expectations, which were manifest in the promises made by mining firms but which did not always come to fruition. Firms referred regularly to their fear of the community's reaction and its effect on mining operations. And governments became visible primarily when conflict arose. As a result of these observations, I began drawing out the interactions among relevant groups (i.e. those groups integral to shaping the range of outcomes near mines). I outlined between five and eight different models, but settled on three that I carried with me on my next journey into the field. While there, I posed questions to the proposed relevant actors, observed the environment, and combed through archives of media and policy documents in order to first decide on the model that best captured the general interaction, and then to calibrate the actors, preferences, and interactions in that model to best reflect my field experience.

In sum, the goal of the model that follows is to detail the mechanisms that lead to different outcomes in regions of natural resource extraction by providing a formal representation of the theory detailed in the previous chapter. The model describes the strategic interaction between a firm, government, and local population in an extractive region to understand the conditions under which (a) a firm invests in mitigating environmental consequences and providing compensation to a local population, (b) a local population engages in protest in response to firm operations, and (c) the government represses the local population in the event of protest. Field work, including interviews with employees of extractive firms, consultants, local residents, and government officials, in four African countries informs the assumptions underlying the model, as well as the preferences and beliefs of the government, firm, and local residents.

MODEL OVERVIEW

In the one-shot game that follows, three actors interact with incomplete information about each other. A common assumption in comparative and international politics is that conflict is costly to all parties to it. Given these costs, explanations about when conflict occurs tend to fall into two categories: conflict resulting from the existence of private information or conflict resulting from commitment problems. Regions of natural resource extraction are often regions of limited state presence, especially at the time of firm investment and, thus, constitutes an environment of limited information.[4] The context is best characterized as one of uncertainty derived from the existence of private information about the costliness of protest to the local population, and the costliness of government response to such resistance. The decision to model this as a game of incomplete information, as opposed to an enforcement problem, is the result of my empirical observations in the field. Actors' beliefs about the risks of protest and repression were central in my conversations with them, and as such they are central in the model. It is the actors' beliefs that matter in shaping the relevant cut points of the parameters. A shift in parameters or a shift in beliefs yields different cut points, at which different outcomes may emerge.

Formal models of protest and repression are somewhat limited in the strategic contexts they depict, but they present a useful departure point. While such models typically consider two actors, and seek to understand the effect of repression on protest, this literature demonstrates that repression can in fact carry political costs, in addition to the monetary costs modeled in other canonical models of larger-scale phenomena (such as Acemoglu and Robinson (2001)). I am interested precisely in when governments employ repression to protect access to revenue from natural resources, given that repression has political costs, which might vary. In the next section I lay out the parameters and actors, and then I outline the order of play and the outcomes that result.

Parameters

Consider three actors in a region of natural resource extraction: the government (G), the extractive firm (F), and the local population (LP). The firm makes profit, π on extraction. The profit parameter, π, takes into consideration the known cost structure of the project at the time of investment. Such cost structures are likely to vary across projects, ensuring that the profit margin differs at each project site. The firm must pay $\tau\pi$ (where τ is a general tax rate on resource revenue) to the government.[5] Once the firm begins extracting the resource, it produces

---

[4] This does not necessarily preclude the potential for commitment problems to emerge in the long run, but an asymmetric information foil captures the absence of local knowledge that is an overarching characteristic of the regions in which I am interested in explaining at the time of investment.

[5] In this model, τ is a parameter determined before the game, and the government cannot alter the tax rate during the game.

environmental externalities, L, which affect the local population negatively if the firm does not incur costs to mitigate or prevent them. For
example, toxic run-off from a mine may affect the local population's
capacity to grow crops. Alternatively, local populations may be displaced
as a result of the mining activities. As a result, the firm may choose to
make a transfer, T, which may be some combination of goods and services and monetary compensation to the local population in order to
compensate them for this loss.[6] Such transfers by the firm often include
infrastructure, local training for employment, social services such as a
medical clinic or school, and in the case of resettlement, new housing
and land allocation. There may be direct positive consequences of some
of these transfers for the firm. For instance, the building and maintenance of roads is both a good for the local population and lowers the
cost of operations for the company, and thus may not be a net cost to
the firm. The transfer includes those goods and services that represent an
investment that the firm would not otherwise make if there was no local
population in the area.

The environmental externalities of extraction differ across space. For
example, mines that require significant areas of land for mine construction, overburden piles, and tailings ponds are likely to impose greater
costs on local communities, especially if much of that is arable land
on which local communities rely. Alternatively, mines require varying
degrees of water for the leaching process, and regions of water scarcity
will face significant competition over access to scarce water resources.
Consequently, the cost to mitigating L, and thus the cost of providing
transfer T varies with the local externalities of extraction, and thus the
cost to the firm of making transfer T is $\chi(T)$.[7] Note that when the
local population receives the transfer, it also avoids the externalities of
extraction, and similarly, when the local population does not receive the
transfer, it endures adverse consequences of extraction. Thus, the parameters L and T are linked, and may be considered the local population's
"stake." Furthermore, the parameter $\chi(T)$ can be thought of as the local,
realized transaction cost to the firm in order to continue extraction and
production.

If the local population protests, it destroys some amount $r \leq \pi$ of revenues from extraction at some cost to it, c. The firm and the government
are aware of the externalities that may affect the local population, L, and

[6] The payment might also be a lump sum transfer without altering the model dynamics.
[7] $T \geq 0$, $\chi'(T) > 0$, and $\chi(T)$ is twice differentiable and convex.

the financial and political costs that will accrue if the local population protests. However, neither the firm nor the government is aware of how costly it is for the local population to protest. LP can take one of two types: LP_l and LP_h where the cost to protest to $LP_l = c_l$, and the cost to $LP_h = c_h$ ($0 \leq c_l \leq c_h$). One can think of this as the degree to which local communities face barriers to collective action, or, alternatively their perceived effort costs to engaging in protest. Neither the government nor the firm knows whether it is dealing with a local population that has a high cost of protesting or one that has a low cost.

How much the local population can destroy in protest, r, is a measure of the monetary costs the local population can impose on the firm (and the government for that matter). One empirical measure of r is the value of the resource that is extracted per day.[8] It is important to note that the resource does not need to have value in the hands of the local population. This is in contrast to the importance of lootability in the civil war literature described by Weinstein (2005), Snyder (2006), and others. In this case it would be an added bonus for the local population if it has high liquidity.

Whether protest occurs or not is contingent not only on the local population's type, but also how easily it can destroy r. The parameter $0 < m \leq 1$ expresses the level of *interruptibility* of natural resource extraction. The level of interruptibility is inversely defined by m, and thus the lower m is, the more interruptible the revenue stream is. One may think of m as the effort required to interrupt the resource and destroy r. For example, underground mines with a single point of entry or exit are relatively easy to interrupt in comparison to open pit mines with multiple access point. Mines with limited access points or singular transport routes require fewer resources, less organization among fewer people, and less time to interrupt. In the next chapter, a case analysis of coal in Mozambique demonstrates how only a single railroad that takes coal from mines in Tete to the port of Beira is particularly vulnerable. If there is a single avenue for transporting the extracted resource to market or a processing facility (or limited redundancies in the transportation network), then m is closer to 0 than to 1.

---

[8] In addition to financial costs of protest, one might expect reputation costs to accrue to the firm when protest occurs. However, they are unlikely to affect firm behavior strategically because in order to do so they must be observable to consumers and stakeholders, which might be signaled by protest. When this is the case, the reputation cost accrues whenever the local population protests and thus only makes the value of protest worse for the firm but does not change the dynamics of the game.

If the local population protests, both the government and the firm incur some financial cost, as the destruction of r reduces the firm's taxable revenue stream. In addition to these monetary costs, the government may also incur a political cost if the local population protests. If the state represses the protest, it incurs some political cost, γ_R, for having done so. If the government compels the firm to follow through on its promise, enforcing the agreement, the government incurs enforcement cost E. One way of thinking of E is as a measure of the government's reliance on the firm for investment. It is the effect of forgone revenue in the form of future investment should the government compel the firm to make transfer T (at firm cost $\chi(T)$). Alternatively, one might view it as foregone side payments that the government might otherwise receive in gifts or bribes.

Though the government may incur political costs for repressing a protest, it may also gain political support from compelling the firm to follow through. The political gain to the government, γ_E, is manifest in the government's capacity to claim credit for the firm's transfer. For instance, a political party interested in consolidating support in a region can tout its role in ensuring the firm provided employment opportunities.

There are two sources of information asymmetry. First, at the moment at which it is deciding to protest, the local population is not certain whether, should it protest, the government will side with the firm (and repress the protest), or whether it will side with the local population (and compel the firm to make the transfer). Second, while both the firm and the government know the value of E, and thus whether the state will repress a protest or compel the firm to make a transfer, the local population does not have complete information about the value of E. Though this is a strong assumption of asymmetrical information, it is reasonable to consider that firms have more information than local populations do about the extent to which the government relies on continued investment. Firms with the resources to invest in large-scale mining projects also invest in gathering information about the national context of extraction – including the likelihood of government enforcement. Furthermore, firms are aware of alternative extractive sites in other countries, which affect the availability of exit options to them, and consequently government incentives to retain their business.[9]

If the local population protests and the government represses, the local population incurs an additional violence cost, v. A protest that the

---

[9] I do not address here the effect of competition of firms on the cost of enforcement parameter for simplicity, as it is outside the scope of the model.

government represses costs the local population $c + v$. Consequently, the local population must decide to protest based on the cost of protesting, and its belief about the government's likelihood of repression. In other words, the local population is not sure whether the firm has the government's support (by repressing protests that threaten the mine's operations) or whether the government will support the local population by upholding the firm's promise.

Sequence of Play

The game consists of a realization of a random variable followed by three decision nodes, each made by a different actor. The sequence of play and payoff specification is represented in Figure 3.1.

Prior to any actor making a choice, the firm realizes the cost $(\chi(T))$ of an agreed-upon transfer of goods, services, and monetary transfers (T). At this point the firm decides whether to follow through (FT) and make the promised transfer, producing the outcome labeled **Adhere**, or to renege $(\neg FT)$. If the firm makes the transfer, the firm receives the revenue

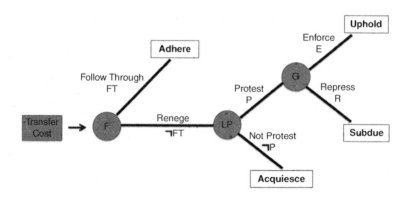

Payoffs			
Outcome	*Firm*	*Local Population*	*Government*
Adhere	$(1-\tau)(\pi-\chi(T))$	T	$\tau(\pi-\chi(T))$
Acquiesce	$(1-\tau)\pi$	$-L$	$\tau\pi$
Subdue	$(1-\tau)(\pi-r)$	$-L-(cm+v)$	$\tau(\pi-r)-\gamma_R$
Uphold	$(1-\tau)(\pi-r-\chi(T))$	$T-cm$	$\tau(\pi-r-\chi(T))-E+\gamma_E$

FIGURE 3.1: Order of play and payoffs

from extraction less the cost of the transfer, taxed at rate τ. The local population receives the promised transfer, and the government receives tax revenue from extraction (less the cost of the transfer). This is the outcome most preferred by the local population as externalities are mitigated and they receive compensation for lost livelihoods.

If the firm chooses not to follow through on the contract, the local population then decides whether or not to protest. If the local population does not protest, they endure the unmitigated externalities of extraction, experiencing a loss of L. I label this outcome **Acquiesce**, in which the firm receives the revenue from extraction after taxation at rate τ and the government receives taxes on the revenue yielded from extraction by the firm. This is the outcome most preferred by the firm, and (short of a sufficiently large political benefit from compelling the firm to follow through) by the government.

If the local population decides to protest, then the government decides whether or not to uphold the contract. If the government does not uphold the contract, it represses the protest. I label this outcome **Subdue**, in which the government receives the tax revenue from resource profits (less the value lost in the protest) but loses political support in the region as a result of repressing the protest. In this outcome, the local population endures the externalities, as well as the cost of protest (scaled by interruptibility), which is increased by a violence cost (v) that results when the government represses. This is the local population's least preferred outcome. The firm receives the value of extractive revenue less what is destroyed in protest, taxed at rate τ.

If the government upholds the contract, the government receives tax revenue from extraction (less what was lost in the protest and the firm's cost of the transfer) and the political support for compelling the firm to make the transfer. However, it endures the cost of enforcement. I label this outcome **Uphold**. The local population receives the value of the transfer less the cost of protest (scaled by the interruptibility of the resource). In this outcome, the firm receives the revenue from extraction less the amount destroyed in protest and the cost of the transfer, taxed at rate τ. This is the firm's least preferred outcome, since it suffers both the loss from the protest and the cost of the transfer. Payoffs for all four outcomes are shown in Figure 3.1.

Recall that at the time of the offer, neither the firm nor the government is aware of the local population's type (whether $LP = LP_h$ or $LP = LP_l$). However, the firm is aware of whether the government will repress, siding with the company, or whether it will uphold the agreement. Additionally, at the point at which the local population decides to protest, it is uncertain whether the government will uphold the contract or repress the protest.

The firm's first move is to decide to make the promised transfer or not, which suggests a pre-game bargaining stage. However if we assume that the firm has knowledge of the local context and the value of a transfer that would adequately compensate the local population for externalities of extraction, the value of the transfer would be exogenously set at this amount. Recall that RAPs and EIAs are conducted, once the contract has been awarded to a firm, detailing the demographics, environmental risks, and potential effects on local livelihoods at the level of the individual in an affected village.[10]

Additionally, note that the local population only considers protesting if they do not receive an offer they were promised. If the firm follows through with an offer, even if the offer is small, the local population does not protest. While this is a strong assumption, communities in several African mining regions have indicated that failure to deliver what was promised to them was more directly linked to their sentiment about the firm's operations than the size of the offer itself. While the observable presence of a large mining company entices local populations to ask for some level of distribution of benefits from extraction, the World Bank and IMF guidelines (in conjunction with the EIAs and RAPs) provide the information relevant for the firm to know the value of a transfer that will compensate the local population for consequences of extraction. Thus the value of T is predetermined, and consequently, it is never in the firm's interest to promise a transfer that is larger than it plans to deliver, since the population will respond to the firm's failure to deliver what it promised, not the actual size of the transfer.

ANALYSIS

The model supports all four possible outcomes: **adhere, acquiesce, subdue,** and **uphold**. Below I describe the conditions under which each outcome is sustainable. The outcomes hinge on the beliefs of each actor, and the parameters of the model determine the relevant cut points of each actor's beliefs (depicted in Figures 3.2 and 3.3) that constrain their

---

[10] I am primarily concerned with the provision of some localized transfer – the parameters affecting the size of the transfer generally and the combination of public and private goods are a subject for farther research, but are outside the scope of the current model.

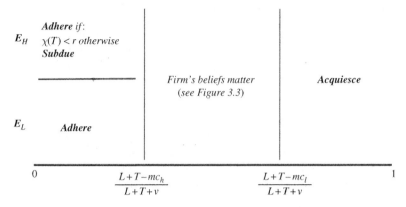

Local population's beliefs that Gov will Repress (μ)

FIGURE 3.2: Belief constraints of local population

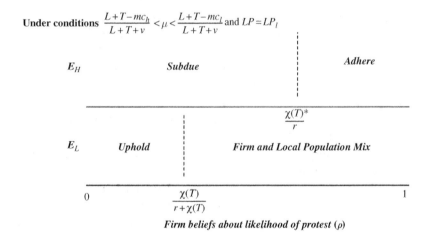

Firm beliefs about likelihood of protest (ρ)

FIGURE 3.3: Belief constraints of firm

behavior. The figures convey the extent to which extreme values of the local population's beliefs about repression (μ) are sufficient to determine the observed outcome, but that when μ is in a middle range, the firm's belief about the local population's type (ρ) becomes relevant for determining the outcome.

First, consider how the local population's beliefs influence the outcomes. If the local population believes that the probability of repression is sufficiently low, and therefore is likely to protest, the firm will make the transfer, leading to the **adhere** outcome. That probability decreases as the local population's stake $(L + T)$ increases, the violence cost falls, or the resource revenue stream becomes more easily interruptible.

If the local population believes that the probability of repression is sufficiently high, the firm will renege, but the local population will not protest, resulting in the outcome of **acquiesce**. That probability increases as the local population's stake $(L + T)$ increases, the violence cost increases, or the resource revenue stream becomes less interruptible. However, as demonstrated in Figure 3.2, between these sufficiently high and low probabilities, there is a middle region expanded in Figure 3.3, where the firm's and government's beliefs about the likelihood of protest matter a great deal.

Figure 3.3 demonstrates how the beliefs about the likelihood of protest affect the outcome. If the firm believes with sufficiently low probability that the local population will protest, and it is sufficiently costly for the government to enforce the contract, the government represses a protest from a local population, resulting in the outcome **subdue**. The probability decreases as the value lost in a protest increases, and as the cost of the transfer $(\chi(T))$ grows. The point at which it is sufficiently costly for the government to enforce the contract decreases as the political relevance of the local population increases, and as the costs of the transfer and the tax rate decrease.

In the event of a protest, the government will compel the firm to make the transfer if there are sufficient political costs to repression. Similar to the **subdue** outcome just discussed, the opportunity for protest will only arise if the firm believes with sufficiently low probability that the local population will protest. Again, that probability decreases as the value lost in a protest increases, and as the cost of the transfer to the local population grows. However, the effect of these two parameters on that probability is weaker than in the **subdue** outcome just described. However, if protest does occur, an increase in the value of the mine makes repression more likely.

This is not to suggest that the parameters in the model do not matter, but only that they matter by way of affecting the degree to which beliefs constrain behaviors. The parameters shape the relevant cut points of the actors' beliefs. There are several parameters that are particularly relevant. First, perhaps not surprisingly, regions where the externalities are the most costly to mitigate are more likely to experience both protest and repression. Consider that when the cost to the firm of providing the transfer is high relative to the value of the transfer to the local population (i.e., mitigation costs might be particularly high), the firm's belief about the likelihood of protest is less restrictive.[11] We are therefore less likely to observe the outcome of **adhere**. Since the cost of the transfer cuts into government revenues, it also affects the government's decision to subdue or to uphold the contract. Consequently, when the cost of the transfer leads the firm to renege, the government is also more likely to repress a protest if it occurs.

Relatedly, the interruptibility of the resource revenue stream (m) and the value of the resource that is extracted (r) affect the likelihood of the contracted outcome. As the value extracted increases, we are more likely to observe the outcome **adhere** (relative to the other outcomes) since this makes protest more costly to the firm and government. As the interruptibility of the resource increases, the local population is more likely to protest, since the local population's prior belief about the government's type becomes less restrictive (at the same time making the firm more likely to make the promised transfer). Finally, and interestingly, higher tax rates create a greater stake for the government in an extractive region. As a result, the government is more willing to repress to protect that stake. In addition, the firm is more likely to renege when it is being heavily taxed, since it is less likely that the government will compel it to make the transfer.

Given that the actors' beliefs about each other shape the likelihood of each outcome, it is important to consider what incentives there might be for each actor to misrepresent its type. The strategic context is such that the local population does not often have an opportunity to send a signal about its type. The local population observes the firm's failure to compensate it, and only then decides whether to incur the cost of protesting.[12] If the local population had the opportunity to send a signal to the firm, it would indeed wish to convey it was the type to engage in protest if it could credibly do so. Figure 3.2 conveys the extreme sets of beliefs (μ) where the local population never protests, or always does. It is only between those extreme values of the beliefs about the likelihood of repression that it would make sense for the local population to misrepresent its type. However, behaviors available to local populations that would constitute costly signaling are difficult to imagine. Many local

---

[11] Furthermore, the $*$ in Figure 3.3 denotes that if if the cost of the transfer is greater than the amount destroyed in protest, $\chi(T) > r$, the region to the right of the dotted line, "Adhere" is not possible.

[12] Thus, the context diverges from a traditional bargaining model.

populations voice demands of the firm, but the consequences for doing so are minimal. Even those local communities with high costs of protest are likely to vocalize dissatisfaction with firm behavior, ensuring such a signal amounts to little more than cheap talk.

The firm, on the other hand, is able to convey some actionable information about whether the government will repress if it reneges, but only to the extent that the local population can update its belief about the likelihood of repression from the firm's decision.[13] The only context in which the firm is potentially better off when the local population protests is if the government will repress a protest, which would in turn make the local population less likely to protest. The firm would wish to renege in order to lead the local population to believe the government will repress, even if that is not the case. In fact, the firm would only ever renege when the government would enforce its promise if it does not believe protest is sufficiently likely. This would look much like the scenario in which the firm observes the local population's beliefs about repression to be high, but it does not know if they are high enough to deter protest. Thus, the firm (and the government for that matter) might wish to manipulate the local population's belief about the likelihood of repression in order to make it less inclined to protest.

Notably, we should only expect to see protest once in a given region, since the information asymmetry will have been resolved, ensuring that firms would incur the cost of the transfer when local residents are the type to protest, but that local residents will not protest when governments are the type to repress. However, firms are not in the development business *per se*, consequently, there may be error in the translation between the effort to follow through on the part of the firm and the observed transfer by the population. Efforts to provide the promised goods and services may be misguided, or have unintended negative consequences that may lead local residents to protest anyway. As a result, we would expect that, on average, protest should be unlikely to occur more than once among a given firm, government, and local population, but that occasionally, protest may occur in spite of the firm's earnest attempt to prevent it.

When the government sides with the firm, repressing social mobilization on the part of the local community, it is tempting to suggest that this is no different from regulatory capture. However, in regulatory capture (in its simplest form), interest groups manipulate the state so as to

---

[13] Consider the semi-separating equilibrium in the Appendix A.

influence the nature and extent of regulation. While the outcome in which the government represses is similar in that the government must manage trade-offs between the producer and the consumer (as is pointed out by Dal Bó (2006)), in this case the government's potential behavior is not actually able to be manipulated by the firm. Instead, it is decided by an inequality among parameters (the monetary cost of enforcement/regulation, the political costs/benefits of repression/enforcement, and the tax revenue lost if the government enforces). If the firm were able to manipulate the government cost to enforcement, then it might look more like a regulatory capture scenario, but even still, the firm does not have the capacity in the model to mitigate political costs or tax revenue lost. Ultimately, the government can rely on the firm's potential monetary cost if protest occurs, and the firm's uncertainty about the likelihood of that protest in order to get it to do things like provide social services, while claiming credit for enforcement.

Summary

The model here unpacks the strategic interactions of firms, governments, and local populations in and around natural resource extraction and lends the consistency of formal logic to the theory provided in Chapter 2. The model suggests several general tendencies. First, natural resource extraction in regions where compensating communities is costly, are likely to see more conflict and more repression. The effect of extraction on the livelihoods of the local population is greater, as is the firm's costs to mitigating such an effect. Such regions may have higher population densities who rely primarily on the natural environment for livelihoods. One implication of this is that it is not only the environmental degradation resulting from mining that may result in a lower likelihood that the firm follows through, but that those communities who occupy particularly valuable land (well irrigated and fertile) and are displaced by mining will be more costly to compensate. Thus, comparatively *better-off* rural communities are actually *more* likely to mobilize, since firms will be less likely to follow through. Second, extractive regions in countries where government take from natural resource extraction is large (relative to other countries) are also likely to see more protest and repression, since this places additional financial burden on firms, and creates a larger stake for the government. Third, increased value of a particular mine should increase the likelihood of a repressive outcome if the community protests, as the interruption of more lucrative mining operation will yield greater monetary costs. Of course, this could be countered if political support in the region was particularly important to the leader at the time of protest. These tendencies are elucidated with additional clarity in Chapter 5.

More generally, the model outlines conditions under which a non-state actor, in this case an extractive firm, has incentives to engage in the provision of goods and services in a defined region. It also outlines how a government can benefit from ensuring that the firm does so. The infrastructure required for extraction and the locational rigidity of the asset make the firm vulnerable to protest by local populations living in the region. The government recognizes this, and though it may lose out on revenue it collects from the firm in the event of protest, it has the added calculation of the effect of protest on its political support base. Under the assumption that the government has limited and finite resources, it can take advantage of firm presence in these areas since it can be less costly for the government to compel the firm to provide goods and services than to incur the costs of protest should they not be provided. *The government can thus leverage the potential costs of protest to the firm in order to garner support resulting from goods provision in the region.* As the model indicates, a government's capacity to do so depends on the relative costs (monetary and political) of protest and each actor's beliefs about each other.

The model presented in this chapter provides a set of strict assumptions that govern a set of precise interactions among three actors, and results in four relatively clear and discrete outcomes. However, the world is messier than that. The orderly presentation here is a helpful guide to the more detailed, dynamic, and complicated lived experience on the ground. The next part of the book introduces some of this messiness, and in doing so provides detail of space, place, and agency to the sparse logic presented here.

PART II

LOCAL POLITICS ON THE GROUND

4

On Comparative Case Analysis

The formal logic of the last chapter specified the preferences, beliefs, and action that lead to one of four different outcomes in regions of natural resource extraction: firm transfer, local population acquiescence, government enforcement, and government repression. But to what extent does this formal model capture the variance predicted, if we zoom in to a few case studies that exhibit this variance? To what extent can we observe the proposed mechanisms playing out on the ground? In this chapter I bring this stylized model to life, by tracing the mechanisms it specifies in specific case studies. Doing so provides validation of the proposed theory and demonstrates plausibility of the mechanisms elucidated in the model.

I conduct two comparative case studies, one comparison of resource concessions within the same country (Mozambique) managed by two different foreign firms, and one comparison of resource concessions owned by the same foreign firm but occurring in two countries (Zambia and DRC). A structured, paired case comparison entails asking the same set of questions in multiple case settings to ensure comparability. This paired case selection strategy has two advantages, particularly in lending internal validity to the proposed theory over competing theories. First, comparing cases within a single country allows me to hold the national institutional context constant. A primary competing theory is that variation in state capacity (or some other characteristic of the central government) is a primary driver of the variation in outcomes. Demonstrating variation in governance outcomes within a single country ensures that national characteristics, which do not vary, cannot be the primary driver of this variation in outcomes. Holding several of the model parameters that characterize the national government constant allows me to focus on the parameters in the model – both the structural parameters such as the cost of the transfer and the tax rate, as well as the actors' beliefs about each other – that vary. Within Mozambique, the coal concessions owned by Vale and Rio Tinto were of particular interest because of their proximity to eachother. As I will detail in the next chapter, the two coal concessions are adjacent to each other, both in the northwest province of Tete, far from the capital, Maputo. The close proximity of these concessions ensures some level of similarity in ethnic composition of the communities, local experience with the state, and geographic conditions. The two firms are two of the largest exploration and mining firms in the world, ensuring relatively similar capacity.

The Mozambique case comparison does not allow me to reject the theory that firm characteristics are the primary driver of the variation in outcomes, since two different firms manage the concessions in this first comparison. As a consequence, a second comparison is warranted – one in which the firm is held constant while the national institutional context varies. This comparison ensures that firm culture is not the primary or sole driver of these outcomes. In this second comparison, I compare copper concessions in the Copperbelt, a region rich in copper that straddles the Zambia–DRC border. Copper mines are in operation on both sides of the border, and some of the same firms operate in both countries. While I focus on copper mines held by South African firm Metorex,[1] I refer to additional copper mines in both countries for two reasons. First, it provides a broader understanding of how the government's type shapes outcomes across mine-community interactions within a single country. While the government's response to firm – community interactions is conditional on the local context (the value of the mine, for example), these local factors are in part shaped by national characteristics of the government, such as the government's share of mining revenue, and the political cost of repression. Thus there will be some similarity in the way the Zambian government responds to firm–community interactions across mines within the Zambian Copperbelt, and some similarity in the way the government of DRC responds to firm–community interactions across mines in Katanga province in DRC.

Second, including reference to additional copper mines allows me to mitigate some of the asymmetry in data availability shaped by conditions on the ground. Conducting field work in this part of Africa

---

[1] The firm has since been bought by the Chinese government, but at the time of study, was still based in South Africa.

COUNTRY	Within-Firm Comparison (Metorex)
DRC	Ruashi
Zambia	Chibuluma

FIRM	Within-Country Comparison (Mozambique)
Vale	Moatize
Rio Tinto	Benga

FIGURE 4.1: Research design

can be challenging for several reasons. First, state capacity often limits the availability of data, both at the national and subnational level. This is particularly true of countries that have faced civil war and violent conflict, which can destroy existing data and limits the availability of resources for collecting data. Second, a strong security state can limit access to particular kinds of data. This is especially true in DRC, where the national intelligence service, l'Agence National Renseignement (ANR), is suspicious of researchers in the area of industrial mining or those researching political phenomena more generally. Even with the appropriate paperwork and permissions for research, firms were often unwilling to speak with me, and the government was suspicious of my activities. This is all the more true in Katanga, where historical attempts at secession[2] and the concentrated mineral wealth have made security forces all the more suspicious. As a consequence, communities are less willing to speak with strangers, and as a researcher, I was more constrained in my capacities.

In both the within-country and cross-country comparative cases, I hold the natural resource constant. In Mozambique I compare two coal concessions, and in Zambia and DRC I compare copper concessions. Holding the resource constant minimizes the role played by characteristics particular to a specific resource such as the cash costs of extraction, the generalize environmental consequences of extraction, the rate of return, and the form of the mine.

As a result of this paired comparative case strategy, I can demonstrate that neither firm nor national government is the single driver of

---

[2] In my conversations with them, locals often cited the American CIA's involvement in these attempts, further hampering any trust in American foreigners.

the outcomes in question. Instead, they are the result of the interaction of these actors with local residents in particular local contexts. In these cases, I rely on the analysis of a series of events in and around the mining concession to trace the behaviors of each of the actors. In general, these cases focus on the events occurring within the several years following allocation of the concession. This time period is particularly revelatory because it is when information asymmetries have not yet been rectified, and because it is often when the events of the proposed model most commonly play out.

The case analysis presented here is the result of field research during the summers of 2012 and 2015 in Mozambique, Zambia, and DRC. In Mozambique, I traveled around the dusty roads of Tete province, as well as down to the port city of Beira and to interview government officials in Maputo. In Zambia, I traveled throughout Copperbelt province, as well as to Northwestern Province, spending time in the towns of Kitwe, Chingola, Konkola, Chililabombwe, Solwezi, Kalulushi, and the capital, Lusaka. And in DRC, much of my time was spent in Lubumbashi and surrounding areas, with trips up to Kolwezi.

In total, I conducted approximately 60 semi-structured interviews with current and former government officials, local residents living in and around mining concessions, natural resource firm employees, and members of civil society. I also conducted archival research at newspaper offices, government environmental agencies, and NGO offices in each country.

5

Two Firms, One Country: Coal in Tete, Mozambique

Significant coal reserves were discovered in northwest Mozambique in 2006, including what was estimated to be the largest reserve of high-grade coking coal in the world. Known reserves in the northwestern Tete province are more than 20 billion tonnes,[1] and the coal seam has attracted tens of mining companies. The first mining licenses were given to the Brazilian iron company Vale for its Moatize Project and to the joint venture by Riversdale and Tata for its Benga Project (later owned by Australia's Rio Tinto). Vale and Rio Tinto conducted EIAs and completed RAPs, as villagers lived within the concession boundaries and required relocation for the firm to begin construction of the mine and extraction of the coal.

Vale is a Brazilian logistics, exploration, and mining company, and in 2011, its total revenue was approximately US$60 billion. Rio Tinto is an Australian exploration and mining company with total annual revenue (in 2011) of US$65 billion. The year before operations for each firm began in Tete, both companies were among the top three largest mining companies in the world. Each had operations around the world, but mining operations on the continent (outside of South Africa), and particularly in Mozambique, were new to both firms. Each saw the new coking coal deposit as an opportunity for expansion beyond iron and copper. At the time, Vale's Moatize concession was one of six coal operations managed by Vale. While a coal project in Colombia had been sold that year, Vale continued to operate coal mines in Australia and China (where Vale is a minority partner). Rio Tinto had wholly owned or joint venture coal

---

[1] Intellica (2014).

operations in Australia in addition to its concessions in Mozambique. For both firms, Mozambique was a new venture that held the potential to significantly expand each company's share of the coal production market. The total approved capital cost of the Benga Project, as of 2012, was $600 million.[2]

The two firms' engagement in the region yielded different outcomes: the villagers relocated by Vale protested the firm's activities, barricading the railroad and interrupting the transport of coal from the mine to the port, while Rio Tinto was able to avoid this kind of costly resistance. Furthermore, while the government retained a limited state presence in the region after allocation of coal licenses, it intervened to enforce promises made by the firm to the residents near their operations. In what follows, I first describe the different governance outcomes in the two coal concessions in Tete. Then, I explore how firm expectations and costs to obtaining local support through goods provision shaped their behavior. I then discuss how the state's historically limited claim to legitimacy and timing of the protest shaped the government's engagement.

One Resource, One Country, Two Outcomes

Brazilian iron ore company Vale was one of the first firms to invest in coal in Tete Province, signing a mining contract in 2007 and developing its feasibility report for mining operations in 2008. Its Moatize coal concession is about 17 km northeast of the city of Tete, the provincial capital, and rights to extraction last for 35 years. Development of the Moatize coal mine was estimated to cost US$1.7 billion.

Shortly after Vale began construction of the Moatize project in 2009, Riversdale (later Rio Tinto) obtained a license for the development of the nearby Benga concession with leasing rights for 25 years. The Benga project is just west of Vale's Moatize project, still 14 km east of Tete City, bordering closely the Revuboe River. The proximity of the two concessions ensures a shared historical and environmental context. Initial investment by Rio Tinto in the Benga project was US$1.2 billion and it began production in 2011, though export did not begin until June 2012.

On December 20, 2011, local leaders in Cateme, a village resettled by Vale for the construction of its mine, addressed a letter to Vale and the local government enumerating the complaints that members of the resettlement had concerning the structure of the new houses, limited access to arable land, a local market, and water. They requested that these

---

[2] Rio Tinto (2012).

demands be met by January 12.[3] When January of 2012 arrived, more than 500 families gathered at the railroad to block the passage of freight trains carrying coal from Vale's mine at Moatize to the port of Beira. In total three trains failed to reach the port as a result. Each train had about 42 wagons, and carried about 2500 tons of coal[4] (over US$1 million expected loss in one day).[5]

Protesters stated they were barricading the railroad because of the failure of Vale to carry out a promised resettlement package when they were moved to the town of Cateme to make way for the new coal mine in Moatize. They accused the firm of

> downgrading the quality of the houses by not sticking to the model house design that was negotiated with the government and shown to communities. The quality of the houses is also not what was promised... the communities also claim that other pledges – such as paved roads, running water, ambulances, land for farming and employment – have not been fulfilled.[6]

Those resettled in Cateme complained about the lack of foundation in the houses, the poor quality of land in and around Cateme (relative to the old village), the greater distance to the markets (the new settlement was more than 40 km from the nearest market), limited government-provided services, and insufficient grazing grounds.[7] Furthermore, Vale promised two hectares of land per family, only one had been allocated, and while the firm had provided food aid briefly during 2009 and 2010 given the interrupted harvesting season, it failed to do so after 2010. In response to the January protest in Vale's concession, a rapid response team arrested fourteen of the protesters. Production and transport of coal was restored within twenty-four hours.

Caught off guard by the protest, district-level officials refused to address questions about the protest in a press conference. While Vale did not make a public statement about the protest at the Moatize site, it did issue a formal response to a report conducted by a regional NGO about the effects of coal mining on communities in Tete. The initial response from the government to the protest was minimal, but in the aftermath, the government compelled Vale to address the complaints. Less than a

[3] Rodriquez (2012).
[4] Campbell (2012).
[5] Resenfeld (2012).
[6] Kabemba and Nhancale (2012).
[7] Mosca and Selemane (2011).

month after the protests, the head of the local government's "Tete Provincial Resettlement Commission" changed the required specifications on
the houses. According to firm employees, the commission was of limited
local significance up until this point (one employee did not even know it
existed).

As a result, Vale resumed the delivery of food aid to Cateme in March,
two months after the protest by Cateme residents,[8] and engaged in a
publicized campaign to fix the houses. Six months after the January 2012
protest, Vale signed an MOU with the government of Mozambique and
representatives of the resettled communities, which includes, according to
Vale, approximately 40 commitments to maintain infrastructure in and
around the villages. Immediately after the demonstrations, Vale worked
to renovate the houses in Cateme as well as in its more urban resettlement
including fixing flooring, roofing, wooden frame, and electrical wiring,
on over 80 percent of the houses in Cateme, and just under 15 percent
of the houses in the village 25 de Septembro, where other residents from
the concession had been resettled.[9] Furthermore, on December 11, 2012,
the government publicly stated that a portion of mineral revenues would
be directed toward the community of Moatize, in 2013. By 2014, a law
was passed, ensuring the region was to receive 2.75 percent of revenues,
amounting to approximately US$1 million.[10]

In the nearby Benga coal concession, Australian firm, Rio Tinto, was
in the process of implementing its resettlement action plan. In the short-
term, thirty-nine families that required relocation by Rio Tinto were to
be temporarily settled in the town of Moatize, where the firm promised
to pay rent, up to 250 kilowatt hours of electricity per month (generous
relative to average consumption),[11] and up to 15 cubic meters of water
per month. An announcement was made at a meeting with Rio Tinto
and residents of Capanga, for whom the new requirements would be
relevant that "Rio Tinto has promised the people, the Provincial Resettlement Commission and the Moatize District Government that it will
comply with the agreements it has reached with the Capanga population
and with the government" and that the population had agreed to the
proposal.[12] Residents already resettled to Rio Tinto's Mualadzi village

---

[8] Human Rights Watch (2013).

[9] *Mozambique: Vale Renovates 576 Houses in Cateme* (2013).

[10] Salemene (2013).

[11] Based on Bensch, Peters, and Schraml (2010).

[12] *Mozambique: Tete Govt Changes Resettlement Strategy* (2012).

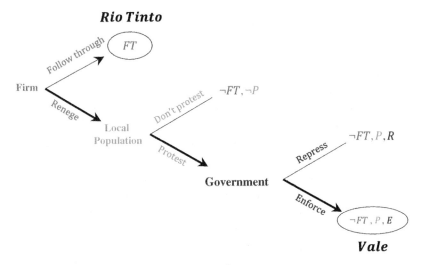

FIGURE 5.1: Mozambique outcomes

received a monthly package of dried fish, maize, flour, rice, cooking oil, and soap from Rio Tinto as of early 2013.[13]

In sum, the two firms were awarded adjacent coal concessions, however, their engagement in the region yielded different outcomes. The villagers relocated by Vale protested the firm's activities, barricading the railroad and interrupting the transport of coal from the mine to the port, and the government of Mozambique intervened on behalf of the protesters. Rio Tinto was able to avoid costly resistance altogether. To understand these two outcomes, which occurred in such close proximity to each other, it is necessary to explore the firm's beliefs and the costs of securing local support to explain the initial difference in firm strategy.

Local Support: Firm Costs and Expectations

The costs to obtaining support and the firms' beliefs about the consequences of failing to do so shaped the firms' behavior in their respective concessions. In this section I elaborate the promises that firms made to local population to demonstrate that firms did in fact aim to obtain local support initially. I will also show that fulfilling these promises was costly for both firms, though more so for Vale than for Rio Tinto. However, because Rio Tinto was able to observe the consequences that Vale faced

---

[13] Human Rights Watch (2013).

when it failed to fulfill those promises, it was able to update its beliefs and expectations about the likelihood that its operation would be threatened if it failed to fulfill its promises.

Before the events of January 2012, both firms made explicit promises to local residents about the compensation that would be provided, and the steps that would be taken to mitigate the adverse consequences of extraction. These promises were communicated, as is often the case, in several stakeholder meetings in order to obtain buy-in from the local residents and set expectations. Vale's resettlement process for the Moatize mine occurred between November 2009 and April 2010, and included the relocation of over 5,000 people. Those relocated included members of the Chipanga, Bagamoyo, Mithete, and Malabwe villages, and resettled villagers were split up into two populations: approximately 700 households were considered rural and resettled in the village of Cateme, approximately 40 km from the town of Tete, while the other group of approximately 600 families were considered urban and resettled into a neighborhood in the town of Moatize.[14]

Vale's community relations liaisons made promises to those relocated residents that they would receive compensation,[15] including water pumps at each house, refurbishment of a primary school as well as a hospital, and the construction of housing for those families (269) that were relocated to the outskirts of Moatize. For those families relocated to the rural settlement of Cateme, a new house was to be constructed for each family, neighborhood pumps were to be provided, an elementary and secondary school and health clinic were to be built, and two hectares of farmland per family were promised. For a third group, the firm promised financial compensation to allow villagers to purchase new housing.[16]

In comparison, Rio Tinto's Benga project required the resettlement of 679 families from the Capanga, Benga, and Nhambalualu villages. The Australian firm planned to resettle 588 families to the village of Mualadzi,[17] adjacent to the village of Cateme, and another 75 families in more urban areas (though the exact location is not specified in the firm's Resettlement Action Plan).[18] The resettlement and compensation plan, which was expected to take approximately two and a half years to complete,

---

[14] Mosca and Selemane (2011).

[15] According to NGOs, the company's EIA, and a letter from members of the local population relocated to the town of Cateme.

[16] Consultec Consultoria Associados, Diagonal Urbana, and ERM Brasil Ltda (2006).

[17] Mosca and Selemane (2011).

[18] Golder Associates (2009).

was developed by Riversdale, whose license was later bought out by Rio Tinto. At the time of the acquisition, Riversdale had already built over 100 of the houses and begun resettling residents in the nearby villages. Rio Tinto was bound (both legally, and by way of the deterring cost of conducting another RAP) to carry out the plan developed by Riversdale, and according to a representative at Rio Tinto, began an analysis in 2012 to identify any gaps in the existing plans for resettlement.[19] The firm promised the resettled residents of Mualadzi new houses, a primary school, two hectares of land per household, and several water pumps. Similar to Vale, Rio Tinto also promised those non-farming households financial assistance in purchasing a house in or near Moatize or Tete.[20]

These promises, and particularly their communication to the local residents, demonstrated the firms' interest in at least paying lip service to international norms and guidelines regarding stakeholder involvement. The firms may have even had the initial intent on following through. However, the cost of fulfilling these promises, and thus securing a social license in the area, was shaped by the local context in which the firms were operating. The operations of both firms disrupted the livelihoods of residents in the concessions, particularly those that relied primarily on small-scale agriculture. Agriculture employs at least 70 percent of the population in Mozambique.[21] The cost to the firms to compensating them was significant given the number of mining licenses already allocated in the area to other firms. Furthermore, this competition for land only increased as more firms bid on and received mining concessions in the area. Residents in both concessions relied on small plots of land and access to water for the harvesting of maize and other staple crops, as well as the proximity of the towns of Moatize and Tete for selling these crops. Both firms were constrained by the limited availability of arable land for the resettlement of the local population (in fact water and land availability in Tete was a problem even during the 1980s).[22] The many small rivers are empty during the dry season, and droughts are common throughout the year, thus the access to water that local residents had before the resettlement was particularly valuable.

While limited land and water resources characterized the surrounding areas of both Vale's Moatize and Rio Tinto's Benga concessions, it

---

[19] Human Rights Watch (2013).
[20] Golder Associates (2009).
[21] This is a conservative estimate for regions like Tete.
[22] Coelho (1998).

was particularly constraining for Vale, who had many more families to relocate from its significantly larger concession (240 km^2) than did Rio Tinto, whose concession was 50 km^2. As a result, the cost to fulfilling all requirements of the resettlement action plan to the firms differed as many more villagers lived in Vale's concession than in Rio Tinto's. The actual monetary cost to Vale was expected to be approximately US$40 million[23] while the initial estimated cost to Rio Tinto for resettlement was estimated to be US$26.1 million,[24] making honoring the promise more costly in absolute terms for Vale.

It might be argued that Vale made all attempts to honor its promises, and that protest was a result of grievances of the local population that would have erupted regardless of the strategy of resettlement and amount of local investment. To be fair, Vale acknowledges that it is not in the business of local development and as early as 2011, the firm recognized that improvements were required on some of the infrastructure in the new settlements.[25] It claimed that it had already begun to repair homes and maintain drainage systems and roads. Additionally, the firm indicated that the government altered the agreement, requiring that Vale compensate the families financially, in place of allocating a second hectare given the emerging land scarcity as a result of the multiplying concessions.[26] However, the firm did not live up to even those promises that remained unaltered. Specifically, it failed to provide foundations for the new houses it built for resettled residents. Residents claimed that the firm presented different model houses to them, ones with foundations, than those that were ultimately constructed at the resettlement site.[27] Not expecting the costly protest that would result, Vale failed to follow through on its promise.

At the start of mine construction in 2009, the firms did not expect to face resistance – they had no historical experience in the region that could accurately inform their beliefs about the likelihood of social mobilization against them. In a report by Riversdale to investors in 2010 (before the site was acquired by Rio Tinto and before the protest in Cateme), key

---

[23] Consultec Consultoria Associados, Diagonal Urbana, and ERM Brasil Ltda (2006).
[24] Golder Associates (2009).
[25] Vale (2011).
[26] Human Rights Watch (2013).
[27] While Vale does employ several contractors and thus it might be argued that this failure was an oversight by the contractor building the house, the failure to monitor the construction by the firm, and the presentation of a model that was different from those that were eventually built, suggests more than an oversight.

risks did not include any mention of resistance by the local community living in the concession. This is noteworthy because local discontent and violence for surrounding communities is a risk that is often explicitly noted in mining project internal documents. But a Rio Tinto employee claimed that once the protest against Vale occurred, he began to worry about the potential for protest by the residents of his firm's resettled communities, and noted the importance of avoiding Vale's strategy.[28]

The actual costs of the Cateme protest amounted to approximately US$1 million, which was not significant relative to the expected returns over the life of the entire mining project. However, it demonstrated the potential for much greater revenue loss once production was at its height, if protest continued over time. Furthermore, this is approximately the amount that Vale stated it intended to spend on community investment during 2009.[29]

While some sources suggest that the residents of Cateme were protesting against the firm, others indicate the protest was against the government.[30] The limited infrastructure presented an opportunity for local populations to impose costs on both, regardless of the explicitly stated target (as Scott (1987) would suggest). In this way, the nature of the industry ensured that sabotage did not require targeting of the firm or the government specifically in order to impose costs on both. As a result of the protest and vulnerability that it highlighted, Vale began construction of a US$5 billion railroad from Tete to the port of Nacala through Malawi, in partnership with the government of Mozambique,[31] and Rio Tinto has proposed an additional new rail line and a deep-water port at Macuze to mitigate these risks (as well as reduce the transportation bottleneck).

In sum, both firms were aware of the consequences of their operations on the residents in their concessions. The effects are detailed in the EIA and RAP of each concession and dictate the promises made to the residents. However, Rio Tinto was able to observe how the local population would respond if the firm failed to adequately provide compensation that was promised. Rio Tinto was still in the midst of its relocation process when it observed the protest in Cateme. As a result, it was particularly wary of the likelihood of protest, should resettlement and compensation

[28] Interview (2012*a*).
[29] Vale (2009).
[30] Campbell (2012).
[31] Resenfeld (2012).

provision not meet the expectations of the local residents. Consequently, Rio Tinto delayed resettlement, ensuring that its houses were better constructed, that agricultural projects were underway, and even that the utility poles erected to carry electricity current were in better condition to ensure it avoided potential interruptions.

Government Trade-offs: Frelimo, Political Support, and Revenue

The government's perception of the potential value of the industry in the region weighed against the timing of the protest to shape the government's response. Both the Vale and Rio Tinto coal concessions presented significant revenue potential for the government, which would be at risk if events like the Cateme protest repeated.

Tax revenue was expected to reach US$700 million per year when production was fully underway.[32] Revenue from extractives in Mozambique was 12 percent of all revenue collected by the state. Tax revenue from extractive industries in 2009 amounted to about US$12.5 million, and of the 96 companies, 24 of them represented 92 percent of payments.[33] In 2010, the natural resource sector contributed only US$11.4 million to the national budget, and though in 2011 it was approximately US$24 million (a nearly 100 percent increase, in comparison to energy production, oil exploration, and "other," which saw significant decreases), it was still only a small fraction of its potential capacity.[34] In 2010, the Mozambique Coal Development Association reported that the Moatize project resources were about 2,286Mt,[35] but the first 35,000 tonnes of coal did not leave Vale's Moatize mine until in August 2011, traveling the 575 km by rail to the port of Beira.[36]

In spite of this potential, significant revenue from Vale's coal operations had yet to materialize at the time of the protest, and the short-term concern about political costs related to the protest outweighed the immediate revenue from the mine. The revenue potential of Tete, and the Moatize and Benga projects in particular, was countered by the political salience of local support at the time of the protest.

The northwestern province of Tete is historically a region of limited state presence in which the ruling party, Frelimo, has sought to

[32] World Bank International Development Agency (2013).
[33] IDA (2013).
[34] Ministry of Finance. Government of Mozambique (2011).
[35] MinAxis Pty Ltd (2010).
[36] African Development Bank (2012).

build legitimacy. Frelimo had both fought for independence from the Portuguese, and won the civil war against Renamo, and as a result, perceptions were such that, in effect, the party and state were synonymous. However, it has historically sought to gain political legitimacy at the local level. These attempts included a development strategy that entailed the villagization of rural Mozambique, resulting in the resettlement of peasants into villages and the transformation of the means of production into collective farms. The district of Moatize saw one of the largest concentrations of these villages in the 1980s. These villages were developed far from the provincial capital, without sufficient transportation infrastructure, which limited state presence. Because Tete was a "backward province based on household agriculture," there was minimal state investment.[37] In other cotton-producing regions of the country, the state was better able to build local legitimacy. Pitcher (1996) details how Frelimo involved itself in the day-to-day operations of the newly privatized cotton industry. Privatization of the cotton industry resulted in "opportunities for Frelimo to gain badly needed political legitimacy on the local level and to create a new constituency of supporters for its economic agenda as a result" (Pitcher 1996, p. 51) in cotton-producing regions. However, absent the cotton industry, in which significant joint ventures and lower capital costs invited state involvement, Tete remained of limited interest and presence of the state.

Legislation in 1994 called for a stronger role for traditional authorities, known as regulos, and a decentralization of government functions was expected to lead to greater state presence in peripheral provinces like Tete. The law devolved control over social welfare, education, roads, health, development, environmental protection, land management, and public and private markets to an elected administrator and assembly at the district level. The role of traditional authorities included maintenance of social stability,[38] management of land, tax collection, and secondary road management. Frelimo officials wished to pay chiefs for these tasks, ensuring they acted more like enforcers than independent representatives of local communities. Indeed, it is reported that Frelimo representatives held high-profile meetings with chiefs of regions in which government presence was weak. Alexander (1997) notes "that for officials, chiefs seemed to offer a cheap, willing and apolitical means of

---

[37] Coelho (1998).
[38] Alexander (1997).

extending state authority, and thus redressing the quandaries produced by multi-partyism and an inability to mobilize resources or labour by other means." However, soon thereafter, in 1996, this decentralization was reversed after Renamo performed unexpectedly well in subnational elections. Many of the provinces far from Maputo, and Tete in particular remained regions of chronic state weakness, and the state remained absent other than quite minor involvement in Moatize's early coal industry. This absence of the state ensured first that local residents had limited, recent experience with the coercive apparatus of the state, and thus were unlikely to have strong prior beliefs about the likelihood of repression. It also demonstrated a legitimacy deficit, shaping the Frelimo's response once the protest around Vale's concession occurred.

The protest at Vale's concession provided an opportunity to build legitimacy and support, by allowing the government a clear regulatory role. The context and timing of electoral politics ensured an increased focus on the importance of building and maintaining political order in Tete. Frelimo was able to capitalize on opportunities to cement support at the local level. The majority (two-thirds) of Frelimo's Central Committee as well as two-thirds of the congressional delegates are elected at the provincial level. The Frelimo congress was set to meet and elect the members of the Political Commission, the party's central ruling body during 2012, when most of the events of interest transpired. Though Tete is a traditional stronghold for the ruling Frelimo party (in 2009 Frelimo won provincial assembly elections handily), the convergence of the provincial conference and party congress, and the local response to Vale's resettlement and local investment ensured that the government sought a resolution to the protests that was likely to yield some political favor. One firm official in Tete explicitly noted that the government's decision to compel Vale to follow through was the result of the Frelimo party elections, claiming that the public directive toward Vale was the best way to maintain order while potentially building support.[39] Indeed, Frelimo did claim credit for attracting the firms to the region and the provision of housing and compensation to the residents.[40] The Congress resulted in the election of Tete's governor Viegas to the party's Political Commission and, as a result, President Guebuza replaced the Prime Minister with him. Consequently, nearly two decades after privatization, Pitcher's claim

[39] Interview (2012a).
[40] Davies Private Interview (2012).

that the party curries favor with local constituencies through regulatory engagement is particularly relevant in Tete.

After the protest against Vale at Cateme, Rio Tinto worked to ensure that it appeared to be living up to its remunerative commitment through the provision of well-constructed houses, livelihood projects, food packages and subsidized rent in the interim, and even superficial dressings such as the aesthetics of utility poles. The potential for protest drove Rio Tinto to make its attempts at building local support visible, and more durable. Interestingly, those relocated by Rio Tinto to Mualadzi had similar complaints except for those related to the housing, which has become the symbol for the different ways in which the communities perceived the companies.[41] Rio Tinto was able to update its beliefs about the capacity of the residents to organize collectively to impose costs on the firm by interrupting the transportation of coal. In a region in which the state had retained limited presence since villagization, and the firm and government had limited experience with significant extractive projects, little information existed about the likelihood of resistance to firm operations before the protest in Cateme.

International norms and regulations, as well as operational feasibility ensured that Vale promised local investment to those living in and around its concession. Until the protest, the resettlement was largely the purview of the firm, compelling no initial reaction by the government, which remained a mere passive recipient of written grievances. The protest led the government to intervene directly in the firm's interactions with local communities. After an initial response to ensure the preservation of revenue from the coal projects, the government compelled Vale to fix the houses, issuing a public statement about new specifications and ensuring that Rio Tinto would also adhere to the new requirements. Vale engaged in a visible campaign to fix the houses in Cateme.

In sum, the firms engaged in the provision of goods and services in and around its mining site in order to protect its assets in a particularly vulnerable context, once they updated their beliefs about the likelihood of resistance from the communities. The government was able to claim credit for compelling Vale to follow through, building local legitimacy (as an enforcer and conflict mediator), even in the face of limited capacity, without engaging in many of the traditional state functions. The local population's protest served as an opportunity for the government to build

---

[41] The importance of building structure, the primary complaint of the residents in Tete, dates back to the villagization of Tete.

support at a relatively low cost. The government was able to leverage the potential monetary costs incurred by the firm to minimize any potential political costs. It benefited from revenue from the firm's extractive operations as well as the firm's provision of goods and services to a population during an election year.

6

Two Countries, One Firm: Mining the Copperbelt in Zambia and DRC

The case of coal in Mozambique offered a comparison across two different firm concessions, demonstrating the way beliefs, local costs to the firm of local investment, and the government's preference for political support shaped outcomes. I now turn to the case of copper extraction in Zambia and DRC, in which the same firm operates a copper and cobalt mine on both sides of the border, to understand outcomes of regulatory versus security governance in mining regions.

The Copperbelt in Africa is a region approximately 280 miles long and 50 miles wide that straddles the Zambian–DRC border.[1] Copper ore grade is some of the highest in the world in this region, and there is a long history of industrial copper mining on both sides of the border. Cobalt is generally found alongside copper, and thus mines constructed for the extraction of copper are also used for the extraction of cobalt.[2] For both Zambia and DRC, government-owned mining enterprises dominated the Copperbelt landscape until the mid-1990s, though the government of DRC was not a proponent of the socialist rhetorical and economic platform that characterized Zambia's government. Both countries rely on the natural resource sector for government revenue, and DRC's southeastern Katanga Province and Zambia's northern Copperbelt Province contain the most significant resources for industrial-scale foreign mining companies in each country. In 2010, Zambia accounted for 8 percent of African cobalt production, and 56 percent of African

---

[1] Birchard (1940).
[2] KPMJ (2013).

copper production. Mining comprised approximately 11 percent of Zambia's GDP, and copper exports accounted for approximately 78 percent of the country's merchandise exports. The same year, DRC accounted for 86 percent of African cobalt production, and 30 percent of African copper production.[3]

Two copper and cobalt mines, one on the Zambian side and the other on the DRC side of the border, are owned by the same firm, each in a region where a history of mining has left a legacy of expectations about the provision of social goods and services to populations living in and around the mine. However, the two regions demonstrate significantly different governance outcomes. In Zambia's Chibuluma Mine, the firm provides a range of goods and services, and the government exercises regulatory enforcement on extractive firms. In contrast, in DRC's Ruashi copper mine, the local population has briefly protested the firm's failure to engage in similar behavior and the government has largely ignored this failure. Instead, it has made the state's coercive apparatus available to firms operating in the area. The outcomes here demonstrate how the firm's, government's, and local residents' beliefs about each other, and relative political salience and revenue imperative shaped firm-government-community interactions. In the next section I describe the different governance outcomes across the firm's extractive sites. I then demonstrate the beliefs that actors had about each other at the time, and how these shaped the outcomes in each region.

Ruashi Mining, Katanga Province, DRC. South African firm Metorex[4] operates industrial copper and cobalt mines on both sides of the Zambia–DRC border. In DRC, Metorex holds 80 percent equity in the Ruashi copper mining project, which is approximately 10 km east of Lubumbashi, the provincial capital of Katanga. In 2005 Ruashi Mining, a subsidiary of Metorex, acquired its mining concession where reserves were estimated to be 1,244,000 tons of copper, and 160,000 tons of cobalt. By 2009, Ruashi Mine produced 21,372 tons of copper, and 2,186 tons of cobalt,[5] and by 2011, the company was the fourth largest company in the Katangan Copperbelt in terms of export value. By 2016, the country was the world's leading producer of cobalt.

---

[3] Yager et al. (2012).

[4] The firm was recently acquired by Chinese Jinchuan Group, but at the time of investment and this case study, it was still headquartered in South Africa.

[5] Metorex Limited (2010).

The nearest community to Ruashi Mining is the commune of Ruashi, which includes three villages (Luano, Kalukuluku, and Kawama) built during the heyday of the parastatal extractive, Gecamines.[6] Luano (population 10,900) and Kawama (population 42,810) have been particularly affected by the Ruashi mine as a result of their close proximity to operations. A majority of these residents, though relatively close to the urban center of Lubumbashi, rely on small-scale agricultural plots as a primary source of livelihood. There is also a significant number of artisanal miners, many from outside of Ruashi.

In June 2006, only a year after the concession was allocated to Ruashi, local residents drafted a petition to the mayor of Lubumbashi stating about the Ruashi mining operation, "We don't want money for our houses, we want a house at a site where there is potable water, electricity, transportation infrastructure, schools, hospitals and markets" (Carter Center, 2012). By the end of 2006, Ruashi Mining began identifying the property owners whose land would be appropriated by the firm in order to begin copper and cobalt production. These property owners promised compensation. However, community members complained that many were left out of the process, and that the company was slow in fulfilling this promise. Only a subset of the population whose land had been appropriated by the company was actually compensated.[7] By 2008, the mayor and representatives from the firm established a commission to identify the status of each land parcel, but the MOU with the firm (which estimated each parcel to be worth US$2,500) was never actually signed.

In November 2008, local residents blockaded all access roads to the mine processing plant, demanding the promised compensatory payments immediately. In response, the Director General of the company met with them, promising compensation. Local residents remained frustrated, stating that "through greed or bad faith you opted for camouflaged expropriation, simulating preparatory meetings in May 2007 in which, moreover, the price of US$5000 for unbuilt land came out. However, what has been done is quite different... By reducing ourselves from the status of owner to that of tenant, we ask a question, would it be the same in South Africa?" (Carter Center, 2012). No action was taken on the part of the government, and there was no attempt to ensure that the firm

[6] Carter Center (2012).
[7] Centre for Research on Multinational Corporations (SOMO) and Action against Impunity for Human Rights (ACIDH) (2011).

respected its commitments or even complied with national mining law. There were no further protests in which local residents blockaded access or interruption operations at the mine, though the mine did not follow through. By August 2010, another 125 farmers were stripped of their fields. In total, one NGO estimated that approximately 6,000 households were affected by either eviction or relocation.

There were additional claims that the company allowed tailings runoff to pollute the Luano river, which community members have relied upon for drinking water. Furthermore, in 2009, a local organization[8] accused Ruashi of releasing industrial waste in the water supply used for agricultural irrigation, damaging crops. To compensate those affected, Ruashi constructed two standpipes for access to clean water, though residents claimed that one was not functional soon after installation. While the local organization requested that the spill be investigated, the DRC's Environment Ministry responsible for the investigation never released any findings.[9] The government refused to share a copy of the firm's EIA when requested by local civil society groups, and the company conducted its own version of an RAP. It was difficult to confirm compliance as a result.

The expropriation of land resulted in a brief blockade of the road leading to the mine's processing plant. However, while the firm made a token effort to address the water issue and provide some compensation, the government did not respond to the local complaints – in fact there was limited engagement. Yet, in spite of the government's failure to respond, the local population did not engage in further protest. In fact, other reports indicated that there were actually *no* conflicts between Ruashi Mining and the local communities at all (ignoring the barricading of mine access early on). The series of events above presents a snapshot of the interactions among the local population, firm, and government, and is a manifestation of the broader trend of governance outcomes across mining sites in Katanga.

Though the Ruashi mine is only 10 km from Lubumbashi, the government of DRC has provided limited public goods and social services, and has not compelled the firm to do so. The central government's 2010 budget allocated only 7 percent of domestically financed revenue to Education, Health, Agriculture, Rural Development and Infrastructure, and Public works (8 percent is debt-related payments, and 7 percent to the

---

[8] Group for Support of Malnourished Women.
[9] Carter Center (2012).

provinces, without earmarks).[10] The World Bank noted that in general, "public security was present more often than more essential needs including potable water. In one instance, the state was not a provider at all, and the only providers were mining companies" (Oil Gas and Mining Policy Division Africa Region, 2013) Firms have begun constructing their own roads in Katanga given limited infrastructure, and while railroad lines in Katanga are operated by state-owned SNCC, transport only occurs at 10–35 km/h and one-third of trains derail, costing about US\$20,000 each time. Though the building of roads does affect local communities by way of connecting local markets, most road construction is primarily completed by firms to ensure lower-cost transport routes that move ore to processing plants, and eventually to market. Furthermore, in cases where politicians learn of the size of the local investment by firms in social projects, well-positioned politicians suggest that such investment is too large, and instead, request the value of the investment to be given to the government.[11]

The government failed to regulate extractive firm behavior in and around its operations. In many cases, the government remains unaware of the extent to which firms are compliant with environmental regulations and fulfill socio-economic investment promises. Since 2003, Le Cadastre Minier (CAMI), the mining registry within the Ministry of Mines, has allocated and documented mining permits and licenses. With only one office in Kinshasa, one that was not yet operational in Lubumbashi as of 2010 (it became operational in 2014), and no other operations at the provincial level, CAMI has not been allocated resources to effectively monitor and regulate mining operations and their compliance with licensing terms.[12] The Mining Inspection Services (within the Directorate of Mines) is tasked with monitoring health, safety, and environment in and around mining sites. However, it had a total staff of 30 for all of Katanga Province, and minimal logistical support to carry out inspections, indicating minimal investment in the allocation of resources to ensure regulatory compliance.[13] As late as 2015, a government functionary at Le Departement de Protection d'Environment des Mines (DPEM) acknowledged that he had insufficient staff to carry out required inspections to ensure mines were complying with their EIAs.

[10] Breakdowns of provincial budget allocation were not available.
[11] Anonymous interview, Lubumbashi June, 2015.
[12] Environmentally and Socially Sustainable Development Africa Region (2008).
[13] Environmentally and Socially Sustainable Development Africa Region (2008).

Furthermore, a local mining consultant confirmed that the DPEM is actually supposed to go to the mining site to check compliance, but that for some firms the EIA is just copied and pasted from preexisting ones created for other mining sites. In this case, the form and content of the EIA meet the requirements but have no bearing on the actual mine-specific context.[14] Thus, the EIA might be approved, but because firms know the DPEM is not reliable to monitor and enforce it, they fail to complete one specific to the site.

Though the government allocates limited resources (monetary and personnel) for monitoring of mining operations in Katanga, indicating limited regulatory engagement, the presence of the public security apparatus is much more visible. The security apparatus is clearly developed in the Congolese mining industry, including private security companies, the national Congolese police (PNC), a separate mining police (PM), the judiciary police officers, as well as the national armed forces (FARDC and GR). Mining companies can call on any or all of these in the event of protest, and according to De Goede (2008), every company works with both a private or in-house security company *and* the PNC, PM, and national armed forces. A strong and diversified market for private security exists in Katanga, but none work independently of government. A formal partnership in 2003 allowed private interests to purchase the use of public security for specific tasks related to mining and private protection. Members of the Congolese National Police, the Police Minière et Hydrocarbon, the security agencies Agence National de Renseignement (ANR), the Direction Générale de Migration, as well as from the Congolese army, the FARDC, and the Presidential Guard frequent mining sites, transport routes, and border posts. As Hönke (2009) notes, "the de facto privatization of the police results in the concentration of most capacities of the Police National and the Mining Police around the mines: for patrolling mining concessions, offices and the houses of senior staff of mining companies."

Furthermore, in a report on its operations at Ruashi, Metorex noted that "community representation on the Community Liaison committee seems to be slanted toward government functionaries" (SRK Consulting, 2010). Metorex places visible security around mining sites. Instead of partnering with local communities to build local support through the provision of services, government functionaries in DRC have replaced

---

[14] Anonymous Interview, Lubumbashi, June 2015.

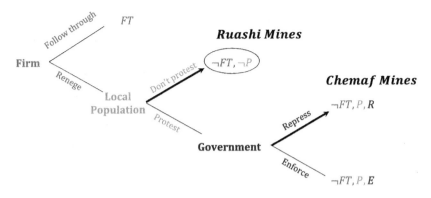

FIGURE 6.1: DRC outcomes

community leaders, excluding them from the process.[15] The limited regulatory environment and strong security presence is in stark contrast to the firm and government's more cooperative management of the Chibuluma mining site in Zambia.

Chibuluma Mine, Copperbelt Province, Zambia. On the Zambian side of the border, Metorex has an 85 percent share in Chibuluma Mines Plc, which owns a copper mine approximately 10 km south of the town of Kalulushi. The Chibuluma South mine has both an open cast and an underground component. The license for the mine was allocated for 1997–2022, and construction began in 2001. Copper production began in 2005, and by 2007, the production was averaging approximately 45,000 tonnes per month.[16] In 2010, more than 17,700 tons of concentrate were produced.[17]

With approximately 3,300 houses, the town of Kalulushi has its own hospital, clinic, school, and recreational facilities. A paved road links the town to the larger city of Kitwe, and the town is on the electrical grid, maintained by the government-owned utility, ZESCO. Water is available through multiple drill holes and a pipeline from the regional hub of Kitwe.

In order to begin production, Chibuluma had to relocate approximately 90 households to nearby villages. The firm did not face any

---

[15] SRK Consulting (2010).
[16] SRK Consulting (2010).
[17] Mobbs (2012).

observable resistance to the relocation, though it noted that the local pop-ulation had expectations about the benefits of the mine that were higher than could be met.[18] The community liaison and director of CSR allo-cation noted, "[W]e cannot ignore the leadership hierarchies, the chiefs (Chief Nkana), headman of villages, I have to go through them. I need their support. There would be a lot of resistance from the headman, and they would make their people not see me, if I didn't go through the headmen" (Mwale Private Interview, 2012). The firm adopts schools in the area, and writes a regular newsletter to update the surrounding community of its activities including water monitoring, school building maintenance, and small business support.

In Chililabombwe, a town near Chibuluma, a local government offi-cial noted that communities are represented by councilors in areas affected by the firm, and they act as liaison with the firm to ensure com-munities demands are heard. She stated that firms do not decide how to invest locally by themselves; the district helps to plan local firm invest-ment. If the community has an objection, the municipal council evaluates it. "When it comes to resettlement, [the firms] can't just build houses without some services for that community" (Interview, 2012b). Further-more, Metorex explicitly recognized that it is indeed the responsibility of local councils to provide goods and services, but the firm works to "fill in the gaps." While the local council receives some tax revenue from mining in the province, it is first collected by the central government of Zambia before it is allocated back to the province. The firm–community liaison viewed the government as helpful, though wished the government would be more explicit in describing to the firm and the communities how taxes paid by firms were being allocated.[19]

In contrast to DRC, the government of Zambia has compelled firms to adhere to the provisions of their EIA and RAP. For instance, at a site in Mufulira, a local community complained of health problems related to acid mist and leaching, as well as noise pollution, dust, and crack-ing in their houses. Upon receiving the complaint from the community of Butondo, the government suspended operations at the portion of the mine, compelling the firm to erect barriers, reduce pollution, and pre-pare an additional environmental and social impact plan for the leaching portion of the mine. The mine's license had been renewed only two weeks before the complaint was launched by the community, just after

[18] Sikamo Private Interview (2012).
[19] Sikamo Private Interview (2012).

the Zambian Environmental Management Agency (ZEMA) approved the site's operations, suggesting that the local community's discontent with the firm's operations provoked a change in policy by the government. The firm suffered a loss of 1.5% of its annual copper production.[20] Under similar circumstances in 2011, the government shut down a portion of Ndola Lime company as well.[21]

In a further indication of differing constellation of government and firm incentives in Zambia, the Mining Union of Zambia (MUZ), the largest mining union in Zambia, expressed public satisfaction with the extent to which many mining companies were providing sanitation and other services to communities near their mines. The union particularly lauded the provision of clean water and sanitation to the township of Konkola in Copperbelt Province,[22] which is located on the border of the Konkola North mining concession owned in part by Vale (who failed to successfully engage with the local population in its coal concession in Tete, Mozambique). Specifically, Vale has publicized its commitments, and specific targets for localized investment around its copper mine in northern Zambia, including the proposed funding and development of a Millennium Village.[23] While the Mines Safety Department monitors the mines' adherence to regulations and Zambia Environmental Management Agency is responsible for evaluation of the mines' EIAs, the Miner's Union of Zambia is involved in monitoring firm compliance with the EIA. MUZ randomly conducts inspections of the mines to assess their impact and compliance. While MUZ advocates specifically for mineworkers, MUZ can act as additional monitor of firm compliance, thus lowering government monitoring costs and resulting in spillover effects for local communities like Chibuluma.[24]

Next I demonstrate that the firm had different expectations about whether it would face resistance from the local population, in spite of some similarities between the extractive contexts in Zambia and DRC. However, these expectations on their own turn out to be insufficient to explain the difference in governance outcomes between Metorex's copper mines.

---

[20] *ZEMA Orders Mopani Mine to Shut Down Part of Its Operation after Complaints from Butondo Community* (2006).

[21] *Ndola lime continues operating* (2011).

[22] Njovu (2012).

[23] *Vale: Another quality addition to mining in Zambia* (2012).

[24] Mushota Private Interview (2012).

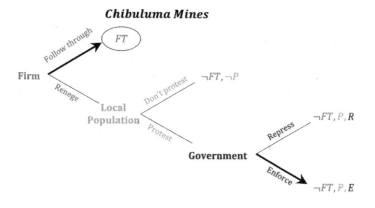

FIGURE 6.2: Zambia outcomes

Costs and Beliefs About Local Protest

Legacy of Industrial Mining. Much like in the case of Vale and Rio Tinto in Mozambique, the local context shaped the cost of meeting local expectations for goods provision. Ruashi and Chibuluma are both in regions with a history of large-scale copper mining and state-owned firm investment. This history has led to a legacy of goods provision by mining operators and resulted in strong expectations for firm compensation and local distribution of benefits. However, the localized landscape shaped the cost of actually meeting those expectations. Consequently, while the firm had different beliefs about the likelihood that they would face resistance, it was the expected costs of obtaining local support and the government's response that led to the different outcomes.

Unlike in the case of Mozambique, where industrial-scale mining was relatively new, and thus firms (and the government for that matter) had limited experience to support any beliefs about the potential reaction of the local population to extractive operations, local populations living near mining sites in the Copperbelt region had strong expectation that a set of goods would be provided by extractive firms. Until privatization in the mid-1990s, Congolese parastatal companies Gecamines, OKIMO, and MIBA operated as a "state within a state," both with respect to regulatory structure and goods and service provision. This included the provision of schools, hospitals, social centers, transportation, energy, water infrastructure, and employment opportunities to residents in the area.[25] Similarly, the Zambian state-owned mining enterprise, ZCCM, engaged in investment in and around extractive sites, including "cradle to grave" welfare programs, as historically, this was a strategy for maintaining a local labor supply for firm operations.

A survey of members of mining communities in DRC conveys the local expectation that mining companies provide localized goods and services. When local chiefs were asked who was responsible for providing services to local residents, nearly 30 percent said the state, about 50 percent said the mining company, while the rest stated either that it was unclear or that it was the responsibility of both the state and the firm. However, many noted that the government was supposed to compel the firm to do so, or that since the government allowed the mining firm to operate in the area, it was the firm that was responsible. In a Zambian village just south of the DRC border, a local chief and village chairman expressed similar sentiments, stating that "the mining company was making a lot of money on taking copper out of the ground" (Chairman Private Interview, 2012). He claimed that the company should not only compensate them for the noise and dust pollution from the mine construction, but also should build another school building, as well as a clinic since that was what ZCCM had done. Metorex's community liaison confirmed this expectation.[26] Similar to the role of Gecamines in DRC, the assumption of responsibility for welfare by mining communities left a legacy of expectations by residents, even after privatization of both enterprises and the deterioration of Gecamines.

Beliefs about Resistance. The region's history of mining led local populations in both Zambia and DRC to expect extractive firms to provide certain welfare services and employment. However, the firm had different expectations about the likelihood it would face resistance at each of its mining sites, should it fail to fulfill those expectations. Addressing its mine in DRC, Metorex acknowledged that "by virtue of the proximity of the community to the [Ruashi] mine and the inherent volatility of communities in an African context, community dissatisfaction and possible unrest represented a potential risk (for example unrealistic expectations with regard to post closure supply of services such as water) to the operation."[27] The firm noted a high level of existing violence in the

---

[25] Oil Gas and Mining Policy Division Africa Region (2013).

[26] Mwale Private Interview (2012).

[27] SRK Consulting (2010).

community, some of which affected mining personnel. The potential for protest and riot was listed as "a key risk and management focus area," and of the 32 risks identified by Metorex at the Ruashi site, the risks presented by the local community fell within the top five. Specifically, the firm viewed it as particularly likely that "the community runs riot and takes their frustration out on the mine."[28] The firm believed that the riot would cause an interruption of production for more than six months.

As a consequence, the firm noted in their annual reports that the Ruashi villages required a high level of engagement with local communities. The firm's stated strategies for managing this risk included the development of a social program, compensation, and maintaining good relationships with the community. While the firm claimed that most of these strategies were already in place by 2010 – five years after the firm's arrival – investments such as ensuring the availability of safe drinking water and facilitation of sustainable social programs had not yet been made.[29]

In contrast, Metorex had significantly different beliefs about the risks posed by local communities around the Chibuluma site in Zambia. In Zambia, the firm did not believe the local population presented a significant threat. Specifically, the firm noted that the local population presented "no potentially material risks." In an assessment of the group's risks (across all of its operations), the community-related risks that are likely to result in business interruption, damage to equipment or property, are listed exclusively for its mine in Ruashi, DRC, not for the firm's Zambian mines.[30] Miners with other firms operating in both countries shared a similar belief. One expressed a particularly strong cultural bias, stating, "Zambians are very kind, they are very non-violent . . . they have never had a civil war. So I don't think it is in the nature of the locals."[31] Furthermore, an official at the Chibuluma mine stated that "in general, the local population will not do anything, they will just stop. They will do nothing physical, they do not destroy anything."[32]

---

[28] SRK Consulting (2010).

[29] Interestingly, at the time of privatization, an agreement between the parastatals and private firms indicates that the private firm is explicitly not responsible for assuming the responsibility of providing social services, according to Oil Gas and Mining Policy Division Africa Region (2013).

[30] SRK Consulting (2010).

[31] Svendlund Private Interview (2012).

[32] Sikamo Private Interview (2012).

The company's perception was that the likelihood of resistance at the Zambian Chibuluma site was significantly lower than at the Ruashi site. However, in spite of this, there was no significant difference in discretionary spending on the community between Ruashi and Chibuluma. According to their own report on social spending, Metorex did not spend any more resources to address risks at the Ruashi site than at its Chibuluma mine.[33]

If the firm believed its assets to be at greater risk from surrounding communities at its DRC mine than in Zambia, why did it fail to address the local population's complaints? Why did the local population in Ruashi not continue to protest? And if the firm did not believe the local population in Zambia would engage in protest that would materially affect their operations, why did they pursue localized goods provision to secure local legitimacy from the local population? Two factors overshadowed the difference in expectations about protest to explain the governance outcome in DRC versus that in Zambia: the material costs of meeting local expectations, and the expected government response to resistance.

Costs of Fulfilling Promises. Though the countries share a history of industrial copper mining along the Copperbelt, the countries' different trajectories through the privatization process resulted in significantly different baseline infrastructure and demographics, which affected the costs to the firm of meeting local expectations. The government of DRC allowed Gecamines to enter into shared agreements with private firms only after bankruptcy and significant deterioration of infrastructure and failure to pay wages for employees of the mine. Gecamines could support all of its social commitments when production was at 400,000 metric tonnes of copper per year, but with the production restored to only 30,000 metric tonnes, the parastatal suggested that the government, NGOs, or the church would assume these responsibilities.[34]

In contrast, Zambia's ZCCM entered into shared equity agreements with private partners before insolubility, and thus secured the continued investment in existing mining regions. Though socio-economic conditions and infrastructure did deteriorate in the interim while ZCCM was being unbundled (between 1992–1997),[35] production soon rebounded.

---

[33] SRK Consulting (2010).
[34] World Bank (2007).
[35] Lungu and Mulenga (2005).

Furthermore, as the community liaison at Chibuluma noted, the local residents are, generally, relatively well educated,[36] making it less costly to train local work force for the mine (instead of recruiting labor from elsewhere).[37] Thus, by the time Metorex began operations at its Ruashi and Chibuluma mines, the baseline landscape of infrastructure and human capital at each country's mining site looked very different. Schools and hospitals built by Gecamines in and around Ruashi were dilapidated, and Ruashi required more investment in human capital to train a local work force than did Chibuluma. Thus, living up to expectations of a community that had historically benefited from mining operations would be more costly near Ruashi than it would be near Chibuluma.

The actual costs of production and anticipated closure liabilities of the mining sites differed significantly too. Metorex's operating and expected closure costs were much greater at Ruashi than at Chibuluma. Chibuluma had one of the lowest costs (per unit production) of the copper mines in Zambia, at approximately half of the cash cost per tonne produced at Ruashi. The firm's anticipated closure liabilities at Ruashi are US$14,950,000,000 while at Chibuluma the firm anticipates spending US$2,624,000,000 to close the mine in accordance with national environmental standards.[38] Such a significant difference, particularly when viewed in light of the higher per unit operating costs, makes the Ruashi mine a significantly more expensive operation, and thus constrained the firm's willingness to allocate significant funds to local communities.

In sum, the costs of meeting local expectations in DRC were greater relative to Zambia. While these costs can explain the firm's perception of risk that could be ameliorated by sustained local engagement and investment, they do not yet provide an understanding of why the local population failed to engage in continued protest, given the firm's failure to meet expectations near the Ruashi site. For this, it is important to understand the expectations about the likelihood of government repression.

Local Beliefs and Repression. The Ruashi mine is only a couple of kilometers from an Indian-owned copper and cobalt mine, CHEMAF.

---

[36] Firm officials elsewhere frequently mentioned the lack of human capital as a justification for non-local labor recruitment.

[37] Mwale Private Interview (2012).

[38] Metorex Limited (2010).

Residents in villages near both the Ruashi and Chemaf mines protested CHEMAF's failure to employ local residents, local displacement, and frustration by artisanal miners. In response to these protests, the firm called the national police, who violently repressed the protests, which resulted in several casualties. Similarly, in Kolwezi, a mining town 200 km northwest of Ruashi, riots led companies to call the police, who repressed the riots.[39] A local NGO noted of the area that "the government seems to come in and protect the companies, I don't have any cases in which the government sides with the local communities."[40]

In yet another example, a Canadian mining company operating near Ruashi, relocated a community. Much like in Vale's coal concession in Tete, the firm built houses of questionable quality, and the community had no access to fields for agricultural or potable water in their new location. The firm organized a meeting with members of the community to tell them of the project, and the firm promised schools, houses, and hospitals. When the firm failed to deliver on these promises, the members of the local population stated that they considered protesting, but they feared the response of the central and local authorities. A member of a local NGO noted that the people living in the area would stop supporting the government, but that was unlikely to matter to them.[41] One respondent noted that "the government did not care if the population existed."[42] These events shaped the local population's beliefs about the likelihood of government repression, so as to limit their engagement in continued protest.

This kind of repressive campaign to protect mining sites has been rare in the Zambian Copperbelt province. In fact it is difficult to identify instances of overt government repression in response to a mining protest in Zambia. Thus, while local populations in both countries had expectations of the provision of some set of social goods and services by those extracting minerals around them, the history of violent repression indicated that expectations about how the government would respond should residents of the Copperbelt protest differed significantly.

In sum, the firm had different beliefs about its operations in the two contexts: it saw local protest as likely near its Ruashi project, but not

[39] Hönke (2009).
[40] Umpala Private Interview (2012).
[41] Umpala Private Interview (2012).
[42] Dweidary et al. (2012).

near its Chibuluma project. Additionally, the local context made the cost of providing goods and services near Ruashi much higher than at the Chibuluma site. Furthermore, while the historical context of copper mining in both places created expectations about the provision of goods and services in and around these sites, the local population had a greater expectation of repression in Ruashi, should it protest, than did those living in the Chibuluma site. I turn now to the primary trade-off that shaped the government's response in each of the mining sites: the political relevance of the local population in each of these sites relative to the economic value of the mining project and sector.

Government Trade-Offs: Kabila's Katanga and Zambia's Mining Unions in the Copperbelt

Both DRC and Zambia have a diverse portfolio of mineral resources. However, while the copper belt represents a significant revenue generator for both the Zambian and Congolese governments, Ruashi is of somewhat greater strategic, monetary importance to the government of DRC than Chibuluma is to the government of Zambia, given its revenue generation relative to other extractive sites in the province, and the importance of that province for taxable industrial mining.

In DRC, the mining sector has consistently contributed between 70 and 80 percent of export revenue.[43] Katanga province, where Ruashi is located, consistently generates the most revenue annually of the mineral-producing provinces.[44] Additionally, in 2009 government revenue[45] from the copper and cobalt projects was expected to increase from 12 percent of GDP to 22 percent of GDP between 2010 and 2016 at the time, further increasing the region's economic value to the state.[46] While DRC's copper production constituted only 2.7 percent of global production by 2011,[47] its cobalt production during the same year was an astounding 53.1 percent of global production.

Katanga's minerals comprise a significant source of revenue for the government, and within it, the Ruashi site is a particularly important

---

[43] Environmentally and Socially Sustainable Development Africa Region (2008).

[44] Oil Gas and Mining Policy Division Africa Region (2013).

[45] It is important to note that these are reported revenues, and both the World Bank and the EITI acknowledge that government receipts constitute only a small percentage of the total amount that could be collected given the legal tax and royalty rates.

[46] Oil Gas and Mining Policy Division Africa Region (2013).

[47] KPMJ (2013).

source. The Ruashi project generated approximately US$200 million in revenue in 2009 and 2010, and its contribution to government revenue was projected to continue to grow with production increases.[48] In 2010, Ruashi was the second largest mineral exporter (by value), exporting a total of over US$510 million.[49] The government declared US$11.8 million in receipts from Ruashi that year, among the top five companies in terms of amounts recovered. The Ruashi site has three times the copper reserves of Chibuluma, in addition to notable cobalt reserves. Though the tax recovery rate is significantly below 100 percent, Katanga province has the greatest concentration of industrial mining concessions of the provinces, and tax collection is significantly higher than in other provinces where artisanal mining is more common. Furthermore, CHEMAF, the mine operating near Ruashi, was also a significant producer.[50]

Zambia, in addition to being one of the top copper producers in the world, has the second largest emerald deposits as well (accounting for approximately 20 percent of global supply). In addition, manganese reserves have significant revenue potential. In 2011, Zambian copper production constituted 4.4 percent of global production, with cobalt production at 5.8 percent; but in contrast to Ruashi in DRC, Chibuluma did not constitute such a significant source of taxable revenue. In 2009, the Zambian Revenue Authority collected approximately US$337 million that year from extractive companies, and the mining sector contributed US$866 million to total exports. However, Chibuluma contributed 2.42 percent of all of the mining contributions to government in 2009, at US$11.5 million, ranking 7th among companies.[51] From Chibuluma, the government collected approximately US$7 million in company and windfall taxes in 2011.[52] While Chibuluma presents a greater revenue source to the Zambian government than Ruashi does to the government of DRC in absolute terms, Zambia's northwest province also has

---

[48] Environmentally and Socially Sustainable Development Africa Region (2008).
[49] Government of DRC (2010).
[50] EITI reports suggest that discrepancies between payments made by CHEMAF to the government and those made by Ruashi to the government are systematically higher by Ruashi. While difficult to confirm, this is not inconsistent with the idea that members of the government who benefited from a particular relationship with CHEMAF were more inclined to repress a protest in order to protect it.
[51] *Extractive Industry Transparency Initiative Report, Zambia* (2009).
[52] Zambia Chamber of Mines (n.d.).

significant industrial mining, and presents opportunities to recover mineral tax revenue beyond the Copperbelt province. Thus while Katanga in DRC constituted the government's largest concentration of revenue, Zambia's emerging Northwest Province, where the largest copper mine on the continent was slated to be built, presented a potentially lucrative alternative.

The Copperbelt region represents a significant revenue generator for both the Zambian and Congolese governments, but Ruashi is of somewhat greater strategic, monetary importance to the government of DRC than Chibuluma is to Zambia. This is a result of its revenue generation relative to other extractive sites in the province, and the importance of that province for taxable industrial mining, relative to others, as noted above. But perhaps more importantly, the political salience of the mineral region's population for the administration differs significantly between the two countries. The government of Zambia faces the potential of significant political costs to repressing resistance in a region with a politically important constituency and an historically strong miner's union, neither of which constrained Kabila's government in Katanga. The difference in regime types cannot be ignored, as it is long recognized that democracies like Zambia provide public goods (including regulatory enforcement) at a greater rate and repress at a lower rate than autocracies like DRC. However, subnational variation in local governance outcomes (as described in the Mozambique cases) cannot be explained by national-level characteristics, short of the interaction of these characteristics with specific, geographic contexts.

In Zambia's Copperbelt province, where the Chibuluma mine is located, support for the administration has been in greater contention. In 2008, Michael Sata of the Patriotic Front (PF) received 56 percent of the vote in the Kalulushi district of the Copperbelt province, with Banda of the Movement for Multiparty Democracy (MMD) receiving 36 percent.[53] While not a particularly close margin, the MMD was the incumbent, and support for the MMD in the Copperbelt Province was not a given. As one miner noted, candidates and government officials perceive electoral benefits to attracting mineral companies, and to compelling firms to provide social services and employment to local communities. He noted, "Whoever got First Quantum to come in, they can

---

[53] Electoral Commission of Zambia (2011).

use it in a political campaign to say, 'I provided so many jobs' " (Svend-lund Private Interview, 2012). If supporters indeed reward incumbents for public works projects in their region (whether the government or a firm provides it) as some literature suggests,[54] then a political leader who enforces or promises to ensure the provision of those projects can better secure support. While this instance of enforcement was ultimately insuf-ficient to ensure victory for the MMD, such enforcement can be seen as a tactic to secure support in the region.

Additionally, the presence of a historically well-organized and polit-ically effective miners union in the Zambian Copperbelt facilitated the coordination of local support for candidates it saw as acting in its interest. As Larmer (2006) notes, "[T]he relative autonomy of mine townships, managed by the mine companies and policed by their own security forces rather than those of the state, provided a relatively autonomous space in which a community-based form of union organiza-tion was able to develop. Local union offices, based in mine townships (where the vast majority of mineworkers were residents) rather than in the mine itself, provided bases for the coordination and mobilization of local campaigns outside the effective control of the state, the mine com-pany and the national union leadership."[55] Unions still retain localized networks to facilitate collective action in order to extract concessions from the management of mining firms, whether the firm is publicly or pri-vately held. During the process of privatization of ZCCM, between 1986 and 2001, labor union membership in the Zambian Congress of Trade Unions declined, but was still 250,000 by 2002.[56] The historical strength and political ties of the mineworkers' union (and limited cooptation) have resulted in its continued, if weakened, relevance, with potential to impose particularly high political and economic costs on leaders during electoral cycles.

Similar miners' unions are not present in DRC's Katanga. A Mining Union of Zambia (MUZ) official explained that he attempted to start a union like MUZ in DRC's copper region, noting "We tried to have a safety training, they have been coming here, we have tried to train them how to organize. It has been difficult because they have so many groups that want to form unions because there are so many minerals. There is internal competition. Each one wants to be on top. Splintering

---

[54] Moser (2008), Min (2009).

[55] Larmer (2006).

[56] Negi (2011).

undermines presentation of united front and demands."[57] As a result, the political salience to President Joseph Kabila of the population living in and around Ruashi was limited relative to that of Zambia's copperbelt, as there were few avenues and manifestations of organized political capital.

Furthermore, the Ruashi project is in Katanga Province, President Kabila's home province. Kabila's home outside of Kinshasa can be seen when driving north on the main road from the Zambian border. Historically, Katanga has experienced several secession attempts, and Kabila's second home is not a particularly well-veiled attempt to monitor any continued efforts. However, Kabila enjoys strong support in Katanga, where social cleavages exist on the basis of regional and historical affiliation. Kabila is from northern Katanga, and in the country's first multi-party election in 2006, he received first 78 percent and then 94 percent of the vote in Katanga Province, relative to 48 percent throughout the country.[58] His support in the province, and in general in the east of the country, is largely uncontested, insulating him from political consequences of protest and repression among local mining communities. Additionally, foreign miners and investors reside primarily in the provincial capital of Lubumbashi, and constitute a foreign elite on which it is suggested that Kabila relies for access to mineral rents (given the low rate of official government collection of industrial mining revenue). As a result, incentives for Kabila to compel the firm to address local complaints about pollution and unfulfilled promises are limited. The neo-patrimonial networks that ensure the direction of mineral rents among a select number of political elites (detailed in Global Witness (2006)) and confirmed in my interviews suggest that there is little incentive for any government official to ensure the firm complies with an EIA or follows through on promised compensation.

[57] Mushota Private Interview (2012).
[58] Weiss (2007).

7

Comparative Implications

In the cases discussed in the last two chapters, I demonstrate variation in local governance outcomes across states and across firms. In Mozambique, Vale's failure to follow through on promises made to the local community led to protest by those adversely affected by its operations. The result was that both Vale and Rio Tinto ultimately provided a set of material goods and services, while the government provided regulatory enforcement. In an attempt to ensure continued operations, the firm made efforts to build local support through visibly redoubling its investment efforts. The protest provided a relatively low-cost opportunity for the Frelimo government to secure local support in a region with a traditional legitimacy deficit during a time at which it was particularly valuable for the party to do so. The cases of Vale and Rio Tinto highlight two important aspects of the strategic context: the importance of the firms' beliefs about the likelihood of protest, and the political salience of the local population relative to the interruptible revenue stream at the time of the protest. Table 7.1 provides a shorthand for the differences that shaped the outcomes in the two concessions.

In both DRC and Zambia, the history of industrial mining ensured strong local expectations that mining activity brought local development in the form of social goods provision by firms. However, in both countries, trade-offs among revenue and political support dictated different strategies for indirect outsourcing of state functions to companies in areas of extraction. The firm's annual reports suggested that it believed that protest was extremely likely near Ruashi. Beliefs about the likelihood of protest mattered in ensuring the firm made at least a token gesture toward the local residents, but the firm had little incentive to ensure they

123

TABLE 7.1: *Within country case comparison*

	Moatize Mine	Benga Mine
Resource	coal	coal
Country	Mozambique	Mozambique
Infrastructure	single rail	single rail
Firm	Vale	Rio Tinto
Transfer Cost	High	Low
Belief of Protest	Low	High

met local expectations in the Ruashi communities. The knowledge that the government would repress any serious threat to operations meant that social investment that met local expectations was not required, especially if it was too costly. Given the government's repression in response to events near CHEMAF, the local community's beliefs about the likelihood of repression was sufficiently high so as to undermine the likelihood of a protest. Thus, the firm's beliefs about the likelihood of protest did not ultimately matter in determining the outcome – as is suggested in Figure 3.2 in Chapter 3. Furthermore, because the firm could rely on the police and military to repress any protest that did occur, there was no reason to invest significant amounts in local development to stave off such protests. The relative importance of the Ruashi mining site (for cobalt as well as copper) for state revenue and the presidential base in the mining heartland ensured Kabila's preference of continued extraction by way of repression and deterrence over costly monitoring and ensuring firm compliance. In DRC, the government was more willing to trade domestic support, particularly in a region that has always supported the incumbent, for continued access to mining revenue.

In contrast, in Zambia, the firm believed protest to be relatively unlikely, yet engaged continuously with the local population to provide a set of social goods. Doing so was less costly near the Chibuluma mine than near Ruashi in DRC, given a more educated local population, and better existing infrastructure. The firm is more willing to incur those costs given the political relevance of the local population which would lead the government to support them if the firm failed to live up to its commitment. Specifically, the history of labor unions in combination with electoral contestation for presidential support ensured a regulatory role from which the government could profit. Table 7.2 provides a comparison of the two copper extractive regions managed by Metorex.

TABLE 7.2: *Within firm case comparison*

	Chibuluma Mine	Ruashi Mine
Resource	copper/cobalt	copper/cobalt
Firm	Metorex	Metorex
Country	Zambia	DRC
Infrastructure	roads	roads
Pol. Relevance	High	Low
Belief of Repression	Low	High

While the cases in Mozambique highlighted the importance of firm beliefs for understanding different outcomes when the costs of meeting local expectations differed only slightly between firms, the cases in Zambia and DRC demonstrated how the relevance of those beliefs was limited by the cost of meeting local expectations and the expected government response. In all four of the cases the local population is of strategic consideration to the firm, but local engagement is shaped by the firm's beliefs about the likelihood of protest, the government's response to firm behavior, and the relative costs of avoiding protest. Thus both firms and governments may have incentives to secure local support in these regions, but these incentives are shaped and potentially constrained by the costs and expectations of doing so, as well as beliefs that the firm, government, and local population hold of each other.

PART III

BEYOND MOZAMBIQUE, ZAMBIA, AND DRC

8

Generalizing the Theory

Recall that Chapters 2 and 3 detail a theory that explains the local politics of natural resource extraction, providing conditional arguments about when we should expect to see firms providing local transfers to communities, when communities might mobilize against the firm, and how the government might respond. I described a logically consistent, if abstract and stylized, set of propositions and conclusions about the way local politics of natural resources play out in extractive regions. In the case studies of Zambia, Mozambique, and DRC that followed I provided evidence of the plausibility of these mechanisms, demonstrating how the actors, beliefs, and parameters interact on the ground to yield the different outcomes predicted by the model. In particular, the case work suggested how and when beliefs of the firm, government, and local population about each other are important for understanding the comparative outcomes. However, we do not yet have a sense of whether the theory travels more generally.

In the next two chapters, I turn to an quantitative test of the generalizability of the geographic and structural characteristics shaping the likelihood of the different outcomes described in the model. To test the broader applicability of these claims, I first operationalize a set of hypotheses derived from the model. After laying out these hypotheses, I provide an empirical test of their generalizability.

The quantitative tests in Chapters 9 and 10 build on existing studies of social mobilization in and around mines,[1] but my empirical strategy

---

[1] Haslam and Ary Tanimoune (2016).

diverges from existing quantitative work[2] in order to reflect the specific claims derived from the theoretical model. The theory presented in Chapters 2 and 3 yields claims about the likelihood of social mobilization, but also about the likelihood of government repression in response to instances of social mobilization around mines. Existing quantitative work and the majority of qualitative work focuses on the process of mobilization and the various characteristics of the mine and firm that lead to mine-related protest as the outcome of interest. While these works provide a rich exploration of how and when local groups living in and around large-scale mines overcome collective action problems to engage in protest, a more holistic understanding of the local politics around natural resource extractive sites should include an evaluation not only of the likelihood of mobilization near a mine, but also of government repression of that protest. In line with the theoretical model, Part III provides insight not only into the behavior of the local population living in and around regions of natural resource extraction, but also of the government's willingness to use repression in ways predicted by the theory. Evaluating both the likelihood of protest, as well as the likelihood of repression advances our understanding of mobilization around mineral extraction by taking into consideration the strategic nature of these locales, and thus the relevance of the behavior of the government as well as that of the local population.

The theoretical model presented in Chapter 3 suggests two types of constraints on actors' behavior: actors' beliefs about each other, and structural characteristics about the local geographical, economic, and political context. The cases described in Part II elucidated the existence of beliefs in shaping firm, community, and government behavior and the constraints on their importance in shaping outcomes. In this quantitative test, the structural characteristics of the local geographical, economic, and political context are the focus. To evaluate the generalizability of the claims derived from the formal model, they are formalized into two groups of hypotheses: (1) hypotheses about the likelihood of social mobilization[3] near a mine and (2) hypotheses about the likelihood that a mobilization event near a mine is repressed by the government. Given the sequential nature of the model (in order for repression of a protest to

---

[2] Arce (2014), Arce and Miller (2016), Bebbington, Humphreys, Bury, Lingan, Muñoz, and Scurrah (2008), Arellano-Yanguas (2011).

[3] As I have throughout the book, I use protest occasionally in place of social mobilization for the sake of brevity.

be a possible outcome, a protest must first occur), it is useful to evaluate these two outcomes separately.

The unit of analysis in both of these analyses is the industrial mine. To be clear, the theory in this book seeks to understand variation of outcomes across mines, *not* which outcomes are *caused* by the existence of a mine. As a consequence, the mine is the appropriate unit of analysis for evaluating the hypotheses. Furthermore, I focus on industrial mines, where concessions are large enough to affect communities, firms have invested significant sunk costs and have limited exit options, and governments benefit from the rents that accrue as a result. Thus they are best suited for the test of my theory, as artisanal mining relies less on foreign investment and the concessionary arrangement that shapes and constrains the interaction among the firm, government, and community.

The analysis is restricted to the years between 1990 and 2014. Practically, this is the range for which there is good spatial coverage of social conflict data in Africa. Additionally, as noted in the introduction, 1990 marks a time at which implementation of the policies of the Washington Consensus was in full swing, specifically privatization of major industries including natural resources. While not all natural resource industries were fully privatized in Africa, the trend is toward private and independent enterprise, presenting a natural point of departure for developing a dataset to understand the role of these firms as emerging non-state actors in sovereign African states.

Part III is split into two sets of analyses. Chapter 9 presents an analysis of the likelihood of social mobilization near mining sites, and Chapter 10 provides an analysis of the conditions under which these instances of protest are repressed by the government.

9

On Social Mobilization Near Mines

In this chapter I provide a quantitative empirical test of the likelihood of social mobilization near a mine in Africa, according to the theory laid out in Chapters 2 and 3. While the quantitative study of protests near mining sites is in its early stages, it has burgeoned in the last five years.[1] This recent scholarship builds on earlier, region-specific, qualitative explorations of the dynamics of protest around mines.[2] Though existing work has paid somewhat more attention to Latin America (given greater data availability), more scholars have begun to consider these mechanisms in the African context.[3] In addition to testing the specific hypotheses derived from the theory I have laid out, adding this regional context provides another set of cases from which to infer generalizability of existing and new theories about when and how mining can result localized mobilization.

Hypotheses

As detailed by the theory and model, the local context of the mine shapes the expected costs and benefits of localized mobilization for the firm, government, and local population. In particular three specific characteristics about the local context that shape these costs and benefits are the interruptibility of the resource, the expected costs to firms of providing

---

[1] Arce (2014), Arce and Miller (2016), Haslam and Ary Tanimoune (2016).
[2] Amengual working paper, Bebbington (2010), Bury (2005).
[3] Arce and Miller (2016).

a promised transfer to the local communities, and the government's take of firm revenue. Recall from the theory that the interruptibility of the resource shapes the likelihood of social conflict near the mine. Specifically, as it becomes easier to disrupt mining operations, local populations incur less cost to do so. While point resources, like mining, are particularly easy to disrupt relative to diffuse natural resources (like forests), even within this category of natural resources, there is variation in the extent to which mining operations can be easily interrupted. As we saw in the case of Tete in Mozambique, firm reliance on a single railroad for transporting iron ore to the port was a particular vulnerability. The local community was able to block the railroad, stalling the transport of the ore to the port of Beira, and creating significant costs for the firm and the government. The local community needed only to overcome relatively low collective action costs to impose monetary costs on both the extractive firm and government. Interrupting the transport of the ore to the port caused shipments to be delayed, costing the firm.

H1: Communities weigh their relative effectiveness in terms of their ability to interrupt a commodity to market. As a result, the more interruptible mineral extraction is, the greater the likelihood of mobilization near a mine.

In addition to the interruptibility of the resource, the expected cost of the promised local transfer shapes the likelihood of each outcome. Recall that the firm promises the local residents a transfer, often including farmland, monetary compensation, or access to potable water sources. The size of this transfer is contingent on the expected social and environmental impact of the mining project, so the cost of providing this transfer is shaped by the local context. A community that lives within or along the boundaries of a mining concession are part of the group promised this transfer, either by way of their physical resettlement or by way of economic compensation for assets affected by the existence of the mine. Factors that may increase the cost of the transfer include population density at the mining site, since this indicates more people will require compensation. Additionally, higher average wealth and asset ownership is likely to increase the cost of this transfer. If the community members' assets are valuable, the cost of compensation is greater. But when the cost to the firm of providing the promised transfer is high, the firm is less likely, on average, to provide it in its entirety. As a consequence, mobilization is more likely. An interesting point of note here is that the cause of social mobilization is the result not immediately of grievances related to externalities from mining, but of the expectations resulting from the promised transfer.

H2: Firms weigh the cost of providing the promised goods and compensation to communities against the potential cost of community mobilization. As a result, as the cost of the promised transfer to the local population increases, firms are less likely to provide it. Consequently, protest near the mine becomes more likely.

In addition to these geographic determinants of protest suggested by the model, there are political and economic ones as well. Recall from the model that the government's take of the firm's revenue stream shapes both the firm's and the government's incentives. The government's take is determined by the tax and royalty rate on minerals in the country, as well as additional fees associated with licensing and permit acquisition. Different taxation structures distribute risk across the firm and the government differently (taxes on fixed inputs tend to favor the government, while profit-based taxes tend to favor firms). However, most governments rely on some combination of these taxation instruments, and the combination of these is often called the effective tax rate, which can be considered the government take. An increase in the government's take cuts into firm revenue and profits. Recall the mining executive in Zambia who noted that such an increase in government's take made him less inclined to provide local compensation in the form of goods and services. While it is the case that mining companies receive relief from fees, royalties, and taxation during the early exploration phase, initial losses are often carried forward, and expected taxation is incorporated into firm expenditure. As a consequence, an increase in government take ensures that the firm is less willing to provide the transfer. The firm calculates that when the government is taking a significant portion of its revenue stream, then the government should assume the role of local distributor.

H3: Because an increase in the government's take of natural resource rents decreases firm resources and willingness to provide the promised transfer, as the government's take increases, the likelihood of protest increases.

Data and Measurement

To evaluate the likelihood of social mobilization near a mine, I create a spatial dataset of large mining projects and instances of social conflict. The mines that constitute the unit of analysis are drawn from a dataset of industrial mineral, metal, and coal mines existing in Africa since 1990, collected by individual consultants at S&P Global Data.[4] The majority of projects in the dataset are mines of the following minerals and metals: coal, copper, gold, iron, lead, nickel, phosphate, platinum, potash, silver, tin, and zinc.[5] These are industrial mining sites – the dataset does not include artisanal mining sites. As noted earlier, reliance on industrial mining sites ensures the presence of the concessionary arrangement on which the theoretical interaction among these actors relies.

Social Mobilization and Conflict. I measure protest around mines as distinct and discrete events of social mobilization, as defined by Tilly and Tarrow (2006). The theoretical model does not make explicit claims about the type and level of violence of social mobilization around mining sites, as doing so is not the focus of this study. It does suggest that communities engage in social mobilization if they expect to be able to impose costs on firms and governments. Such forms of social mobilization might include property damage, protests blocking transport routes or mine entrances, and localized strikes, particularly by local workers with families living nearby.

As has been well documented in the social movements and microdynamics of conflict literature, episodes and even specific events within episodes of contentious politics are dynamic. Individual events escalate and de-escalate over the course of hours or days, as the result of repressive responses by the government, the flow of information over social networks, and in response to perceived changes in the cost and likelihood of success of the event.

However, for the narrow test at hand, which seeks to test the correlates of the outcomes proposed by the theoretical model, it is the likelihood of the occurrence of a discrete social conflict event and its location that is of interest. Conflict events are drawn from the Social Conflict in Africa Dataset (SCAD),[6] which collects and codes instances of social conflict and geo-codes each event from newspaper and media sources. The SCAD dataset includes a wide range of types of social mobilization that vary in intensity and tactic as well as issue. These conflict events include organized or spontaneous demonstration, organized or spontaneous violent riots, strikes, and pro/anti-/extra-/intra-government violence.

---

[4] Formerly of SNL Financial (formerly IntierraRMG) (2014).

[5] Other materials mined include diamonds, fluorspar, uranium, gypsum, manganese, salt, ilmenite, bauxite, lithium, cobalt, rutile, graphite, chromium, limestone, titanium, tantalum, niobium, tungsten, sandstone, vanadium, scandium, and zircon.

[6] Hendrix et al. (2012).

The dataset is well suited for testing these hypotheses because it captures social conflict events of low intensity. Other conflict event datasets, such as Armed Conflict Location and Event Dataset (ACLED),[7] or Uppsala Conflict Data Program (UCDP),[8] have minimum fatality thresholds for inclusion. However, social mobilization around mining may successfully shut down a mine without causing any fatalities at all. Therefore, it is important that broader forms of social mobilization that do not meet a predetermined threshold of violence are included. This is a better characterization of the kind of event that is likely to occur near a mining site absent a pre-existing armed rebellion.

The SCAD dataset is still a coarse measure of social conflict, and in particular it does not allow differentiation between mining-related conflict and non–mining-related conflict. While it does differentiate between types of conflict events, in particular their degree of organization and whether the event involves violence or not (protest, strike, riot, armed violence), the expressly stated grievances are broad ranging and unreliable.[9] Ideally, the list of social conflict events could be easily separated according to specific grievance, and those conflict events that specifically relate to resource extraction or the mine would be identified. However, even this ideal dataset would suffer flaws. First, as discussed earlier, the effects of mining on local residents may vary – they may include increased cost of living, increased competition over agricultural land, water contamination, noise pollution, and resettlement. While the theoretical basis for the social conflict event is one in which the firm fails to live up to expectations, the way in which it fails to do so and the expressed grievances by community members may not correspond. For example, a SCAD event may be described as a protest over food prices. While the coding will not mention the mine, the economic and social effects of mining are wide ranging and often indirect, including increased population yielding upward pressure on food prices. Limiting the list of conflict events to those explicitly referencing a mine would ignore instances of social mobilization that are related to the mine in a more indirect way.

In order to evaluate the likelihood that a conflict event occurs near a mining site I create a variable that takes on 1 if a conflict event occurred

---

[7] Raleigh et al. (2010).

[8] Hallberg (2012).

[9] Conversations with SCAD coders revealed significant skepticism in trustworthiness of the SCAD issue area description.

within 20 km of a mining site, and 0 otherwise. While this distance is somewhat arbitrary, it is a conservative estimate of a radius within which it is reasonable to expect that local populations might be affected by observable impacts of the mining operation. Mine areas range significantly in their size, from 1 to 12 square kilometers in the current dataset. Because the areas of most of the mining concessions are not available, I cannot control explicitly for the fact that the longitude and latitude of the mining site might be in the middle of a firm's concession, which may extend several kilometers from that point. Furthermore, local ecological conditions that vary by season and year are likely to effect the maximum radius of environmental consequence of extraction. Soil effects have been found to deteriorate at about 20 km by Dudka and Adriano (1997) while water contamination has been identified up to 60 km away from the mine by Ashley and Lottermoser (1999) – though this is not significantly indicative as the presence of surface water is a precondition, and a variety of other geographic factors are likely to affect the radius of environmental consequence of mining. Given the combination of the size of the mine (up to 12 square km), and the outer bound of the environmental externalities of the mines, 20 km is a conservative distance.[10]

Interruptibility. In order to measure the interruptibility of the resource, I focus on the transportation infrastructure around the mine. Firms rely on both rail and road networks to transport mineral ore over land to port, processing plant, or market. Rail is perceived to be a cheaper method of transport for the transport of bulk materials for their weight. Much of the existing rail networks across the continent were constructed by colonial administrators, before the wave of independence in the 1960s. Railroad networks were often constructed for the purpose of transporting extracted minerals to newly constructed ports on the coast.[11] Because of the cost of constructing new roads that could bear the weight to allow transport of raw materials to port in regions where there are limited paved road networks, existing rail networks are a particularly common way of transporting raw materials over long distances.

Mines that rely on railroads to transport ore are likely to be more vulnerable because they are more easily interruptible. Rail in sub-Saharan

---

[10] See Appendix B for a robustness test with distances of 15 km and 25 km – all results are robust to these minor changes in distance threshold.

[11] Hilling (1969).

Africa is particularly susceptible to interruption by dissatisfied local community members because significant redundancies in rail networks are less common than in road networks. As a consequence, rail transport provides a lower cost way for local community members to impose monetary costs on the firm and government. As seen in Mozambique, blocking the railroad required relatively few people, and costs the firm millions of dollars in revenue by keeping the coal freight from reaching the port. This is more likely to be effective than barricading a road, which is much more likely to have network redundancies, ensuring trucks can simply take a different route. Rail is thus more vulnerable to protesters interested in imposing costs by disrupting the transport of valuable ore to processing plants or to market. Because rail is, on average, a cheaper way to transport raw material, in the presence of a railroad I assume firms are relying on rail for transport, but in its absence, they are relying on roads. While this presents the possibility that firms could simply switch to a road if the railroad is blocked, shifting from one transportation method to another is costly for the firm. To measure interruptibility, I calculate the distance between the mine and the nearest railroad. The variable is coded dichotomously and takes on a 1 if there is a rail line within 20 km of the mine, and 0 if not.

The Cost of the Local Transfer. The externalities of mining matter significantly in shaping the likelihood of protest. The cost to mitigating the negative consequences from mining (labeled L in the model) and thus the cost $(\chi(T))$ of providing transfer (T) to the local population varies with local environmental characteristics. Mines often require a significant parcel of land to ensure space for construction of the actual infrastructure of the mine, but also for the removal and storage of overburden. Concessionary allocations to firms may include existing agricultural land, or they may abut against it. If the concession includes agricultural land, the cost of compensating local communities in the area who rely on that land is likely to be high, since either additional land will have to be found for the displaced population, or they will have to be compensated through the allocation of cash or other transfers. The cost of compensation is likely to be particularly high if a large proportion of the population relies on agriculture, as the presence of a mine will cause agricultural land to grow more scarce, and thus more costly to locate and provide to locally displaced residents. The percentage of land in and around the mining site that is devoted to agriculture provides an indicator of the degree of reliance on the land by the local community. In contrast, mines that occur in regions not characterized by large percentages of agricultural land will not face the problem of locating suitable land with which to compensate the local population.

Furthermore, it will be particularly costly to compensate local communities who rely on this agricultural land if the quality of the soil is high. The use of soil productivity (a weighted measure of the suitability of the soil for the best suited crop) is not new in spatial studies of socioeconomic outcomes. In an exploration of the effects of geographic characteristics on local poverty rates, Okwi et al. (2007) found that soil quality reduced the level of poverty. Wantchekon and Stanig (2015) explores the possibility of a curse of good soil – in that it undermines investment in human capital. As in these studies, I consider high-quality soil to be increasing the value of the agricultural land held or farmed by local residents. Relying on the UNEP's soil productivity index,[12] soil productivity is recorded at approximately 10 km resolution.

Government Take. Recently collected data on resource taxation measures the revenues collected by governments, but does not yet include the portion of firm profits that this constitutes. Between 1990 and 2010 the number of African countries reporting resource taxes doubled from 9 to 18.[13] However, there is still insufficient data indicating the effective tax rate on mining activities in African countries. While the average mineral royalty rate across most African countries is between 2 and 5 percent, this does not take into consideration additional fees and taxes including licensing fees, property taxes, land use fees, income taxes, payroll taxes, and other county-specific taxes. To measure government take I rely on the IMF's Doing Business Survey[14] recorded total tax rate. The variable is the total tax rate as a percentage of profits reported by domestic firms to the IMF. This is a rough proxy, as it does not specifically include the natural resource sector, which is generally dominated by foreign firms. However, it does have the benefit of indicating an average tax burden on firms, instead of the total revenue collected by the government. As such, it can provide a proxy for how extractive the government is from the firm's perspective. There is significant missing data here, and thus, I average the available data over the country years in the dataset. An evaluation

---

[12] United Nations Environment Programme (accessed on Dec.2013).

[13] Mansour and others (2014).

[14] IMFdbi.

of those countries for which there is sufficient data suggests that these values are relatively stable over time.

Control Variables. Beyond the characteristics of the government and local context that I outline above, I include several control variables that have been suggested to increase the likelihood of conflict. First, regions that are particularly poor are likely to be more prone to social unrest. Consistent with grievance-based theories about protest, I control for the level of poverty in the subnational unit in which the protest occurs. I use the infant mortality rate provided by USAID's Demographic and Health Surveys as an indicator of the level of poverty in the subnational unit of the mining operations.

I control for the distance between the conflict event and the political capital. In much of the empirical work exploring the geography of civil war,[15] distance from political capital is expected to increase the likelihood of violent conflict (unless conflict is primarily about regime change). One suggested mechanism is that hinterlands have limited state presence, and thus lower deterrence to those with sufficient grievances and organizational capacity to rebel. It is reasonable to expect this mechanism to hold true for lower-intensity conflicts as well, as preemptive and covert forms of repression are less likely to extend to these regions,[16] so there will be a lower organizational barrier to mobilization.

However, there are other reasons why distance to capital might matter. Protesters might consider that mobilization that occurs far from a capital is unlikely to yield significant response or concession on the part of the government, since it may be less visible. Thus I rely on road density using Columbia SEDAC's road atlas[17] to convey the logistical capacity of the state, and distance to capital as a measure of visibility of the protest and potential threat to the capital.

I also control for whether the majority equity stake in a mining project is held by a national or a foreign company. Anecdotally, foreign firm ownership or management has been suggested to lead to more resistance from local communities. Specifically, communities may see foreign firms as more exploitative, and if foreign firms fail to integrate employees into the

[15] Buhaug and Rød (2006).
[16] Sullivan (2015).
[17] Center for International Earth Science Information Network – CIESIN – Columbia University and Information Technology Outreach Services – ITOS – University of Georgia and NASA Socioeconomic Data and Applications Center (SEDAC) (2013).

local communities or learn the local language, such a perception is likely to be exacerbated. While systematic empirical evidence of this claim is not yet available, it is reasonable to control for foreign ownership.

Additionally, I control for the population density. Population density is likely to shape whether a protest occurs, but also whether it is recorded or not. Events data such as the SCAD database commonly exhibits an urban reporting bias. Including this measure is helpful in mitigating selection effects.

Because the outcome variable is a measure of the distance between an instance of social conflict and the mine, I control for the size of the country in kilometers to account for the fact that the 20 km is a comparatively larger radius in Burundi than it is in DRC. I also include a dummy variable for South Africa. There are spatial clusters of mines in South Africa, and the close proximity of these mines to each other makes attributing protest to specific mines difficult, and less accurate than in other countries. Finally, I control for the country's level of democracy as measured by the Polity IV score. The degree of democracy shapes the political opportunity structure for participation.[18] I also control for the type of mineral extracted as each has a different environmental footprint, and is thus likely to affect both the cost of the transfer and the likelihood of protest.

Note on Data. Unfortunately, the mining data in this dataset suffers from significant missingness related to the year in which the mines opened or closed. Of the total number of mines, only approximately 10 percent have data for the year in which they opened, and even fewer have a listed date of closure, making it impossible to sufficiently consider the temporality of the data. This makes it difficult to assess the temporal dimension of my argument.

However, there are a few things to keep in mind in considering this gap in the data. The mine usually opens several years after the contract has been allocated and construction has begun. This means there is a significant buffer of time during which social mobilization near a mine might occur that would be consistent with the argument. The average lifetime of a mine is approximately 20–30 years, during which the firm has sunk costs in the investment, and the time frame of the data is 1990–2014. Finally, structural adjustment programs that were adopted broadly

---

[18] Marshall, Gurr, and Jaggers (2014).

across Africa lead to the privatization of mining, and the attraction of foreign investment in the extractive sector. Much of this up-tick occurred in the early 1990s, suggesting that many of these mines were active at or near the start of the dataset.

This missingness will be somewhat less of a problem when we turn to the likelihood that an instance of social mobilization near a mine is repressed, since any conflict event that occurs within several years around the start of production is still likely to be perceived as a potential threat to mining revenues by the government and the firm, and thus is still likely to be part of the same data-generating process.

Summary Statistics. The complete dataset of mines includes 2,497 mines, in operation between 1990 and 2014. Of these, approximately 23 percent (566) experience conflict within 15 km of the mining site, approximately 27 percent (684) experienced conflict within 20 km of the mine site, and 33 percent (820) within 25 km. For the following analysis, I use a distance threshold of 20 km, but my results generally hold across thresholds of 15 km and 15 km as well (see Appendix B).

Of the 41 countries with mines included in the dataset, South Africa experienced the largest number conflicts within 20 km of a mine. However, the clustering of the mines in South Africa can account for this, given that of the total number of mines in the dataset 607 of them are in South Africa. Other countries with significant number of mines include Burkina Faso (151), Mali (150), Ghana (123), Democratic Republic of Congo (120), Tanzania (129), Ghana (123) Namibia (88), Botswana (111), and Zambia (99).

The mean distance between a mine and conflict event was approximately 72 km, with a minimum of less than 1 km, and a maximum of 627 km. Of the 120 mines in DRC, 43.33 percent saw social mobilization within 20 km. In Mozambique, nearly 30.91 percent of mines saw conflict within 20 km, and in Zambia 32.3 percent. Additional summary statistics are presented in Tables 9.1 and 9.2, and Figure 9.1 conveys a map showing the spatial distribution of mines and conflict events.

Analysis

To evaluate the likelihood of social mobilization within 20 km of a mine, I estimate a series of logit models, appropriate for binary outcomes. I include six models to demonstrate the effects of country and year fixed

TABLE 9.1: *Descriptive statistics for discrete variables*

Variable	# Observations	%
SCAD within 20 km	Yes (1) = 684	27.39
	No (0) = 1,813	72.61
Rail under 20 km	Yes (1) = 1,177	47.14
	No (0) = 1,320	52.881
Foreign Owned	Yes(1) = 1,923	77.01
	No (0) = 574	22.99
Soil Productivity	(1 = low, 6 = high)	
	1 = 78	3
	2 = 66	3
	3 = 414	17
	4 = 1,332	54
	5 = 523	21
	6 = 37	1.4

TABLE 9.2: *Descriptive statistics for continuous variables*

Variable	Mean	Std. Dev.
SCAD Distance to Mine (km)	71.78	82.33
Average Tax Rate (% company profits)	51.84	51.93
Population Density (ppl/km^2)	113.73	365.92
Infant Mortality Rate (/1000)	81.19	39.2
Mine Distance to Capital (km)	367.88	332.4
Road Density	81.04	24.69
Land Area (km^2)	846.65	564.78
Polity IV	6.62	2.4
N	2,497	

effects, as well as clustered standard errors. The magnitude of the effects of the relevant variables is not easily interpreted, so interpretation will focus on the direction and significance of the hypothesized predictors.[19] My strategy draws heavily on that of Haslam and Tanimoune (2016) in that I am looking at the correlates that make mining sites likely to

[19] The use of a linear regression model, while easier to interpret, can result in probabilities less than 0 and greater than 1 when the event in question occurs with a sufficiently low or high probability. While this is not the case in this dataset, I present logit results because of the more common tradition of doing so for binary outcomes. The models were run with a linear probability estimation technique for robustness, and the results do not differ significantly.

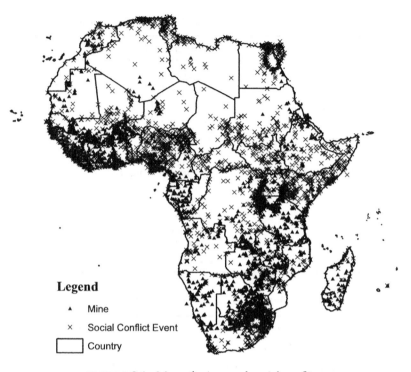

Legend

   ▲   Mine

   ×   Social Conflict Event

   ☐   Country

FIGURE 9.1: Map of mines and social conflict

experience protest nearby. As in their analysis, I test each hypothesis separately, not against the others (though I do include all of the relevant predictors in the final models to get a sense of their comparative effect). Unlike their analysis, which is an analysis of a general set of hypotheses derived from the qualitative literature of the likelihood of protest (taking place in Peru), I test the specific hypotheses derived from the theory presented in Chapters 2 and 3. Thus, the hypotheses tested here reflect the specific, observable implications of the theoretical model.

To ensure transparency in model specification and assumptions, I include results from the following models: (a) base model, (b) year fixed effects, (c) country and year fixed effects, and (d) standard errors clustered at the country level to account for possible country-level heteroskedasticity. I include various post-estimation test results to provide an indication of model specification and goodness of fit including chi-squared likelihood ratio test (for non-clustered standard error models) and the link test.

Table 9.3 presents the results of the logit test of whether proximity of a mine to a railroad makes protest more likely. In all versions of the model, the presence of a railroad within 20 km of the mine significantly increases the likelihood of protest. On average, the odds of having a protest within 20 km of a mine are two and a half times greater if there is also a railroad within 20 km than if not. These results lend reasonably strong support to the claim that the infrastructural context surrounding the mine matters in shaping the likelihood of protest. Rail, as transport infrastructure that often has few redundancies (in Africa) and serves as a primary method of transport for ore from the mine, presents a particularly vulnerable target for communities to impose costs on the firm and the government.

Table 9.4 provides results of the logit test of whether highly productive agricultural land makes protest more likely. A larger portion of highly productive land near a mine suggests a higher cost of compensating local communities for displacement or environmental damage to the land. The graph of the interaction between percentage of agricultural land and soil quality presented in Figure 9.2 demonstrates that an increase in the percentage of cropland that has productive soil increases the likelihood of protest. Note that an increase in cropland of less suitable soil decreases the likelihood of protest. Specifically, a 1 percent increase in the portion of land that is cropland decreases the likelihood of protest by 67 percent when soil productivity is low. However, at higher levels of soil productivity, a 1 percent increase in cropland increases the probability of protest by 14 percent (this number increases to 27 percent if soil productivity is at its highest). An increase in the geographic desirability of the land around the mine is likely to increase the cost of the transfer. As the tables show, high-quality soil that is used for cropland is a significant predictor of protest near the mine. These results are inconsistent with a purely environmental grievance mechanism, whereby local residents protest because a fragile environment is made worse off by the consequences of the mine. Since *better* agricultural soil makes protest more likely. , it is more plausible that residents who are better off are more costly to compensate, which may make firms less likely to follow through, making protest more likely.

Table 9.5 presents the results of the logit test of the effect of government take on the likelihood of protest. Measured by the average effective tax rate, government take increases the likelihood of protest except those in which both country and year fixed effects are included (Models 15 and 18). For a 1 percent increase in average tax rate, the probability of protest near a mine increases by approximately 58 percent. Notably, this result slips out of the range of significance with country fixed effects because

TABLE 9.3: *Probability of social conflict within 20 km, interruptibility*

	Model 1	Model 2 yFE	Model 3 cyFE	Model 4	Model 5 yFE	Model 6 cyFE
Railroad within 20 km	1.231***	1.185***	1.221***	1.231***	1.185***	1.221***
	(0.13)	(0.14)	(0.15)	(0.23)	(0.23)	(0.25)
Population Density (l)	0.632***	0.671***	0.669***	0.632***	0.671***	0.669***
	(0.04)	(0.04)	(0.05)	(0.08)	(0.10)	(0.11)
Infant Mortality Rate	0.007***	0.008***	−0.001	0.007*	0.008*	−0.001
	(0.00)	(0.00)	(0.01)	(0.00)	(0.00)	(0.01)
Distance to Capital (l)	−0.280***	−0.294***	−0.258**	−0.280*	−0.294*	−0.258
	(0.06)	(0.07)	(0.08)	(0.12)	(0.12)	(0.16)
Road Density	−0.004	−0.005+	−0.005	−0.004	−0.005	−0.005
	(0.00)	(0.00)	(0.00)	(0.01)	(0.01)	(0.01)
Country Area	0.000+	0.000*	−0.000	0.000	0.000	−0.000
	(0.00)	(0.00)	(0.00)	(0.00)	(0.00)	(0.00)
Polity IV	0.120***	0.135***	0.094	0.120*	0.135*	0.094
	(0.03)	(0.04)	(0.07)	(0.06)	(0.06)	(0.10)
South Africa	0.269	0.271		0.269	0.271	
	(0.23)	(0.26)		(0.32)	(0.30)	
Foreign Owned	−0.007	−0.007	0.137	−0.007	−0.007	0.137
	(0.14)	(0.14)	(0.15)	(0.12)	(0.12)	(0.13)
Coal	0.000	0.000	0.000	0.000	0.000	0.000
	(.)	(.)	(.)	(.)	(.)	(.)
Copper	0.343	0.181	0.084	0.343	0.181	0.084
	(0.25)	(0.26)	(0.30)	(0.26)	(0.24)	(0.30)
Gold	−0.101	−0.082	0.160	−0.101	−0.082	0.160
	(0.18)	(0.19)	(0.21)	(0.20)	(0.23)	(0.16)
Iron	0.329	0.242	0.080	0.329	0.242	0.080

	(1)	(2)	(3)	(4)	(5)	(6)
Lead	1.115	0.750	0.364	1.115+	0.750	0.364
	(0.27)	(0.28)	(0.31)	(0.24)	(0.27)	(0.25)
Other	-0.023	-0.128	-0.116	-0.023	-0.128	-0.116
	(1.27)	(1.18)	(1.06)	(0.64)	(0.68)	(0.66)
Nickel	-1.262*	-1.297*	-2.133**	-1.262+	-1.297*	-2.133***
	(0.18)	(0.19)	(0.21)	(0.17)	(0.16)	(0.15)
Phosphate	-1.140+	-1.300*	-1.639*	-1.140*	-1.300+	-1.639
	(0.63)	(0.63)	(0.78)	(0.70)	(0.66)	(0.64)
Platinum	-0.494	-0.539	-0.487	-0.494***	-0.539*	-0.487*
	(0.61)	(0.65)	(0.81)	(0.58)	(0.68)	(1.22)
Potash	0.000	0.000	0.000	0.000	0.000	0.000
	(0.32)	(0.34)	(0.35)	(0.13)	(0.24)	(0.20)
Silver	-0.338	-0.301	0.070	-0.338	-0.301	0.070
	(.)	(.)	(.)	(.)	(.)	(.)
Tin	0.590	0.400	0.306	0.590	0.400	0.306
	(0.93)	(0.93)	(0.92)	(0.67)	(0.74)	(0.81)
Zinc	-0.828	-0.898	-0.504	-0.828	-0.898	-0.504
	(0.78)	(0.83)	(0.91)	(0.54)	(0.60)	(0.40)
Constant	-1.859*	-1.641+	-1.115	-1.859	-1.641	-1.115
	(0.73)	(0.73)	(0.85)	(0.56)	(0.59)	(0.57)
Pseudo R Sq	.25	.265	.291	.25	.265	.291
Chi-Sq Test	706.5	750.8	815.0	(.)	(.)	(.)
Log-Likelihood	-1064.8	-1042.6	-993.6	-1064.8	-1042.6	-993.6
Linktest (htsq)	.04	.019	.012	.04	.019	.012
Observations	2402	2402	2402	2402	2402	2402

$+ p < 0.10, * p < 0.05, ** p < 0.01, *** p < 0.001$

TABLE 9.4: *Probability of social conflict within 20 km, cost of transfer*

	Model 7	Model 8 yFE	Model 9 cyFE	Model 10	Model 11 yFE	Model 12 cyFE
Soil Productivity	-0.352***	-0.415***	-0.412***	-0.352**	-0.415***	-0.412**
	(0.08)	(0.09)	(0.10)	(0.11)	(0.11)	(0.13)
Percent Cropland (l)	-4.867*	-5.351*	-6.820**	-4.867*	-5.351*	-6.820*
	(2.09)	(2.19)	(2.57)	(2.30)	(2.09)	(2.66)
Soil Productivity × Percent Cropland (l)	1.187*	1.280*	1.515*	1.187*	1.280*	1.515*
	(0.49)	(0.51)	(0.59)	(0.50)	(0.51)	(0.61)
Population Density (l)	0.725***	0.775***	0.761***	0.725***	0.775***	0.761***
	(0.04)	(0.05)	(0.05)	(0.10)	(0.13)	(0.13)
Infant Mortality Rate	0.003	0.003	-0.002	0.003	0.003	-0.002
	(0.00)	(0.00)	(0.01)	(0.00)	(0.00)	(0.01)
Distance to Capital (l)	-0.352***	-0.373***	-0.422***	-0.352**	-0.373**	-0.422*
	(0.06)	(0.07)	(0.09)	(0.12)	(0.12)	(0.17)
Road Density	-0.005+	-0.006*	-0.007+	-0.005	-0.006	-0.007
	(0.00)	(0.00)	(0.00)	(0.01)	(0.01)	(0.01)
Country Area	0.000**	0.000***	-0.000	0.000	0.000*	-0.000
	(0.00)	(0.00)	(0.00)	(0.00)	(0.00)	(0.00)
South Africa	0.542*	0.598*		0.542	0.598+	
	(0.23)	(0.26)		(0.33)	(0.31)	
Polity IV	0.116***	0.124***	0.086	0.116*	0.124*	0.086
	(0.03)	(0.04)	(0.07)	(0.06)	(0.06)	(0.10)
Foreign Owned	-0.062	-0.048	0.077	-0.062	-0.048	0.077
	(0.14)	(0.14)	(0.15)	(0.14)	(0.14)	(0.17)
Coal	0.000	0.000	0.000	0.000	0.000	0.000
	(0.00)	(0.00)	(0.00)	(0.00)	(0.00)	(0.00)
	(.)	(.)	(.)	(.)	(.)	(.)
Copper	0.466+	0.229	0.189	0.466+	0.229	0.189
	(0.25)	(0.26)	(0.30)	(0.25)	(0.27)	(0.25)

	(1)	(2)	(3)	(4)	(5)	(6)
Gold	-0.377*	-0.367+	-0.040	-0.377	-0.367	-0.040
	(0.19)	(0.20)	(0.22)	(0.27)	(0.33)	(0.23)
Iron	0.219	0.039	-0.053	0.219	0.039	-0.053
	(0.27)	(0.28)	(0.31)	(0.28)	(0.32)	(0.28)
Lead	1.238	0.880	0.367	1.238*	0.880	0.367
	(1.20)	(1.11)	(1.06)	(0.61)	(0.72)	(0.77)
Other	-0.189	-0.339+	-0.299	-0.189	-0.339	-0.299*
	(0.19)	(0.20)	(0.22)	(0.18)	(0.22)	(0.15)
Nickel	-1.535*	-1.648*	-2.277**	-1.535*	-1.648*	-2.277***
	(0.63)	(0.64)	(0.80)	(0.61)	(0.66)	(0.64)
Phosphate	-1.159+	-1.377*	-1.444+	-1.159*	-1.377*	-1.444
	(0.60)	(0.64)	(0.77)	(0.58)	(0.69)	(0.96)
Platinum	-0.779*	-0.879*	-0.758*	-0.779***	-0.879**	-0.758**
	(0.33)	(0.34)	(0.35)	(0.17)	(0.32)	(0.27)
Potash	0.000	0.000	0.000	0.000	0.000	0.000
	(.)	(.)	(.)	(.)	(.)	(.)
Silver	-0.608	-0.586	-0.099	-0.608	-0.586	-0.099
	(0.88)	(0.92)	(0.94)	(0.68)	(0.78)	(0.83)
Tin	-0.689	-1.033	-0.892	-0.689	-1.033	-0.892
	(0.93)	(1.01)	(1.11)	(0.65)	(0.83)	(0.58)
Zinc	-1.063	-1.088	-0.637	-1.063+	-1.088+	-0.637
	(0.79)	(0.78)	(0.90)	(0.60)	(0.59)	(0.60)
Constant	1.227	1.682	3.821**	1.227	1.682	3.821
	(0.92)	(1.03)	(1.39)	(1.68)	(1.60)	(2.47)
Pseudo R Sq	.22	.24	.27	.22	.24	.27
Chi-Sq Test	610	671	738			
Log-Likelihood	-1081.6	-1051.2	-1001.1	-1081.6	-1051.2	-1001.1
Linktest (htsq)	.018	.014	.031	.018	.014	.031
Observations	2356.0	2356.0	2310.0	2356.0	2356.0	2310.0

+p < 0.10, * p < 0.05, ** p < 0.01, *** p < 0.001

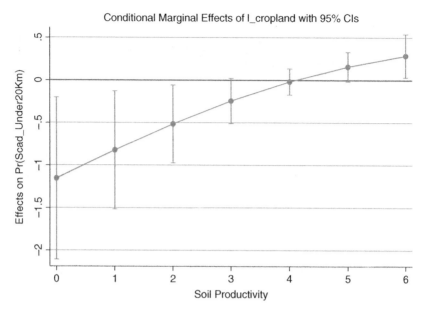

FIGURE 9.2: Conditional effects of suitable cropland percentage on protest likelihood

adding country fixed effects soaks up much of the variation that is of interest.

This is consistent with the theoretical claim that an increase in the portion of the firm's natural resource revenues going to the government decreases the likelihood that firms will provide a local transfer. Given the measurement error here and the somewhat tenuous causal path because of the indirect nature of the relationship, it is all the more surprising that the result is significant at all.

In Table 9.6, all three hypotheses are included in a logit model and perform similarly to their independent evaluation. In addition to these primary results there are some additional findings that bear mentioning. As expected, population density makes protest near a mine more likely. Infant mortality is significant across some models but does not remain a consistent predictor of protest. Surprisingly, distance to capital is consistently negative and statistically significant, suggesting that mines near a capital are *more* likely to see protest than those farther away. While mines that are in close proximity to the capital account for a small portion of the mines, the result may be explained by the fact that governments are less likely to repress protests that occur in close proximity to the capital.[20]

---

[20] Steinberg (2018).

TABLE 9.5: *Probability of social conflict within 20 km, government take*

	Model 13	Model 14 yFE	Model 15 cyFE	Model 16	Model 17 yFE	Model 18 cyFE
Avg Effective Tax Rate (l)	0.410**	0.461**	−0.064	0.410+	0.461*	−0.064
	(0.14)	(0.15)	(0.57)	(0.24)	(0.21)	(0.70)
Population Density (l)	0.681***	0.716***	0.734***	0.681***	0.716***	0.734***
	(0.04)	(0.04)	(0.05)	(0.09)	(0.11)	(0.13)
Infant Mortality Rate	0.000	0.000	−0.003	0.000	0.000	−0.003
	(0.00)	(0.00)	(0.01)	(0.00)	(0.00)	(0.01)
Distance to Capital (l)	−0.376***	−0.382***	−0.378***	−0.376**	−0.382**	−0.378*
	(0.06)	(0.07)	(0.08)	(0.12)	(0.12)	(0.16)
Road Density	−0.007*	−0.009**	−0.005	−0.007	−0.009	−0.005
	(0.00)	(0.00)	(0.00)	(0.01)	(0.01)	(0.01)
Country Area	0.000	0.000	−0.000	0.000	0.000	−0.000
	(0.00)	(0.00)	(0.00)	(0.00)	(0.00)	(0.00)
South Africa	0.550*	0.471+		0.550+	0.471	
	(0.22)	(0.25)		(0.32)	(0.30)	
Polity IV	0.146***	0.175***	0.088	0.146*	0.175**	0.088
	(0.03)	(0.04)	(0.07)	(0.06)	(0.06)	(0.10)
Foreign Owned	0.032	0.051	0.138	0.032	0.051	0.138
	(0.14)	(0.14)	(0.15)	(0.14)	(0.11)	(0.14)
Coal	0.000	0.000	0.000	0.000	0.000	0.000
	(.)	(.)	(.)	(.)	(.)	(.)
Copper	0.408+	0.236	0.175	0.408	0.236	0.175
	(0.24)	(0.25)	(0.29)	(0.32)	(0.30)	(0.26)
Gold	−0.349*	−0.302	−0.005	−0.349	−0.302	−0.005
	(0.18)	(0.19)	(0.21)	(0.26)	(0.29)	(0.21)
Iron	0.204	0.089	−0.038	0.204	0.089	−0.038
	(0.26)	(0.28)	(0.30)	(0.27)	(0.30)	(0.29)

(continued)

TABLE 9.5: *(continued)*

	Model 13	Model 14 yFE	Model 15 cyFE	Model 16	Model 17 yFE	Model 18 cyFE
Lead	1.083	0.722	0.315	1.083+	0.722	0.315
	(1.11)	(1.05)	(1.05)	(0.63)	(0.73)	(0.74)
Other	-0.219	-0.328+	-0.239	-0.219	-0.328+	-0.239+
	(0.18)	(0.19)	(0.21)	(0.17)	(0.19)	(0.14)
Nickel	-1.736**	-1.792**	-2.245**	-1.736***	-1.792***	-2.245***
	(0.63)	(0.64)	(0.78)	(0.51)	(0.52)	(0.62)
Phosphate	-1.308*	-1.536*	-1.612*	-1.308*	-1.536*	-1.612+
	(0.60)	(0.64)	(0.75)	(0.55)	(0.65)	(0.90)
Platinum	-0.832**	-0.834*	-0.712*	-0.832***	-0.834**	-0.712**
	(0.32)	(0.34)	(0.35)	(0.15)	(0.27)	(0.24)
Potash	0.000	0.000	0.000	0.000	0.000	0.000
	(.)	(.)	(.)	(.)	(.)	(.)
Silver	-0.693	-0.670	-0.115	-0.693	-0.670	-0.115
	(0.88)	(0.92)	(0.93)	(0.69)	(0.81)	(0.88)
Tin	-0.031	-0.243	-0.102	-0.031	-0.243	-0.102
	(0.72)	(0.78)	(0.87)	(0.43)	(0.50)	(0.29)
Zinc	-0.915	-0.942	-0.529	-0.915+	-0.942	-0.529
	(0.71)	(0.71)	(0.80)	(0.54)	(0.58)	(0.51)
Constant	-0.939	-0.839	1.804	-0.939	-0.839	1.804
	(0.86)	(0.96)	(2.25)	(1.53)	(1.63)	(3.01)
Pseudo R Sq	.22	.24	.27	.22	.24	.27
Chi-Sq Test	623	681	749			
Log-Likelihood	-1105.2	-1076.1	-1026.5	-1105.2	-1076.1	-1026.5
Linktest (htsq)	.03	.007	.024	.03	.007	.024
Observations	2398.0	2398.0	2356.0	2398.0	2398.0	2356.0

+$p < 0.10$, *$p < 0.05$, **$p < 0.01$, ***$p < 0.001$

TABLE 9.6: *Probability of social conflict within 20 km, complete model*

	Model 19	Model 20 yFE	Model 21 cyFE	Model 22	Model 23 yFE	Model 24 cyFE
Railroad within 20 km	1.208***	1.151***	1.198***	1.208***	1.151***	1.198***
	(0.13)	(0.14)	(0.16)	(0.23)	(0.24)	(0.25)
Soil Productivity	−0.347***	−0.387***	−0.378***	−0.347**	−0.387**	−0.378**
	(0.09)	(0.09)	(0.10)	(0.13)	(0.13)	(0.14)
Percent Cropland (l)	−3.903+	−4.268+	−6.706*	−3.903	−4.268+	−6.706*
	(2.17)	(2.26)	(2.62)	(2.52)	(2.38)	(2.77)
Soil Productivity × Percent Cropland (l)	0.991*	1.076*	1.437*	0.991+	1.076+	1.437+
	(0.50)	(0.53)	(0.60)	(0.54)	(0.57)	(0.63)
Avg Effective Tax Rate (l)	0.306*	0.356*	−0.325	0.306	0.356	−0.325
	(0.14)	(0.15)	(0.60)	(0.24)	(0.24)	(0.73)
Population Density (l)	0.657***	0.699***	0.700***	0.657***	0.699***	0.700***
	(0.04)	(0.05)	(0.05)	(0.08)	(0.11)	(0.12)
Infant Mortality Rate	0.004	0.004	−0.000	0.004	0.004	−0.000
	(0.00)	(0.00)	(0.01)	(0.00)	(0.00)	(0.01)
Distance to Capital (l)	−0.301***	−0.318***	−0.308***	−0.301*	−0.318**	−0.308+
	(0.06)	(0.07)	(0.09)	(0.13)	(0.12)	(0.17)
Road Density	−0.007*	−0.009**	−0.007+	−0.007	−0.009	−0.007
	(0.00)	(0.00)	(0.00)	(0.01)	(0.01)	(0.01)
Country Area	0.000	0.000	−0.000	0.000	0.000	−0.000
	(0.00)	(0.00)	(0.00)	(0.00)	(0.00)	(0.00)
South Africa	0.299	0.332		0.299	0.332	
	(0.23)	(0.27)		(0.31)	(0.30)	
Polity IV	0.142***	0.159***	0.089	0.142*	0.159**	0.089
	(0.03)	(0.04)	(0.07)	(0.06)	(0.06)	(0.10)

(continued)

TABLE 9.6: *(continued)*

	Model 19	Model 20 yFE	Model 21 cyFE	Model 22	Model 23 yFE	Model 24 cyFE
Foreign Owned	-0.037	-0.036	0.076	-0.037	-0.036	0.076
	(0.14)	(0.14)	(0.15)	(0.14)	(0.13)	(0.16)
Coal	0.000	0.000	0.000	0.000	0.000	0.000
	(.)	(.)	(.)	(.)	(.)	(.)
Copper	0.330	0.148	0.077	0.330	0.148	0.077
	(0.26)	(0.27)	(0.31)	(0.31)	(0.28)	(0.29)
Gold	-0.147	-0.148	0.128	-0.147	-0.148	0.128
	(0.19)	(0.20)	(0.22)	(0.22)	(0.27)	(0.19)
Iron	0.254	0.151	0.075	0.254	0.151	0.075
	(0.27)	(0.29)	(0.31)	(0.25)	(0.28)	(0.24)
Lead	1.078	0.679	0.422	1.078+	0.679	0.422
	(1.25)	(1.15)	(1.07)	(0.63)	(0.69)	(0.68)
Other	-0.124	-0.245	-0.195	-0.124	-0.245	-0.195
	(0.19)	(0.21)	(0.22)	(0.16)	(0.19)	(0.16)
Nickel	-1.376*	-1.474*	-2.185**	-1.376*	-1.474**	-2.185**
	(0.64)	(0.66)	(0.81)	(0.59)	(0.55)	(0.67)
Phosphate	-1.390*	-1.538*	-1.529+	-1.390*	-1.538+	-1.529
	(0.63)	(0.69)	(0.83)	(0.70)	(0.86)	(1.26)
Platinum	-0.544	-0.638+	-0.550	-0.544***	-0.638*	-0.550*
	(0.33)	(0.35)	(0.36)	(0.16)	(0.27)	(0.24)
Potash	0.000	0.000	0.000	0.000	0.000	0.000
	(.)	(.)	(.)	(.)	(.)	(.)

	(1)	(2)	(3)	(4)	(5)	(6)
Silver	−0.375	−0.371	0.069	−0.375	−0.371	0.069
	(0.92)	(0.92)	(0.94)	(0.64)	(0.70)	(0.75)
Tin	−0.298	−0.596	−0.723	−0.298	−0.596	−0.723
	(0.98)	(1.06)	(1.18)	(0.88)	(0.96)	(0.61)
Zinc	−1.113	−1.167	−0.646	−1.113+	−1.167+	−0.646
	(0.82)	(0.82)	(0.95)	(0.66)	(0.65)	(0.69)
Constant	−0.880	−0.600	2.269	−0.880	−0.600	2.269
	(1.00)	(1.11)	(2.42)	(1.82)	(1.83)	(3.44)
Pseudo R Sq	.25	.27	.29	.25	.27	.29
Chi-Sq Test	699	747	799			
Log-Likelihood	−1036.2	−1012.2	−970.5	−1036.2	−1012.2	−970.5
Linktest (htsq)	.046	.022	.027	.046	.022	.027
Observations	2352.0	2352.0	2310.0	2352.0	2352.0	2310.0

+$p < 0.10$, *$p < 0.05$, **$p < 0.01$, ***$p < 0.001$

Interestingly, in nearly all the models, nickel mines are statistically less likely to experience a protest within 20 km of the mine, however it is not clear that this statistical regularity is anything more than an artifact of the data.[21]

Finally, a particularly interesting result is that mines that are foreign owned are no more likely to see protest than those that are not foreign owned. This is contrary to many existing narratives about the extent to which foreign entities extracting African wealth make mining related mobilization more likely.

Selection and Endogeneity. One might argue that there is the potential for selection bias in the dataset. For example, firms may only invest in mining in a country with low levels of protest. However, while ongoing civil wars or insurgencies or other forms of large-scale organized collective violence might deter mining investment, it is unlikely that discrete instances of protest might successfully deter investment. They are unlikely to rise to the level of intensity or duration that would be sufficiently destructive. For example, while civil war in Angola did stall existing, large-scale diamond operations in the Lunda regions and arguably prevented additional investment, the multitude of strikes in South Africa have not, on average, prevented firms from investing in diamond mines there. Furthermore, when the cumulative number of conflict events is calculated for each country, there is no negative correlation with the number of mines in that country.

There is the potential that, in many of my proposed hypotheses, the causal arrow goes in the opposite direction – particularly given the data missingness on the mine start dates. First, it could be that the association between railroads and nearby protest is the result of the fact that increased protest led to the construction of railroads, possibly to create additional transportation routes. This is somewhat unlikely, given that the railroad data dates to 1992. While this means the data does not vary

---

[21] In models without country fixed effects or year fixed effects, the effect has a p-value of .044, barely under the .05 acceptable level. It is only when the country and year fixed effects are included that the nickel variable becomes statistically significant. As such, nickel mines make up only 1.4 percent of the total number of mines in the dataset, and only 5 out of 36 mines in the dataset saw protest within 20 km. These mines are well distributed across the countries in the dataset, and nickel mines with protest within 20 km are located in Burundi, Cote d'Ivoire, Madagascar, and Togo (on average, smaller countries). Furthermore, nickel is usually found with other minerals, and a mine is only coded as a nickel mine if the primary material mined is nickel. In reality, many more mining projects include nickel extraction; however, it is much more commonly a secondary resource taken out of a mine.

over time (after 1992), it does make it impossible that new construction of railroads was the result of protest.

Second, it could be the case that soil productivity and cropland are affected by protest. In order for this to be a significant worry, it would have to be the case that an increase in protests led to an increase in the percentage of productive cropland. One possibility is that protests were the manifestation of earlier grievances about the lack of access to productive cropland, resulting in the allocation of more productive land. The correlation coefficient of cropland and likely of a conflict event within 20 km is only .15. Therefore, we can be reasonably confident that soil productivity and cropland are exogenous to protest.

Third, and perhaps most potentially problematic, is that it is possible that protest leads to an increase in tax rates – particularly if protesters are making explicit claims about access to resource revenue. However, similar to the rail data, the tax data does not vary significantly over time, making it unlikely that protest leads to an increase in tax rates.

10

On Repression Near Mines

In this chapter I turn to understanding when governments repress social mobilization near a mine. Fundamental to my theoretical argument is the idea that governments, firms, and local communities interact strategically, and that geography may compel governments to manage locationally specific trade-offs between political support and revenue, given the presence of the extractive firm. To recap, if the economic value of the mine is particularly high, the government will be more likely to use repression to quash a protest, protecting a mining project from a costly interruption of operations. Of course, beyond the stylized confines of the model, the real world carries with it other options that governments may choose from. Yet the formal theoretical frame provides some generalizable expectations as to when we should expect to see repression specifically. The government's repressive response rests on a couple of important assumptions that it is necessary to revisit.

Intuitively, repression constitutes the government siding with the firm, as coercive force is imposed on local community members to protect the firm's assets. Inherent here is the assumption that the government expects that the strategy of repression is more likely to protect the asset than some other form of action (indeed, than compelling the firm to follow through). Why can we assume this?

Repression is only one of a menu of options governments can use in response to a perceived threat. It is well established that governments are more likely to rely on repression if social mobilization is perceived to directly threaten the political system.[1] It is clear that repression is

[1] Muller (1985), Davis and Ward (1990), Aflatooni and Allen (1991), Davenport (1995), and Valentino (2013).

often used in response to a perceived threat to a political system, but Davenport (2007) has argued that we have a muddled understanding of how location affects threat perception. The geography of civil war literature, for instance, argues that armed, violent conflict events that occur in close proximity to the capital are perceived to be of greater threat to the political system than those that occur in the hinterlands. In these works, governments use repression in response to a perceived threat to territory or political power.

There is limited work to date that links the location of fixed assets, such as natural resources to government repressive behavior at the subnational level. In other work,[2] I find that governments are actually *more* likely to repress an instance of social mobilization if it occurs in close proximity to a mining site in Africa, especially if the mine is far from the capital. Additionally, in a quantitative, subnational study of violence in the Democratic Republic of Congo, Maystadt et al. (2014) demonstrate that since violence decreases the profitability of a mine, mining companies attempt to keep violence sufficiently far from the extraction site. While low-intensity social conflict events do not present the same level of direct and immediate threat as these episodes of armed conflict, this does not imply that they may not result in costs that draw the attention of potentially coercive governments. Social mobilization in close proximity to a significant and geographically fixed source of revenue has the potential to make governments "trigger happy" on average, with respect to their use of repression in response to low-intensity events such as protests. The immediate economic costs of social conflict near such a concentrated source of fixed revenue may outweigh any long-term political cost of repression (which may include additional mobilization). However, repression does not occur at all mining sites, and thus there is still variation yet to be explained.

Hypotheses

Returning to the theoretical model, recall that the alternative to repressing a protest is that the government may compel the firm to live up to its promises to provide a transfer to the local community – an outcome that is difficult to measure for reasons I explain later in this chapter. However, there are parameters that should make the government relatively more or less likely to repress an instance of social mobilization near a mining site.

---

[2] Steinberg (2018).

Here the model suggests clearly that two parameters are likely to matter: political relevance of the local population, and economic value of the asset. In the theoretical model, the potential political cost is labeled γ_R and is characterized as the amount of political support the government might lose by resorting to repression in response to low-intensity social mobilization. This assumes two things: first, that repression has a negative effect on the level of local support for the regime; and second, that the regime in fact relies on this support and cares if it loses it. Surprisingly little has been written on the effect of geographically specific repression on political support – likely because preference falsification is a common consequence,[3] making it difficult to evaluate true preferences in the aftermath of repression. However, it is not far-fetched to assume that the targets of repression are less likely to support the incumbent leader.

As for the second assumption, the nature of the geographically specific political relevance of a given group is contingent on the political regime structure (and the geographic distribution of leader support). In particular, by definition consolidated democracies rely more explicitly on the support of the populace, and thus are more likely to feel any political costs of repression. A large literature on the domestic democratic peace suggests that on average, consolidated democracies are less likely to use repression in response to perceived threats.[4] Davenport (2007) summarizes most clearly: "Democratic institutions are believed to increase the costs of using repressive behavior because, if state actions are deemed inappropriate, authorities can be voted out of office." While there is little systematic evidence demonstrating decreased voter support for a repressive incumbent, implicit in Davenport's claim is that the use of coercive force by a democratic incumbent is likely to cause her to lose sufficient support to retain office in the next electoral cycle.

However, even autocratic regimes are not entirely immune to the loss of political support.[5] Autocratic regimes or anocracies often rely on the support of particularly geographically concentrated populations,[6] though some debate remains as to whether incumbent leaders are likely to target such groups with distributive benefits to retain their

---

[3] Bratton and Masunungure (2007).

[4] Davenport and Armstrong (2004), Regan and Henderson (2002), Henderson (1991), and Carey (2010).

[5] Weeks (2008).

[6] Ngoy-Kangoy (2008).

support.[7] As Bhasin and Gandhi (2013) point out, even autocratic regimes are unwilling to resort to indiscriminate repression when their tenure is uncertain.

H4: Governments weigh the potential political cost of repressing an instance of social mobilization when deciding if or how to respond. As the political relevance of the local population increases, repression of a nearby conflict becomes less likely.

However, governments responding to protest near mining sites are mitigating a trade-off between political support and revenue. They are weighing the importance of political support against the value of revenue extracted from the mine. When revenue from the mine increases, it is more likely to offset the importance of political support of the local population. Recalling the qualitative observations of Downey, Bonds, and Clark (2010) and quantitative analysis of African mines I conduct in earlier work, governments are likely to engage in repressive campaigns if they believe doing so will protect assets. As the cases in DRC and Zambia showed, the more valuable those fixed assets are to a leader relative to any political costs they might endure by engaging in a repressive campaign, the more likely the government is to repress. Conflict events that occur in close proximity to extractive sites can threaten government access to revenues from extraction. The greater those revenues are, the greater the loss from interruption of extractive operations. While repression may lead to more social mobilization in the long run, in the face of an immediate, if uncertain, threat to a valuable mine, governments are likely to rely on coercive power. As a result, governments may act to prevent that possibility by repressing the conflict.

H5: Governments rely on repression to protect a mine whose productivity may be threatened by social mobilization. The benefit of repression increases with the value of the mine. As a result, as the value of the mine increases, repression of a nearby conflict event becomes more likely.

Data and Measurement

Repression. Still using the mine project as the unit of analysis, I restrict this analysis to the subset of mines that experienced a social conflict event within 20 km. To capture whether the event was repressed or not, I employ an existing variable in the SCAD dataset, *repress.* Repression is considered to be the coercive use of force by the government or an agent

[7] Kasara (2007).

thereof in response to a social conflict event. The SCAD dataset is the only geo-coded conflict event data at the time of this writing that systematically records whether an event was repressed by the government. In the SCAD dataset, an event is coded as repressed if the government used non-lethal (such as tear gas or arrests) or lethal force to quell or stop a protest event. A SCAD event is coded with a value of 1 if the government used repression in response to the event and 0 otherwise.

Political Relevance. As noted earlier, repression carries with it potential political costs. If political support is particularly important, governments should be less likely to use repression in order to avoid losing support. The relative value of political support depends, in part, on the extent to which an incumbent leader relies on political support at any given point in time. Leaders are likely to be particularly interested in maximizing their support base, and ensuring the support even of marginalized groups in peripheral mining areas if they believe their leadership tenure to be under threat. As a consequence, given the political costs associated with repression, uncertain leader tenure should make repression less likely.

Indicators of leadership tenure uncertainty differ in autocracies in comparison to democracies, in part because the relative importance of the political support of the population is likely to be different in democracies than in autocracies. Consistent with other studies of leader tenure,[8] I rely on the occurrence of national, executive elections as an indicator of uncertainty of leadership tenure, using data from Salehyan and Linebarger (2015). Elections constitute a clear, observable indicator of the opportunity for leadership change, thus increasing the uncertainty that a leader will retain power. Elections are likely to be particularly (though not exclusively) important in democratic countries. Leading up to the 1990s, few African countries were considered democratic, as Cold War alliances drove support for even the most dictatorial regimes, so long as they professed support for the West. However, in the 1990s Africa experienced a third wave of democracy. Countries that were not yet democratic began to hold multi-party elections, primarily between 1989 and 1993, and while many African countries were autocratic for a portion of the years included in the dataset, 562 protests out of 673 occurred in countries that scored greater than 5 on the normalized Polity IV scale during the year of the protest. Furthermore, the number of African democracies increases steadily throughout the time period between 1990

---

[8] Hafner-Burton, Hyde, and Jablonski (2014).

and 2014. I interact the Polity IV score (normalized from 0 to 10), and whether there was a national executive election that year.

Since political costs of repression are likely to be different in democracies than autocracies, elections do not indicate the same kind of leader tenure uncertainty. Instead, one measure of leader tenure in autocracies might be the number of years that the leader has been in power. Bienen and van de Walle (1989) argue that leader tenure becomes more certain the longer a leader has been in office. This would suggest, according to my theory, that repression near a mine (which does not usually present an existential threat but does potentially produce political costs) should be more likely the longer an autocratic leader has been in power. This is because such a leader might be more immune to any potential political costs of repression. I use the Goemans, Gleditsch, and Chiozza (2009) dataset to code the number of years the leader has been in power at the time of the conflict event to proxy for overall non-democracy leader tenure uncertainty. A leader who has been in power for many years is more likely to repress a conflict near a mine because she believes herself to be immune to any political costs of repression.

At the core of the theory is the claim that governments face geographically specific trade-offs between revenue and political support. Ideally, I would measure how important the population in the mining area is for the leader's tenure. Specifically, it would be helpful to know how much the leader relies on the geographically concentrated local population's support in order to remain in power. Understanding the particular political relevance of the local community could provide a more geographically disaggregated and targeted indicator of the government's resolution of the trade-off between political support and revenue. Unfortunately, spatial indicators of the importance of a particular constituency for the incumbent's support are prohibitively costly to obtain.

Value of the Mine. To measure the economic value of the mine, I use the commodity price of the mineral or metal being extracted during the year of social conflict. Commodity price is regularly used in studies of conflict, but it has been associated with contradictory findings, and it has not been applied to the study of repression specifically. Unlike agricultural commodity price shocks, the benefits of which accrue to farmers and individuals, the benefits of mineral price increases generally accrue to the state and extractive firm. Because industrial extractive commodities are relatively easy to tax, increases in the commodity price directly benefit the state. As a result, commodity prices of natural resources like minerals and fuel have a different effect than agricultural commodity prices.[9] An increase in these prices thus increases natural resource rents.[10] As Deaton (1999) points out, it is not well known that high commodity prices do not last, and states are unlikely to be better forecasters than econometricians. As a consequence, if the government observes an increase in the value of the commodity extracted, it often believes this will persist, increasing the value of the mine not only for the particular year in which it is observed, but also for (at least) the near future. Governments are thus likely to see mines as all the more valuable when the respective commodity price is up.

Unfortunately, there is insufficient data on the total volume of the resource extracted from each mine, but the yearly commodity price provides an indicator of the relative value of the resource extracted at the time of the conflict event. The commodity price recorded is drawn from the IMF's commodities price index, and is recorded for the mine's primary mineral extracted during the year of the conflict event. The price is the yearly average, and thus reasonably likely to be observed by the government at the time of the decision to repress.

Control Variables. Several control variables are included. First, I include the type of social mobilization. Governments are more likely to respond to violence with repression than non-violent outcomes, in part because violent response to violence is perceived as justified, and likely to impose fewer political costs on the government. As a result, the nature of the conflict event is likely to shape the likelihood of repression. I control for road density, as in the earlier analysis, as it indicates lower logistical cost to governments deploying coercive apparatus. I also control for distance to the capital, as it is an indicator of how the government might perceive the level of threat from the conflict event. As Herbst (2000) and others suggest, governments are likely to care much more about what is occurring near the capital than what is occurring much farther away (in the periphery of the state). Consistent with existing theories suggesting that resource-rich states are more repressive on average,[11] I include the percentage of GDP derived from coal and minerals. I use a sum of the

---

[9] Dube and Vargas (2013) and Bazzi and Blattman (2014).

[10] Bates (2015) and Fearon (2005).

[11] Ross (2001*b*).

percentages of GDP derived from minerals and coal, as calculated by the World Bank during the time of the protest. I also control for population density, as conflict events in regions of larger population density are expected to be of greater threat to the government. I control for whether a mining project is majority foreign owned, as it sheds additional light on the theoretical claims made in the model. Specifically, if governments are particularly interested in continuing to attract capital, they may be more willing to repress conflict events near foreign-owned mines to demonstrate that they (a) have sufficiently strong coercive apparatus to support firms and (b) on average are willing to support firm activity, even at the potential expense of political support. I also calculate the cumulative number of SCAD incidents in a country at the time of the mining project. Davenport (1995) suggests that governments repress more upon facing more instances of protest.

Summary Statistics. A total of 684 observations are included in this analysis (out of the 2,497 mineral extraction projects). The average distance between a mine and conflict was 8.84 km. Elections occurred in approximately 21 percent of the years with a SCAD conflict near a mine, and the average Polity IV score was approximately 7. Average leader tenure in the dataset is 5.9 years in office. A slight majority of the conflict events were violent. Additional summary and descriptive statistics are provided in Tables 10.1 and 10.2. Table 10.3 demonstrates that of those conflicts that occurred within 20 km of a mine, approximately 31 percent (213) were repressed.

Analysis

As in the analysis in Chapter 9, I estimate a series of logit models with country and year fixed effects, as well as clustered standard errors. Again, this is appropriate for the binary outcome of repression. I also provide the same Chi-squared and link test for fit. Table 10.4 presents the results of a logit model of the likelihood of repression of a protest that occurs within 20 km of a mine in an election year. The results suggest that for democracies, repression of a conflict event that occurs near a mine is significantly less likely during an election year. At normalized Polity IV score of 7, an election decreases the probability of repression by 9 percent over a year without an election, and at a Polity IV score of 9 this is 16 percent. While the direction of this effect holds across all of the models, the significance level varies. It is more instructive to look at the graph

TABLE 10.1: *Descriptive statistics for discrete variables for mines with social conflict within 20 km*

Variable	# Observations	%
Repression	Repressed (1) = 213	31.1
	Not Repressed (0) = 471	68.8
Election	Yes (1) = 113	21.2
	No(1) = 420	78.8
Event Type	Organized Dem. (1) = 97	14.18
	Spontaneous Dem. (2) = 97	14.18
	Organized Violent Riot (3) = 40	5.85
	Spontaneous Violent Riot (4) = 173	25.3
	General Strike (5) = 0	0
	Limited Strike (6) = 58	8.5
	Anti-Gov Violence (8) = 27	3.95
	Extra-Gov Violence (9) = 187	27.34
	Intra-Gov Violence (10) = 5	.7

TABLE 10.2: *Summary statistics for mines with social conflict within 20 km*

Variable	Mean	Std. Dev.
SCAD Distance to Mine (km)	8.84	5.37
Commodity Price	897	1859
Leader Years in Office	5.94	7.22
Mine Distance to Capital	325.98	367.5
Road Density	84.6	22.8
Population Density (ppl/km^2)	280.84	651.83
Mineral and Coal Rents (% GDP)	3.12	4.53
Polity IV (normalized 0–10)	7.12	2.25
Cumulative SCAD events	304.67	374.4
N		684

TABLE 10.3: *Frequency of repression of social conflict events*

	Not Repressed	Repressed	Total
No SCAD within 20 km	1,172	641	1,813
	(64.64%)	(35.36%)	(100%)
SCAD within 20 km	471	213	684
	(68.86%)	(31.14%)	(100%)
Total	1,643	854	2,497
	(68.1%)	(31.9%)	

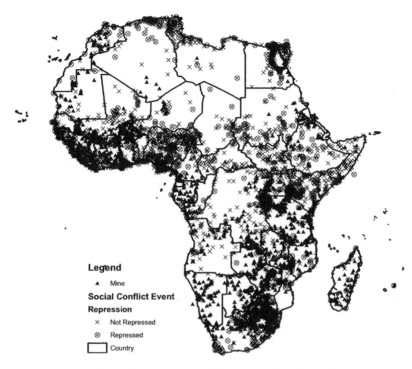

Legend

▲   Mine

Social Conflict Event

Repression

×   Not Repressed

⊗   Repressed

☐   Country

FIGURE 10.1: Map of mines and the repression of social conflict

of the conditional effects presented in Figure 10.2, which demonstrates that elections primarily make democratic leaders less likely to repress a protest near a mine.[12]

Table 10.5 presents the results of a logit model of the effect of a leader's number of years in office (conditional on Polity IV score) on the likelihood of repression. An increase in the number of years a leader has held office increases the likelihood of repression, but this result is significant only after a leader has been in office for 10 years and in the most autocratic contexts, as demonstrated in Figure 10.3. This is consistent with the hypothesis, that as leaders become more secure in their tenure, they care less about any political costs of repression and may use repression to protect the mine. However, only 18 percent of the conflicts near mines occurred at a time when a leader had been in power for more than 10 years.

---

[12] In some alternate specifications, the conditional increase of the likelihood of repression for autocracies in an election year becomes significant.

TABLE 10.4: *Probability of repression of social conflict near a mine, elections*

	Model 1	Model 2 cFE	Model 3 cyFE	Model 4	Model 5 cFE	Model 6 cyFE
Election	0.918	-0.211	6.103+	0.918	-0.211	6.103
	(0.94)	(1.42)	(3.18)	(1.09)	(1.99)	(6.07)
Polity IV	0.174*	-0.010	0.392	0.174	-0.010	0.392
	(0.07)	(0.17)	(0.37)	(0.12)	(0.22)	(0.57)
Election = 1 × Polity IV	-0.222+	-0.094	-1.399**	-0.222	-0.094	-1.399
	(0.13)	(0.19)	(0.51)	(0.16)	(0.26)	(0.97)
Commodity Price (l)	1.499**	4.569***	5.875**	1.499*	4.569***	5.875
	(0.50)	(0.85)	(2.21)	(0.63)	(1.05)	(3.80)
Road Density	0.026***	0.027*	0.023+	0.026*	0.027	0.023
	(0.01)	(0.01)	(0.01)	(0.01)	(0.03)	(0.02)
Distance to Capital (l)	-0.150	0.123	0.411+	-0.150	0.123	0.411+
	(0.10)	(0.15)	(0.23)	(0.19)	(0.27)	(0.23)
Population Density (l)	-0.122	-0.049	-0.016	-0.122	-0.049	-0.016
	(0.08)	(0.10)	(0.13)	(0.10)	(0.08)	(0.09)
Event Type						
Org. Dem.	0.000	0.000	0.000	0.000	0.000	0.000
	(.)	(.)	(.)	(.)	(.)	(.)
Spont. Dem	-0.552	-1.877**	-2.346*	-0.552	-1.877*	-2.346+
	(0.44)	(0.62)	(1.06)	(0.62)	(0.89)	(1.40)
Org. Riot	-1.297*	-2.931***	-1.497	-1.297+	-2.931***	-1.497
	(0.54)	(0.82)	(1.24)	(0.72)	(0.84)	(0.94)

	(1)	(2)	(3)	(4)	(5)	(6)
Spont. Riot	0.012	-0.542	-0.268	0.012	-0.542	-0.268
	(0.39)	(0.52)	(0.77)	(0.53)	(0.88)	(1.20)
Limited Strike	-3.281***	-4.867***	-5.116**	-3.281***	-4.867***	-5.116+
	(0.83)	(1.00)	(1.68)	(0.98)	(1.47)	(2.94)
Anti-Gov Violence	-3.095**	-3.631*	-0.744	-3.095*	-3.631	-0.744
	(1.13)	(1.44)	(1.58)	(1.43)	(2.35)	(2.21)
Extra-Gov Violence	-1.801***	-1.854***	-1.909**	-1.801***	-1.854*	-1.909*
	(0.39)	(0.46)	(0.68)	(0.53)	(0.77)	(0.80)
Cumulative SCAD to Date	-0.002***	-0.002+	0.008***	-0.002***	-0.002*	0.008**
	(0.00)	(0.00)	(0.00)	(0.00)	(0.00)	(0.00)
Foreign Owned	1.100***	1.154**	0.772	1.100***	1.154***	0.772+
	(0.31)	(0.39)	(0.48)	(0.25)	(0.33)	(0.41)
Coal and Mineral Rents	0.004	-0.146*	-0.179+	0.004	-0.146+	-0.179**
	(0.03)	(0.06)	(0.10)	(0.04)	(0.08)	(0.06)
Constant	-8.151***	-20.457***	-17.896+	-8.151*	-20.457***	-17.896
	(2.15)	(3.89)	(9.16)	(3.24)	(6.10)	(17.76)
Pseudo R Sq	.28	.39	.54	.28	.39	.54
Chi-Sq Test	187	228	305	619	.	
Log-Likelihood	-236.5	-178.6	-128.0	-236.5	-178.6	-128.0
Linktest (htsq)	.086+	.058	. – .035	.086+	.058	. – .035
Observations	513.0	442.0	417.0	513.0	442.0	417.0

+ p < 0.10, * p < 0.05, ** p < 0.01, *** p < 0.001

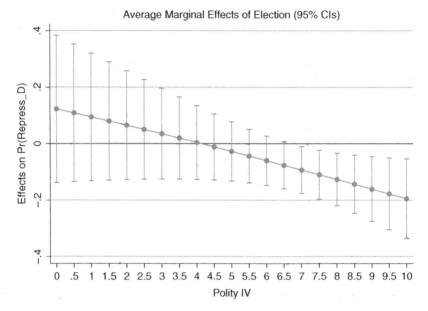

FIGURE 10.2: Conditional effect of elections on repression

Interestingly, a longer tenure in office makes a leader *less* likely to repress a conflict near a mine for transitional and weakly democratic regimes than when the leader has been in power for ten years or less, as shown in Figure 10.4. Transitional regimes might be expected to be the most repressive given their often tenuous hold on power, but since these instances of mobilization near mines do not often present an existential threat to the government, such middling regime leaders may not see repression as worth the political cost. These results are somewhat susceptible to changes in model specification, and therefore should be considered suggestive at best, but they lend some qualified support for the idea that autocratic leaders who are secure in their tenure (i.e., have been in power for many years) grow more immune to any potential political costs of repression, making them more likely to repress an instance of protest near a mine.

Recall that an increase in the commodity price should increase the value of the mine, which, according to the model, should make governments more interested in protecting the mine through coercive means. In both Tables 10.4 and 10.5, commodity price of the mineral extracted is both positive and significant for the majority of the models. In both sets of models, a doubling of the commodity price increases the odds of

TABLE 10.5: *Probability of repression of social conflict near a mine, years in office*

	Model 7	Model 8 cFE	Model 9 cyFE	Model 10	Model 11 cFE	Model 12 cyFE
Years Current Leader in Office (l)	0.057	−1.422*	−1.745+	0.057	−1.422	−1.745
	(0.32)	(0.58)	(1.04)	(0.48)	(0.98)	(1.52)
Polity IV	0.137	−0.276	−0.558	0.137	−0.276	−0.558
	(0.12)	(0.19)	(0.39)	(0.16)	(0.27)	(0.69)
Years Current Leader in Office (l) × Polity IV	−0.054	0.106	0.213	−0.054	0.106	0.213
	(0.05)	(0.08)	(0.14)	(0.06)	(0.11)	(0.20)
Commodity Price (l)	0.721*	1.340**	0.982	0.721*	1.340**	0.982
	(0.33)	(0.48)	(1.06)	(0.33)	(0.49)	(0.90)
Road Density	0.020***	0.025*	0.019	0.020+	0.025	0.019
	(0.01)	(0.01)	(0.01)	(0.01)	(0.02)	(0.02)
Distance to Capital (l)	−0.042	0.081	0.194	−0.042	0.081	0.194
	(0.09)	(0.13)	(0.18)	(0.18)	(0.26)	(0.20)
Population Density (l)	−0.036	0.043	0.122	−0.036	0.043	0.122
	(0.07)	(0.09)	(0.11)	(0.09)	(0.09)	(0.08)
Event Type						
Org. Dem.	0.000	0.000	0.000	0.000	0.000	0.000
	(.)	(.)	(.)	(.)	(.)	(.)
Spont Dem.	−0.331	−0.869+	−2.138**	−0.331	−0.869	−2.138*
	(0.37)	(0.45)	(0.73)	(0.49)	(0.64)	(0.86)
Org. Riot	−0.910+	−1.547*	−1.370	−0.910	−1.547+	−1.370+
	(0.49)	(0.67)	(0.97)	(0.57)	(0.84)	(0.76)
Spont Riot	0.392	0.479	−0.275	0.392	0.479	−0.275
	(0.32)	(0.39)	(0.61)	(0.52)	(0.82)	(0.86)

(continued)

TABLE 10.5: (continued)

	Model 7	Model 8 cFE	Model 9 cyFE	Model 10	Model 11 cFE	Model 12 cyFE
Limited Strike	-2.863***	-3.644***	-3.939***	-2.863***	-3.644**	-3.939**
	(0.68)	(0.91)	(1.11)	(0.65)	(1.22)	(1.39)
Anti-Gov Violence	-1.232*	0.122	-0.408	-1.232	0.122	-0.408
	(0.63)	(0.76)	(1.06)	(1.11)	(1.66)	(1.70)
Extra-Gov Violence	-1.707***	-1.969***	-2.626***	-1.707***	-1.969*	-2.626**
	(0.35)	(0.42)	(0.60)	(0.43)	(0.80)	(1.00)
Cumulative SCAD to Date	-0.002***	-0.002***	0.004*	-0.002***	-0.002***	0.004
	(0.00)	(0.00)	(0.00)	(0.00)	(0.00)	(0.00)
Foreign Owned	0.838**	0.907**	0.804*	0.838***	0.907***	0.804**
	(0.26)	(0.31)	(0.37)	(0.22)	(0.17)	(0.26)
Coal and Mineral Rents	-0.016	-0.039	-0.124*	-0.016	-0.039	-0.124+
	(0.03)	(0.04)	(0.06)	(0.03)	(0.08)	(0.07)
Constant	-5.875**	-4.902+	1.234	-5.875**	-4.902	1.234
	(1.85)	(2.91)	(5.60)	(1.82)	(3.25)	(6.32)
Pseudo R Sq	.26	.37	.5	.26	.37	.5
Chi-Sq Test	217	296	388	755		
Log-Likelihood	-302.2	-250.1	-192.9	-302.2	-250.1	-192.9
Linktest (htsq)	.003	.012	.-.063+	.003	.012	.-.063+
Observations	655.0	633.0	606.0	655.0	633.0	606.0

+p < 0.10, *p < 0.05, **p < 0.01, ***p < 0.001

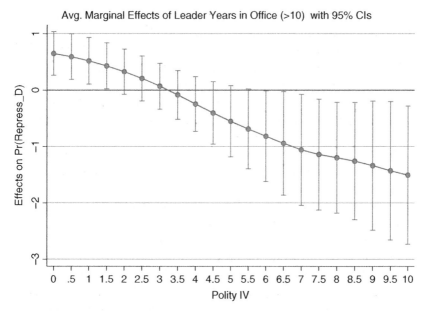

FIGURE 10.3: Conditional effect of leader tenure (>10 years) on repression

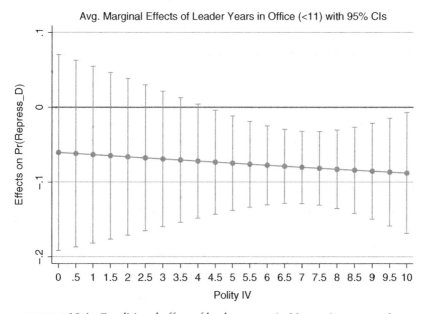

FIGURE 10.4: Conditional effect of leader tenure (<11 years) on repression

repression by 283% (though this ranges slightly across the models). At the commodity's price minimum, the likelihood of repression is only 1.7 percent, while at its maximum, the likelihood of repression is 98 percent. It loses significance in the model that includes both country and year fixed effects and assumes a clustered stand error structure. Given that commodity prices are measured at their global value in a given year, it is unsurprising that year fixed effects reduce the precision of this coefficient estimate.

Beyond these primary results there are some additional results of interest. Consistent with existing theories in which road networks decrease the logistical cost of repression, thereby increasing the ease of access by government coercive forces, road density increases the likelihood of repression, though this result slips in and out of the range of significance. Additionally, the percentage of GDP that comes from mineral and coal rents is not a consistent predictor of repression. This result does not undermine existing findings indicating that resource dependent governments are more repressive on average. Instead, it suggests that local context matters, and governments remain strategic about their use of repression.[13]

Perhaps most interestingly, while being primarily foreign owned does not make a mine any more likely to experience conflict nearby (contrary to anecdotal evidence on the ground), it does make any protests that do occur in close proximity to the mine more likely to be repressed. This finding has several interesting implications. First, the finding that protest is no more likely near a foreign-owned mine than a domestic one in conjunction with the finding that conflicts near foreign-owned mines are more likely to be repressed mitigates selection bias concerns. In other words, it is not the case that repression is simply more likely near foreign-held mines because social mobilization is also more likely.

Second, it is generally the case that foreign-held mining operations are larger projects than domestic ones. As has been described elsewhere in the book, foreign firms are generally larger, and of the mining projects included in the dataset, the vast majority (approximately 77 percent) have headquarters in capital-rich countries with long histories of mineral extraction (Australia, Canada, South Africa, and the United Kingdom). This suggests that governments may consider it more important to protect foreign assets from protest and interruption, since they can leave more easily than domestic ones. Government repression signals to foreign

---

[13] For more on this dynamic, see Steinberg (2018).

investors that the government is interested in and capable of protecting foreign assets from costly local resistance. Furthermore, foreign-owned mines are likely to be larger than domestically held ones, since domestic firms are unlikely to have the capital resources that transnational resource firms have.

SUMMARY OF ANALYSES

The analyses conducted in this and the previous chapter lend general support to the hypotheses derived from the formal model. Consistent with a subset of hypotheses about the likelihood of protest, the analysis in Chapter 9 suggests that there is strong support for the importance of the interruptibility of the resource. In deciding whether to protest, communities weigh their relative effectiveness in terms of their ability to interrupt production, imposing monetary costs on the firm (and government). I find that the more interruptible mineral extraction is, the greater the likelihood of mobilization near a mine. There is sufficient support for the effect of the cost of the local transfer on the likelihood of mobilization near a mine. In deciding whether to live up to promises of compensation and benefits made to the local population, firms weigh the cost of providing them to communities against the potential cost of community mobilization. As the cost of the promised transfer to the local population increases, firms are less likely to provide it and consequently, protest near the mine becomes more likely. Finally, I find qualified support for the effect of government take on the likelihood of social mobilization in close proximity to a mine. Because an increase in the government's take of natural resource rents decreases the firm's resources and willingness to provide the promised transfer, as the government's take increases, the likelihood of protest near a mine increases.

When social conflict does occur in close proximity to a mine, my theory suggests that governments weigh the potential political cost of repressing social mobilization when deciding if or how to respond. As the political relevance of the local population increases, measured by heightened uncertainty of leader tenure, repression of a nearby conflict becomes less likely. Yet governments rely on repression to protect a mine whose productivity may be threatened by social mobilization. Since the benefit of repression increases with the value of the mine, as the value of the mine increases (measured by commodity price), repression of a nearby conflict event becomes more likely. In other words, when the value of the mine increases relative to the importance of political support for leader tenure, repression becomes more likely.

It is important to note some obstacles in testing all of the hypotheses that result from the formal model. First, the model predicts, with relative precision, relevant cut points that shape different outcomes. These cut points are too precise to test at the level of the continent, as existing data is insufficient for this level of granular precision, and the capacity to obtain such data does not exist in most cases. Second, the formal model details how the interaction among three different actors yields different governance outcomes in and around natural resource extractive sites. There are many more simultaneous moving parts than it is possible to test using currently available econometric techniques. Third, obtaining an unbiased measurement of the size of local transfers by firms around mining sites is not feasible. Reports of these transfers usually come from the firm itself, through yearly reports that are not consistently available across firms and across firm operation sites. In cases in which they are available (although they have increased, as it has become a norm to produce such reports), firms have little incentive to report these honestly, or in any standardized way, as any firm that has incurred the cost to provide the promised local transfer will wish to convey this, and any one that has not provided the promised transfer will wish to suggest that they have. Since there is not yet a standardized measurement of this aggregate notion of a local transfer (indeed there cannot be, given the contextual nature of its value), measurement of a firm's provision of the promised transfer using firm reports is likely to be biased and unreliable. As a consequence, the observability of local transfer by the firm is not feasible at the level of the continent. In comparison, the outcomes of social conflict and repression are more easily observable, so the analyses in these chapters test only a subset of the hypotheses.[14]

These quantitative tests present some general support for the hypotheses derived from the theoretical model. The results here provide some bases for their generalizability outside of Zambia, Mozambique, and DRC and supplement the case studies of Part II. More broadly, the

---

[14] Recall from the model that social protest may occur as a result of beliefs about the likelihood of repression, low cost of collective action, or the failure of the firm to provide a local transfer. Unfortunately, testing the likelihood of only a subset of the outcomes (protest and repression) means that protests that do not occur because of the likelihood of repression, high collective action costs, and firm transfer are all observationally the same.

quantitative tests in Chapters 9 and 10 suggest support for the effect of the parameters predicted to matter by the model. It suggests that the characteristics that shaped the governance outcomes described in the comparative cases of Zambia, DRC, and Mozambique travel beyond these countries to the rest of the continent.

11

Conclusion: What Next?

In this book I have proposed and tested a theory about the local politics of natural resource extraction. I have argued that regions of natural resource extraction constitute strategic contexts in which the interaction among extractive firms, local populations, and governments is compelled by the presence of the resource and territorialized by the concessionary allocation of extractive rights. Extractive regions compel extractive firms to engage with local populations in order to secure access to the resource and to continue extraction, but the state's reliance on revenue from extraction ensures that it too experiences costs should the firm fail to secure the support of the local population. The government's response to costly mobilization by the local community reflects its preferences over the trade-off between revenue and political support in the region.

The preceding chapters take seriously the role of geography and the environment in shaping local politics and preferences. Fundamentally, the presence of a mine changes the bargaining power of the local community. The potential to interrupt a geographically fixed revenue source allows the community to impose significant economic costs on the government, as well as the firm. Thus, the presence of natural resources and the geographic context in which they are extracted shapes the emergence and realization of preferences over local distributive outcomes.

This book also elaborates a framework for subnational analysis by introducing a spatially constrained population as an important strategic actor, but ensuring a multi-level approach to understanding subnational outcomes. Local outcomes are determined by the interaction of local, national, and international structural factors as well as the beliefs of the actors.

At the local level, if the cost to the firm of living up to its promises is sufficiently high, it will not do so. The government is likely to repress if mobilization occurs, given the extent to which such a transfer would cut into resource revenues it might receive. Larger or wealthier local communities who rely heavily on the environment around the mine cost the most to compensate, relocate, or provide other goods and services for they therefore are more likely to see conflict and repression.

At the national level, if the government's take of mining revenue (in the form of royalties and taxes) is sufficiently high, firms may be less likely to live up to their promises and governments will be more likely to repress, given the monetary value of the mine. This is interesting, given the tendency for NGOs to lobby for a "fair" deal in which the government gets a sufficiently high percentage of the mine's revenue. The consequence of this lobbying may be that incumbent governments promise to raise taxes leading up to an election (when the call to do so is the highest). If they actually do increase the government's take, the likelihood that firms follow through on localized promises decreases, making protest more likely. Repression is also, then, more likely, except in the event that such a protest occurs during an election year, when the political salience of the community is likely to be high. Conversely, when the population in and around the mining site is of importance for leader tenure, repression is less likely and firm follow through more likely.

Finally, if social conflict is not sufficiently monetarily costly to the firm and government, firms are less likely to care about ensuring they provide promised goods and services. Firms may wish to renege, even if they know protest is likely, because the cost of such protest is not sufficiently high to compel the firm to follow through. This means that if commodity prices, which are often set globally, are relatively low, and firms are uncertain of the likelihood of protest, firms may perceive an opportune time to not follow through, and remedy any information asymmetry.

However, structural conditions on their own are insufficient to explain the range of outcomes observed: these structural conditions interact with actors' beliefs about each other. Given that beliefs are shaped by a history of interaction between the actors, local histories matter in determining outcomes. A historically repressive state translates into shared beliefs among actors that may be difficult to overcome. This is what we observed play out in the DRC around copper mining in Katanga. Social conflict can occur if the firm and government have inaccurate beliefs about the likelihood of protest. A presumption that protest will not occur makes the firm less likely to follow through, and therefore protest more likely. This is what happened to Vale in Mozambique. Similarly, if the government is the type to repress a protest, but local community members have inaccurate beliefs about this, firms are less likely to follow through *and* communities are more likely to protest – only to be met with repression.

Finally, this book reorients the study of governance to emphasize the role of non-state actors in reshaping how the fundamental relationship between the government and the population plays out over space, particularly when it is moderated by the presence of a firm. Constrained by the locational rigidity of the resource, the firm provides the government a low-cost extractor by acting as an alternative, resource-endowed goods provider, thereby changing the calculation of the government. At its core, understanding how the relationship between the government and the population plays out over space, particularly when it is moderated by the presence of a firm, has implications for a more fundamental puzzle that is at the center of political science: what is the role of non-state actors in effecting governance outcomes across space?

One potential outcome is that the strategic interaction between the firm, local community, and government may have implications for the state's legitimacy. Firm provision of goods and services, especially in the absence of the government compelling it to do so, may lead communities to view the firm as the primary provider of a broad range of goods and services usually attributed to the state. The state may become less visible, less relevant, and therefore less legitimate in the long run. Fearing this, governments may, under some conditions, request that firms limit their local transfer so as not to undermine the government. This is particularly to be true of poorer governments, whose administrative capacity to provide goods and services across its territory is more limited. In these cases, the relative credit that governments can claim for enforcement is valuable, but must be weighed against the potential long-term ramifications of abdicating a portion of the development agenda to the private firm.

The preceding chapters demonstrate that there is a unique point after which the concession that has been allocated has long-term consequences. Particular moments in time, often referred to as critical junctures, can shape the order and composition of future events and outcomes. Specifically, the time between when a local community becomes aware of the commencement of a large-scale mining project and the first years after production begins constitutes a critical time frame that may shape the events that follow over the course of the mine. This is because this time frame presents a unique point of information revelation for the government and firm on the one hand, and the local communities on the other. First, firms and governments who may have had inaccurate beliefs about the likelihood that communities would mobilize update these beliefs after observing whether the community members protest or not. Second, local communities are able to update their perceptions about whether the government will respond to mobilization with repression, or whether it will support the firm. A fundamental assumption here is that social conflict emerges in equilibrium because of an information asymmetry – if and when these asymmetries are resolved through this first interaction, we should be unlikely to observe ongoing social conflict in the future.

The absence of social conflict over the lifetime of a mine seems a lofty and naive expectation, and in fact, empirically we do see some mines that experience social conflict repeatedly. But the theory proposed and examined here does not require that other processes and theories are not at work throughout the life of the mine. Additionally, it does not presume that the values of parameters that constrained the relevance of beliefs do not change over the life of the mine. For example, the relative amount that may be destroyed during a protest will most certainly change, given that commodity prices may rise as does the cost of extraction per unit of the resource. When this happens, firms need only to believe that there is a small possibility of costly mobilization in order to ensure that the firm follows through (even if the government would repress a protest). However, when beliefs about the likelihood of mobilization and repression are accurate (i.e., when information asymmetries are removed), the likelihood of conflict decreases drastically.

Obtaining "good" outcomes in which conflict is avoided requires both a resolution of the information asymmetry problem as well as a consideration of existing structural factors. Yet conflict is not the only possible "bad" outcome. A failure of the firm to follow through on its commitment, even if there is no resulting mobilization, ensures that local communities miss out on benefits from extraction and makes environmental degradation more likely (absent other safeguards). This is particularly likely to happen if communities have a high expectation of repression, or if they have a high cost of collective action. As was the case in DRC, a strong expectation of repression may be the result of a local history of government coercion, leading communities to believe that if they mobilize, they are likely to be met with the repressive security apparatus of the state, either directly, or through the private security of the firm. History matters, in that a historically repressive state translates into shared beliefs among actors that may be difficult to escape.

Foreign direct investment in the extractive sector has primarily consisted of (up until quite recently) hosting by resource-rich countries in the global south of firms based in capital-rich countries of the north. When such kinds of investment began, many developing states shared the characteristic of limited state capacity (as Herbst points out, the broadcasting of power over African states in particular has remained limited). In fact, many states invited FDI for the very purpose of increasing state resources, prioritizing capital accumulation, much of which was extracted in regions relatively distant from the political center. In extractive colonies throughout the twentieth century, repression was particularly brutal because the represser experienced few if any political costs for doing so. Particularly where and when political costs of protest to governments are limited, such as in closed autocracies, the density of the local population is likely to matter. But even where local populations were capable of interrupting the revenue stream from the resource (given underdeveloped infrastructure for its transport), the repression of such populations in order to protect the resource has historically carried fewer domestic political costs. Countries that consolidated with significant natural resources developed repressive capacity at the expense of regulatory strength in these regions.

Avenues for Further Research

There are some debates that are advanced by the preceding chapters, and some new ones they bring to the fore. To be sure, there is much more to be written about the local politics of natural resource extraction. The preceding chapters suggest several avenues for additional research that were beyond either the theoretical or empirical scope of this study. In particular, the area is ripe for regional comparisons, as well as a study of diffusion and learning effects.

Much that has been written about mobilization around mining has focused on Latin America. These works link the characteristics of the mine with the likelihood of mobilization,[1] differentiate between the nature of grievances undergirding this mobilization,[2] and qualitatively trace the forms and social movements as struggles over livelihoods in rural territories.[3] It is not yet clear whether the theory developed and

[1] Haslam and Ary Tanimoune (2016).
[2] Arce (2014).
[3] Bebbington, Humphreys, Bury, Lingan, Muñoz, and Scurrah (2008).

tested in the preceding chapters might apply in the Latin American context. The Latin American context is one of stronger states and formal decentralization, and a longer history of mobilization around mining. We might expect this mobilization to shape firm and government expectations – indeed miners I spoke to in Zambia noted that Peru and Chile were seen as hotbeds of protest. Furthermore, formal decentralization might create a greater division between local and central state preferences. Finally, a stronger state might consider intervening to provide public goods or address externalities of mining before protest occurs, or might successfully deter protest altogether.

In addition to the benefits of a regionally comparative study, the theory developed in the preceding chapters suggests the potential for diffusion and learning effects. The theoretical bulwark of the book argues that beliefs matter, and in particular that beliefs about how actors will behave constrain the importance of other more structural factors. In Mozambique, Vale's experience served to provide information for Rio Tinto so that it could change its expectations about the likelihood of social mobilization in its coal concession. It was the proximity of Vale's concession to Rio Tinto's concession that allowed Rio Tinto to easily observe the mobilization against Vale, and consequently update its beliefs. Rio Tinto was then able to act to prevent similar mobilization in its own Benga concession. Given the way in which firms and governments may update their beliefs about the likelihood of protest, it should be the case that firms can observe conflict events happening relatively nearby to evaluate the likelihood of social mobilization near the mine.

We might imagine that these kinds of learning processes will yield additional spatial patterns of conflict and repression related to the capacity and willingness of communities and firms to update their beliefs based on events happening nearby. Mines for which there are social mobilization events that occur somewhat nearby might be less likely to experience mobilization in close proximity to their mine, since just as Rio Tinto was. Firms should be able to observe these nearby events and provide the promised transfer.

However, it is not clear that firms might always learn the right lesson, and it might be the case that some firms are more likely to update than others. What characteristics of a firm make it more likely to change its behavior? Similarly, communities might also change their beliefs given events nearby. In Zambia and DRC, these beliefs were shaped by historical interactions between the communities and the government – whether mobilization and repression had occurred in the past. If communities can observe recent government repression in response to other instances of social mobilization in relatively close proximity or if such instances were otherwise unsuccessful, they may be less likely to mobilize, given the expected higher cost associated with mobilizing. However, this requires additional study of the internal dynamics of the local community to understand the flow of information and the likelihood that it affects the perceptions of community members in a way that shifts the costs of mobilization.

Furthermore, how do the internal dynamics of collective action of local communities near natural resources shift if the community is immediately reliant on the resource as a primary source of livelihoods? Elinor and Vincent Ostrom and coauthors have explored the many ways in which communities self-organize around the management of common pool resources in the absence of either a strong and formal governance structure or a resource-endowed firm. These kinds of resources tend to be more diffuse over space than are mines, making them less excludable though they are still rivalrous (giving them their common pool characteristics). To what extent do the local politics of pointed natural resources, such as mines, travel to resources the community might directly rely upon, such as a forest or fishery? Does this fundamental difference in the nature of the good affect the way in which local communities mobilize?

Finally, the evidence provided to test the theory laid out in this book is observational – it relies on the qualitative observations of the researcher, and on existing data reconfigured and spatially adjoined to understand the spatial patterns suggested by the theory. However, there remains space to take advantage of what has been called the "credibility revolution" – a strong reliance on experimental methods that allow greater proximity to causality. While the random and fixed distribution of natural resources limits the capacity to manipulate the geographic context of extraction, there may be other opportunities for experimental methodologies; for example, quasi-natural experiments in which researchers make use of plausibly random changes in parameters (such as access to information that might reduce information asymmetries, or externally driven influxes of migrants to a mining community, which might drive up the cost to the firm of compensation) to further probe the causal mechanisms here and to develop new theories of the local politics of natural resource extraction. Scholars such as Renard Sexton, Darin Christiansen, Laura Paler, Graeme Blair, and Michael Ross have already begun to advance such an agenda. Furthermore, as more data at the subnational level become available, further research of a selection of country cases could provide further nuance to the arguments presented here.

Implications for Policy

While additional work is yet to be done, it remains the responsibility of any scholar to consider the implications of her findings for policymakers who aim to reduce or mitigate conflict, or ensure that firms live up to their commitments. Given the normative weight of the outcomes at stake, what are the relevant policy levers that can be pulled? The last fifteen years have seen the emergence of new international governance schemes to monitor and mitigate the consequences of natural resource extraction. These emerged out of the recognition by policymakers and NGOs of the prevalence of the resource curse, and a developmental turn toward the local level. The consequence has been a series of initiatives aimed at addressing the local environmental effects of mining, and corruption relating to natural resource revenue.

The most prominent governance scheme to emerge is the Extractive Industry Transparency Initiative (EITI), an outgrowth of the Publish What You Pay initiative. It aims to incentivize firms and governments to publish taxes, royalties, and fees paid by firms and received by governments. It is a voluntary system in which each member country submits a yearly report. By publishing these reports, EITI has the potential to reduce the asymmetric information problem that can make conflict more likely. However, it has been created to ensure that a global public can observe discrepancies between the firm's and the government's accounting of government revenues from natural resources. While the report is publicly available (usually 1–2 years after the subject year of the report), the audience for the report does not often include the local communities who might benefit most from it.

Other efforts have included certification schemes, which are meant to impose market-based pressures on transnational firms to promote higher standards of social and environmental responsibility in production processes (and possibly trade relations). Based on voluntary participation, they require mechanisms for imposing costs when market actors fail to take part. To be effective, the participation of firms in certification schemes must be observable to the relevant actors who can actually impose costs. The Kimberly Process sought to impose this kind of pressure on diamond producers by certifying diamonds were produced without contributing to ongoing armed conflict. While ultimately the Kimberly Process failed to prevent trafficking through circuitous global networks, which eventually undermined the certification process,[4] the certification strategy was well suited to the industry. Specifically, diamonds are a luxury good, and consumers had relatively accessible (and less-expensive) substitutes for diamonds available to them if firms did not buy into the Kimberly Process. Furthermore, the concentration of the diamond market ensured that early on in the process, Global Witness only needed to convince DeBeers to buy into the scheme, lowering the transaction costs and simultaneously affecting a large portion of the market. However, gemstone, mineral, and metal markets that are less concentrated, require more processing, are less substitutable, and are less likely to be easily and successfully governed by certification schemes like the Kimberly Process.

Most certification schemes and voluntary revenue transparency initiatives are aimed at mitigating the resource curse, which has been described until recently as a primarily national-level phenomenon. As a consequence, it is not immediately clear how these strategies might mitigate conflict or maldistribution of extractive costs and benefits at the local level. To be sure, certification schemes or other international governance strategies that result in more transparency would make the relative value of the resource more explicit, and the cost of firm enforcement lower. This would, in turn, reveal whether the government is more likely to prefer political or economic capital. If one of the obstacles to avoiding conflict is the existence of an information asymmetry, then rectifying this asymmetry should decrease the likelihood, and therefore the incidence of conflict.

However, recall that the absence of conflict does not ensure the "good behavior" of firms – conflict may be avoided merely because communities view it as too costly given expectations about repression. Thus, resolving the information asymmetry may be sufficient to reduce the likelihood of conflict, but not necessarily sufficient for improving outcomes for the environment or local communities. Furthermore, the extent to which local communities have access to information revealed as a result of transparency schemes will determine how helpful that transparency is. For mining communities far from the state's political center, with limited access to technology, or with limited NGO presence, the likelihood that communities are able to access relevant information about the mine is relatively low.

Informal guidelines promulgated by international financial institutions have also attempted to guide extractive firm behavior in host countries.

---

[4] Ultimately, its primary sponsor, Global Witness, backed out.

Specifically, the International Finance Corporation's (IFC) performance standards provide relatively clear guidelines for firm behavior with specific reference to assessing environmental and social impacts, land acquisition and involuntary resettlement, indigenous peoples, and other issue areas extractive firms should negotiate with host communities. These guidelines are voluntary, unless the extractive project is supported by a World Bank loan or other financial institution that has signed on to the Equator Principles. Even when a mining project is financed by the World Bank, enforcement of these criteria is not uniform, and is in fact the burden of the borrower.

In addition to global guidelines and certification schemes, policy makers have also taken a local turn. A prolific literature on the benefits and drawbacks of "participatory development"[5] has outlined the ways in which local communities are incorporated or excluded from the process of development, extractive or otherwise. Advocates of the participatory approach laud the community meetings that firm – community liaisons hold in the towns affected by mining, though even they are not wholly convinced of the effectiveness of such participation for ensuring such communities do not receive a raw deal. As demonstrated here, the existence of mechanisms for participation by communities does not neatly map onto the realization of preferences. Since the local context determines some structural parameters that constrain the beliefs and decisions of each group, community participation cannot change many of these.

Acknowledging that mere participation was insufficient to ensure communities benefited from mining, formal Community Development Agreements (CDAs) have become more common since the mid-2000s. While an agreed-upon definition remains elusive, CDAs tend to be agreements between the community and the mining company specifying the local distribution of costs and benefits associated with mining.[6] These agreements often include royalty or profit sharing, the establishment of community foundations, and government revenue earmarking. According to Sarkar et al. (2010), CDAs should help to "avert or mitigate negative project impacts, improve stakeholder relationships, and

---

[5] Nelson, Wright et al. (1995), Shah (1998), Burkey et al. (1993), Mohan and Stokke (2000), and Cornwall (2003) are a few.

[6] Varieties of CDAs include Voluntary Agreements, Indigenous Land Use Agreements, Community Contracts, Landowner agreements, Shared Responsibilities Agreements, Empowerment Agreements, and Community Joint Venture Agreements.

promote mutually beneficial sustainable benefits from the mining industry, including equitable and pro-poor benefits for local communities."

While CDAs have created some optimism, policy makers should
remain cautious about their potential effectiveness. First, in order to
apply to a specific mining project, they must be sufficiently context
specific. They must consider the specific local actors and environment,
reflecting many of the parameters discussed above that structure incentives for firms to follow through on an agreement. This makes identifying
principles of CDAs easy, but specifying the provisions in practice much
more difficult. Second, the most effective CDAs are argued to be those
that exist in partnership with local government which requires sufficient
capacity for enforcement and revenue distribution.[7] Third, regulatory
requirement of CDAs may lead to a least common denominator of firm
practice, thereby minimizing firm incentive to innovate in a given local
context. Fourth, CDAs may absolve the state of any involvement in the
development agenda. Finally, and perhaps most importantly, it is not
clear what it means for a CDA to be effective. Principles for CDAs are
generally vague, and in practice it is not clear whose buy-in is required
and whether fulfilling an agreement active for some portion of the mine's
life span is a sufficient definition of success.

More generally, the very requirements that are likely to make CDAs
effective are the same characteristics that are likely to lead to better outcomes even in their absence. CDAs require local capacity and
accountability of both governments and of communities. Still, mandating
CDAs may be useful in areas where the value of the resource is low, or
where it is difficult for communities to threaten the resource. Since firms
will be less willing to follow through in these cases, mandating a CDA
is more likely to have some sort of effect, so long as it creates costs for
firms that fail to live up to the formal agreement.

Ultimately, the existing collection of policy initiatives suggest that a
normative consensus about the need to improve local governance outcomes around natural resource sites has clearly emerged. However, a
consensus on practical strategies for doing so remains elusive.

Concluding Thoughts

This study takes seriously the role of geography and the environment in shaping local politics and preferences. The presence of natural

---

[7] Sarkar et al. (2010).

resources and the geographic context in which they are extracted shapes the emergence and realization of preferences over local distributive outcomes. Second, in explicitly and systematically analyzing the role of a localized population who can constrain the extractive firm and the state, this study introduces a novel framework for subnational analysis. It demonstrates that local trade-offs and revenue and political support can shape the incentives for governments and firms at the local level, thus exploring the local dimensions of the "resource curse" by emphasizing the agency of local populations. Third, it reorients the study of governance away from the state by emphasizing the role of non-state actors, such as natural resource firms, in shaping governance outcomes. This is particularly important given the existence of competing and alternative sources of legitimacy in weak states, and the potential role of large, transnational firms in performing functions traditionally carried out by the state.

More broadly, it is regularly noted that globalization compels us to reconsider and renegotiate the boundaries of territorial authority of the state, but there has been little work on the territorial implications of globalization, specifically the ways in which state and non-state actors negotiate governance at the subnational level. Regions of natural resource extraction help us to understand this broader puzzle, as they compel extractive firms and governments to interact in a defined space where trade-offs between revenue accumulation and political support are most acute. Revealing these trade-offs and the resulting incentive structure can provide a framework for understanding the localized implications of global capital and its holders on traditional forms of governance.

APPENDICES

Appendix A

MODEL PROOFS (CH.3)

In what follows, I deduce the cut points for the actors' beliefs that determine each of the outcomes, **Adhere, Acquiesce, Subdue,** and **Uphold.** The government will repress if and only if :

$$E \geq \gamma_R + \gamma_E - \tau\chi(T)$$

Otherwise, it will enforce the agreement and compel the firm to follow through. Thus we can portion the set of all values of E into two sets: E_H when $E \geq \gamma_R + \gamma_E - \tau\chi(T)$, and E_L otherwise. Define μ as the probability that the government is of the type $E = E_H$ ($0 \leq \mu \leq 1$). In other words, this is the local population's belief that the government will repress, should it protest.

The local population may have either a high cost of protest (c_H) or a low cost of protest (c_L). Assume $c_H > c_L \geq 0$. Consider the expected value to the local population of protesting and not protesting given that the firm reneges.

For $LP = c_H$:

$$EV_{LP_H}(P) = (1 - \mu)(T - c_H m) + \mu(-L - c_H m - r)$$
$$EV_{LP_H}(\neg P) = -L$$

LP_H protests if $\frac{T - c_H m + L}{T + L + v} \geq \mu$. Call this $\mu = \mu_L$.

For $LP = c_L$:

$$EV_{LP_L}(P) = (1 - \mu)(T - c_L m) + \mu(-L - c_L m - r)$$
$$EV_{LP_L}(\neg P) = -L$$

193

LP_L will not protest if $\frac{T-c_L m+L}{T+L+v} \leq \mu$. Call this $\mu = \mu_H$.

Note that, even if the local population knew the government would compel the firm to follow through on its promise, a local population might choose not to protest if $T < cm$. This case represents a subset of cases in which the transfer is of relatively negligible value, at least relative to the cost of protest. Field work suggests this does not represent a significant portion of the cases, but it is important to note in any case. For the interesting solution of this model, consider the cases in which $T > c_H m$.

Because $c_H > c_L \geq 0$, it must be the case that $\frac{T-c_L m+L}{T+L+v} > \frac{T-c_H m+L}{T+L+v}$. Thus, if $\frac{T-c_H m+L}{T+L+v} > \mu_L$, then $\frac{T-c_L m+L}{T+L+v} > \mu_L$. Similarly, it must be the case that if $\frac{T-c_H m+L}{T+L+v} \geq \mu_H$, then $\frac{T-c_L m+L}{T+L+v} \geq \mu_H$.

Lemma 1 *For all $\mu > \mu_H$, neither type of LP will protest. For all $\mu < \mu_L$, both types of LP will protest.*

Because the firm is aware of this (by way of the Common Prior assumption), the cases of particular interest are those in which $\mu_L \leq \mu \leq \mu_H$.

Define ρ as the firm's belief about the probability that the local population will protest if it reneges ($0 \leq \rho \leq 1$). The firm's expected value to following through is:

$$EV_F(FT) = (1-\tau)(\Pi - \chi(T))$$

If $G = E_H$, then

$$EV_F(\neg FT)|G_{E_H} = \rho(1-\tau)(\Pi - r) + (1-\rho)(1-\tau)\Pi$$

Thus the firm chooses to follow through if:

$$(1-\tau)(\Pi - \chi(T)) \geq \rho(1-\tau)(\Pi - r) + (1-\rho)(1-\tau)\Pi$$

or

$$\rho \geq \frac{\chi(T)}{r}$$

Define ρ^H such that $\rho^H = \frac{\chi(T)}{r}$. Note that if $\chi(T) \geq r$, then the firm never chooses FT.

Lemma 2 *If $\chi(T) \geq r$, and $G = E_H$, the firm has a dominant strategy of playing $\neg FT$.*

If $G = E_L$, then

$$EV_F(\neg FT)|G_{E_L} = \rho(1-\tau)(\Pi - r - \chi(T)) + (1-\rho)(1-\tau)\Pi$$

The firm chooses to follow through if:

$$(1-\tau)(\Pi - \chi(T)) \geq \rho(1-\tau)(\Pi - r - \chi(T)) + (1-\rho)(1-\tau)\Pi$$

or

$$\rho \geq \frac{\chi(T)}{r + \chi(T)}$$

Define ρ^L such that $\rho^L = \frac{\chi(T)}{r + \chi(T)}$.

Separating Equilibria

Consider that a PBE solution specifies a strategy profile in the form of $(F; LP_h, LP_l; G_{E_H}, G_{E_L})$ and prior beliefs for each actor (ρ, μ). Because the firm is aware of the government's type and they share a belief about the local population's probability of protesting, we can simplify the notation to $(F_{G_H}, F_{G_L}; LP_h, LP_l)$.

Consider then that a pure separating equilibrium is one in which a firm that knew the government would repress would pursue one strategy, while a firm that knew the government would compel it to follow through would pursue another. As a result, the local population would update its prior about the likelihood that the government would repress a protest (μ) to reflect the information carried in the signal sent by the firm's decision. A Nash solution concept requires that the firm would not deviate from its strategy once it knows how the local population would respond.

Claim 1 *For all combinations of types of G and LP, and for all beliefs μ and ρ, the set of equilibria that emerge contain no separating equilibria (if $T \geq c_H m$).*

Consider the firm strategy $\neg FT, FT$. If a local population accurately learns it will be repressed from the firm's decision to play $\neg FT$, neither type of local population will play P. As a consequence, neither type of firm would play FT, thus a pure strategy equilibrium in which $\neg FT, FT$ is not a Nash equilibrium.

Consider the firm strategy $FT, \neg FT$. A local population that accurately learns that the government will compel the firm to follow through from the firm's decision to play $\neg FT$ will always protest if it observes

$\neg FT$. If both types of LP will protest, it is never in the firm's interest to renege. Thus a pure strategy equilibrium in which $FT, \neg FT$ is not a Nash equilibrium.

Returning to the earlier assumption that $T > c_H m$, if this is relaxed there is indeed a separating equilibrium that emerges when $c_L m \leq T \leq c_H m$. In this case, the firm with the government support will renege, and LP_L will protest, and LP_H will not protest. The firm's prior beliefs about the local population's type that sustain that equilibrium are $\rho < \rho^L$. If $T < c_L m$, however, the LP will never protest, which means that no type of firm will play FT.

Pooling and Semi-Separating Equilibria

Given Lemma 1, the firm will never play FT if $\mu > \mu^H$, and will always play FT if $\mu < \mu^L$. As a result two pooling equilibria emerge: $(FT, FT; P, P, \mu < \mu^L, \rho \geq 0)$, and $\neg FT, \neg FT; \neg P, \neg P, \mu > \mu^H$, $\rho \geq 0$.

Now consider the cases in which $\mu^L < \mu < \mu^H$. Consider that there are no cases in which LP_h protests, but LP_l does not, given that $c_h > c_l > 0$ and they share the same beliefs about the likelihood of repression. Two additional pooling equilibriums emerge: $(\neg FT, \neg FT; P, \neg P, \rho < \rho^L)$, and $(FT, FT; \neg P, P, \rho > \rho^H)$.

Finally, consider a mixed strategy in which one type of firm plays one strategy, and the other plays each strategy with some probability. Consider the case in which $(FT, FT$ with probability $\delta)$. Given that when either type of local population observes $\neg FT$, it knows the government will repress, neither type will protest. A similar logic dictates that $(FT$ with probability $\delta, FT)$ cannot be sustained as a semi-separating equilibrium. Consequently, only cases in which one type of firm plays $\neg FT$, and the other type plays FT with some probability δ can potentially constitute a PBE.

Case 1: $\neg FT, FT$ with probability δ; $\neg P, P$ with probability $\alpha, \mu^H > \mu > \mu^L, \rho > \frac{\chi(T)}{\chi(T)+r}$. Apply Bayes's Rule to obtain the local population's posterior belief $(\mu*)$ about the likelihood the government will repress given that the firm plays $\neg FT$.

$Prob(G = G_H)|\neg FT =$

$$\frac{(Prob(\neg FT)|G = G_H)(Prob(G = G_H))}{(Prob(\neg FT)|G = G_H)(Prob(G = G_H)) + (Prob(\neg FT)|G = G_L)(Prob(G = G_L))}$$

$$Prob(G = G_H)|\neg FT = \frac{(1)(\mu)}{(1)(\mu) + \delta(1 - \mu)} = \mu*$$

Given the local population's posterior, solve δ such that the local population is indifferent to protest, given $\neg FT$.

$$EV_{LP}(\neg P) = EV_{LP}(P)|\neg FT$$

$$-L = \mu * (-L - cm - v) + (1 - \mu*)(T - cm)$$

$$\mu* = \frac{L + T - cm}{L + v + T}$$

Note that $\mu*_{LP_L} > \mu*_{LP_H}$, that is, the posterior belief about the likelihood that the government will repress must be higher for LP_H than LP_H.

Solve for δ:

$$\delta = \frac{\mu(1 - \mu*)}{\mu * (1 - \mu)}$$

But the strategy $(\neg FT, FT$ with probability $\delta)$ can only render one type of local population indifferent to playing P. Any δ that renders LP_H indifferent would ensure LP_L protested. Consequently, a firm that knew the government was going to enforce the promise would play FT with probability δ such that $\delta = \frac{\mu(1-\mu*_L)}{\mu*_L(1-\mu)}$, ensuring that LP_H does not protest.

The local population plays P with some probability α so as to render the F_{G_L} indifferent to playing FT and $\neg FT$.

$$EV_{G_L}(FT) = EV_{G_L}(\neg FT)$$

$$(1 - \tau)(\Pi - \chi(T)) = \rho(\alpha(1 - \tau)(\Pi - \chi(T) - r) + (1 - \alpha)(1 - \tau)\Pi)$$

$$+(1 - \rho)(1 - \tau)\Pi$$

$$\alpha = \frac{\chi(T)}{(\chi(T) + r)\rho}$$

Recall that to sustain an equilibrium in which the two types of local population would behave differently, it must be the case that $\mu^H > \mu > \mu^L$.

Case 2: FT with probability δ, $\neg FT$; $\neg P$, P with probability α

In order for F_{G_L} to always play $\neg FT$, it must be the case that $\rho < \frac{\chi(T)}{\chi(T)+r}$. However, if this were the case, F_H would never have an incentive to play FT. Consequently, Case 2 does not constitute a PBE.

Appendix B

The following pages provide the following robustness checks: bivariate analysis and placebo tests for key independent variables, and variation in the distance threshold (15 km and 25 km instead of 20 km between conflict and mine). Six variations of each of these tests are provided to include clustered errors, year fixed effects, and country fixed effects.

TABLE B.1: *Bivariate regression on protest within 20 km*

	Model A b/se	Model B b/se	Model C b/se	Model D b/se
SCAD within 20 km				
Railroad within 20 km	1.688***			
	(0.10)			
Soil Productivity		0.189***		
		(0.05)		
Percent Cropland (l)			2.479***	
			(0.33)	
Avg Effective Tax Rate (l)				0.088
				(0.08)
Constant	−1.932***	−1.727***	−1.301***	−1.292***
	(0.08)	(0.21)	(0.06)	(0.29)
Pseudo R Sq	.11	.005	.02	.0004
Chi-Sq Test	315	14	55	1
Log-Likelihood	−1308.3	−1429.6	−1390.1	−1430.6
Observations	2497.0	2450.0	2425.0	2428.0

+ p < 0.10, * p < 0.05, ** p < 0.01, *** p < 0.001

Placebo Tests

Probability of Protest within 20 km – Rail Placebo

	Model 1	Model 2 yFE	Model 3 cyFE	Model 4	Model 5 yFE	Model 6 cyFE
Random Rail under 20km	−0.091	−0.119	−0.106	−0.091	−0.119+	−0.106
	(0.11)	(0.11)	(0.11)	(0.06)	(0.07)	(0.07)
Population Density (l)	0.691***	0.731***	0.735***	0.691***	0.731***	0.735***
	(0.04)	(0.04)	(0.05)	(0.09)	(0.12)	(0.13)
Infant Mortality Rate	0.004+	0.004+	−0.003	0.004	0.004	−0.003
	(0.00)	(0.00)	(0.01)	(0.00)	(0.00)	(0.01)
Distance to Capital (l)	−0.351***	−0.364***	−0.379***	−0.351**	−0.364**	−0.379*
	(0.06)	(0.07)	(0.08)	(0.11)	(0.12)	(0.16)
Road Density	−0.004	−0.006+	−0.005	−0.004	−0.006	−0.005
	(0.00)	(0.00)	(0.00)	(0.01)	(0.01)	(0.01)
Country Area	0.000**	0.000***	−0.000	0.000	0.000*	−0.000
	(0.00)	(0.00)	(0.00)	(0.00)	(0.00)	(0.00)
Polity IV	0.116***	0.133***	0.088	0.116*	0.133*	0.088
	(0.03)	(0.04)	(0.07)	(0.06)	(0.06)	(0.10)
South Africa	0.545*	0.519*		0.545	0.519	
	(0.22)	(0.25)		(0.33)	(0.32)	
Foreign Owned	−0.003	0.013	0.141	−0.003	0.013	0.141
	(0.14)	(0.14)	(0.15)	(0.12)	(0.12)	(0.14)
Coal	0.000	0.000	0.000	0.000	0.000	0.000
	(.)	(.)	(.)	(.)	(.)	(.)
Copper	0.458+	0.264	0.181	0.458+	0.264	0.181
	(0.24)	(0.25)	(0.29)	(0.25)	(0.25)	(0.26)
Gold	−0.326+	−0.279	0.000	−0.326	−0.279	0.000
	(0.18)	(0.19)	(0.21)	(0.24)	(0.28)	(0.21)
Iron	0.282	0.139	−0.036	0.282	0.139	−0.036
	(0.26)	(0.28)	(0.30)	(0.26)	(0.29)	(0.29)
Lead	1.219	0.889	0.306	1.219*	0.889	0.306
	(1.17)	(1.10)	(1.05)	(0.62)	(0.71)	(0.75)

(continued)

(continued)

	Model 1	Model 2 yFE	Model 3 cyFE	Model 4	Model 5 yFE	Model 6 cyFE
MetMin	−0.135	−0.255	−0.237	−0.135	−0.255	−0.237
	(0.18)	(0.19)	(0.21)	(0.17)	(0.18)	(0.14)
Nickel	−1.525*	−1.587*	−2.249**	−1.525*	−1.587*	−2.249***
	(0.61)	(0.63)	(0.77)	(0.59)	(0.63)	(0.62)
Phosphate	−1.106+	−1.336*	−1.604*	−1.106*	−1.336*	−1.604+
	(0.59)	(0.62)	(0.75)	(0.48)	(0.58)	(0.89)
Platinum	−0.767*	−0.792*	−0.710*	−0.767***	−0.792**	−0.710**
	(0.32)	(0.34)	(0.35)	(0.13)	(0.27)	(0.24)
Potash	0.000	0.000	0.000	0.000	0.000	0.000
	(.)	(.)	(.)	(.)	(.)	(.)
Silver	−0.624	−0.588	−0.133	−0.624	−0.588	−0.133
	(0.89)	(0.93)	(0.93)	(0.69)	(0.81)	(0.88)
Tin	0.125	−0.114	−0.107	0.125	−0.114	−0.107
	(0.73)	(0.79)	(0.87)	(0.42)	(0.50)	(0.29)
Zinc	−0.833	−0.887	−0.546	−0.833	−0.887	−0.546
	(0.70)	(0.70)	(0.80)	(0.52)	(0.55)	(0.50)
styr = 1990		0.000	0.000		0.000	0.000
		(.)	(.)		(.)	(.)
styr = 1991		−0.645*	−0.340		−0.645***	−0.340+
		(0.32)	(0.34)		(0.18)	(0.18)
styr = 1992		−0.137	−0.026		−0.137	−0.026
		(0.33)	(0.35)		(0.46)	(0.55)
styr = 1993		0.146	−0.128		0.146	−0.128
		(0.48)	(0.51)		(0.30)	(0.35)
styr = 1994		0.048	0.158		0.048	0.158
		(0.34)	(0.37)		(0.28)	(0.35)
styr = 1995		−0.532	−0.536		−0.532	−0.536
		(0.41)	(0.43)		(0.44)	(0.42)
styr = 1996		1.060+	0.911		1.060***	0.911***
		(0.55)	(0.56)		(0.19)	(0.14)
styr = 1997		0.581	0.335		0.581	0.335
		(0.44)	(0.47)		(0.40)	(0.39)
styr = 1998		−0.358	−0.303		−0.358	−0.303
		(0.35)	(0.38)		(0.25)	(0.26)
styr = 1999		0.237	0.143		0.237	0.143
		(0.45)	(0.49)		(0.31)	(0.41)
styr = 2000		0.090	0.117		0.090	0.117
		(0.41)	(0.48)		(0.43)	(0.54)
styr = 2001		−0.164	−0.041		−0.164	−0.041
		(0.34)	(0.37)		(0.28)	(0.32)
styr = 2002		−0.051	−0.101		−0.051	−0.101
		(0.50)	(0.54)		(0.49)	(0.59)

	Model 1	Model 2 yFE	Model 3 cyFE	Model 4	Model 5 yFE	Model 6 cyFE
styr = 2003		0.437	0.360		0.437	0.360
		(0.46)	(0.52)		(0.54)	(0.73)
styr = 2004		−0.038	0.239		−0.038	0.239
		(0.41)	(0.49)		(0.50)	(0.67)
styr = 2005		0.471	0.089		0.471	0.089
		(0.37)	(0.41)		(0.38)	(0.30)
styr = 2006		−0.200	−0.365		−0.200	−0.365
		(0.41)	(0.46)		(0.58)	(0.61)
styr = 2007		−0.126	0.113		−0.126	0.113
		(0.39)	(0.49)		(0.49)	(0.58)
styr = 2008		−0.173	−0.551		−0.173	−0.551
		(0.38)	(0.43)		(0.61)	(0.46)
styr = 2009		−0.695+	−0.709		−0.695	−0.709
		(0.40)	(0.47)		(0.71)	(0.74)
styr = 2010		−0.392	−0.383		−0.392	−0.383
		(0.53)	(0.60)		(0.39)	(0.63)
styr = 2011		−0.968**	−0.560		−0.968*	−0.560
		(0.34)	(0.39)		(0.43)	(0.44)
styr = 2012		−0.602*	−0.425		−0.602+	−0.425
		(0.30)	(0.34)		(0.32)	(0.28)
styr = 2013		−0.842*	−0.982*		−0.842*	−0.982*
		(0.36)	(0.42)		(0.33)	(0.48)
Algeria		0.000			0.000	
		(.)			(.)	
Angola		0.822			0.822	
		(0.93)			(0.91)	
Botswana		−1.264+			−1.264+	
		(0.70)			(0.72)	
Burkina Faso		−1.362**			−1.362**	
		(0.47)			(0.51)	
Burundi		1.434			1.434	
		(1.00)			(1.04)	
Cameroon		0.000			0.000	
		(.)			(.)	
Central African Republic		2.322+			2.322***	
		(1.28)			(0.69)	
Democratic Republic of Congo		1.964+			1.964*	
		(1.01)			(0.90)	

(continued)

(continued)

	Model 1	Model 2 yFE	Model 3 cyFE	Model 4	Model 5 yFE	Model 6 cyFE
Egypt			0.000			0.000
			(.)			(.)
Eritrea			−0.891			−0.891
			(0.98)			(0.72)
Ethiopia			−0.110			−0.110
			(0.85)			(0.71)
Gabon			1.082			1.082**
			(0.72)			(0.38)
Ghana			−1.026*			−1.026**
			(0.50)			(0.37)
Guinea			−0.127			−0.127
			(0.55)			(0.50)
Guinea−Bissau			0.000			0.000
			(.)			(.)
Kenya			−0.132			−0.132
			(0.70)			(0.63)
Lesotho			−1.985			−1.985*
			(1.27)			(0.98)
Liberia			0.183			0.183
			(0.70)			(1.03)
Libya			0.000			0.000
			(.)			(.)
Madagascar			−0.488			−0.488
			(0.75)			(0.63)
Malawi			−0.973			−0.973
			(0.72)			(1.05)
Mali			−0.741			−0.741
			(0.69)			(0.83)
Mauritania			0.775			0.775
			(0.91)			(0.77)
Morocco			−2.534*			−2.534***
			(1.14)			(0.49)
Mozambique			0.964			0.964
			(0.64)			(0.97)
Namibia			0.306			0.306
			(0.66)			(0.73)
Niger			1.740+			1.740+
			(0.90)			(1.01)
Nigeria			0.544			0.544
			(0.56)			(0.49)

	Model 1	Model 2 yFE	Model 3 cyFE	Model 4	Model 5 yFE	Model 6 cyFE
Rwanda			−0.230			−0.230
			(1.17)			(0.81)
Senegal			0.778			0.778
			(0.73)			(0.77)
Sierra Leone			−0.009			−0.009
			(0.74)			(0.98)
Somalia			0.000			0.000
			(.)			(.)
South Africa			0.658			0.658
			(0.62)			(0.65)
Sudan			0.000			0.000
			(.)			(.)
Swaziland			0.000			0.000
			(.)			(.)
Tanzania			−1.168*			−1.168*
			(0.53)			(0.49)
Togo			−0.264			−0.264
			(1.27)			(0.41)
Uganda			−0.629			−0.629
			(0.79)			(0.54)
Zambia			0.065			0.065
			(0.57)			(0.70)
Zimbabwe			0.000			0.000
			(.)			(.)
Constant	−0.219	−0.000	1.636	−0.219	−0.000	1.636
	(0.83)	(0.93)	(1.23)	(1.60)	(1.66)	(2.35)
Pseudo R Sq	.22	.24	.27	.22	.24	.27
Chi-Sq Test	617	674	750	.	.	.
Log-Likelihood	−1109.7	−1080.9	−1026.1	−1109.7	−1080.9	−1026.1
Observations	2402.0	2402.0	2356.0	2402.0	2402.0	2356.0
vce	oim	oim	oim	cluster	cluster	cluster

$+ p < 0.10$, $* p < 0.05$, $** p < 0.01$, $*** p < 0.001$

Probability of Protest within 20 km – Cropland Perc. Placebo

	Model 7	Model 82 yFE	Model 9 cyFE	Model 10	Model 11 yFE	Model 12 cyFE
SCAD within 20 km						
Soil Productivity	−0.202**	−0.262**	−0.214*	−0.202*	−0.262**	−0.214*
	(0.08)	(0.08)	(0.09)	(0.09)	(0.08)	(0.10)
Log of Random Cropland	0.117	0.179	0.261	0.117	0.179	0.261
	(0.28)	(0.29)	(0.30)	(0.25)	(0.24)	(0.25)
Soil Productivity × Log of Random Cropland	−0.020	−0.036	−0.055	−0.020	−0.036	−0.055
	(0.07)	(0.07)	(0.07)	(0.06)	(0.06)	(0.06)
Population Density (l)	0.694***	0.747***	0.727***	0.694***	0.747***	0.727***
	(0.04)	(0.05)	(0.05)	(0.11)	(0.15)	(0.14)
Infant Mortality Rate	0.002	0.003	−0.002	0.002	0.003	−0.002
	(0.00)	(0.00)	(0.01)	(0.00)	(0.00)	(0.01)
Distance to Capital (l)	−0.349***	−0.390***	−0.392***	−0.349**	−0.390***	−0.392**
	(0.07)	(0.07)	(0.09)	(0.13)	(0.11)	(0.15)
Road Density	−0.006+	−0.008*	−0.007+	−0.006	−0.008	−0.007
	(0.00)	(0.00)	(0.00)	(0.01)	(0.01)	(0.01)
Country Area	0.000**	0.000***	−0.000	0.000	0.000*	−0.000
	(0.00)	(0.00)	(0.00)	(0.00)	(0.00)	(0.00)
South Africa	0.471+	0.619*		0.471	0.619+	
	(0.24)	(0.28)		(0.39)	(0.34)	
Polity IV	0.121***	0.126**	0.138+	0.121*	0.126*	0.138
	(0.03)	(0.04)	(0.08)	(0.06)	(0.05)	(0.10)
Foreign Owned	−0.010	−0.005	0.140	−0.010	−0.005	0.140
	(0.15)	(0.16)	(0.16)	(0.14)	(0.14)	(0.17)

	Model 7	Model 82 yFE	Model 9 cyFE	Model 10	Model 11 yFE	Model 12 cyFE
Coal	0.000	0.000	0.000	0.000	0.000	0.000
	(.)	(.)	(.)	(.)	(.)	(.)
Copper	0.270	0.026	−0.040	0.270	0.026	−0.040
	(0.26)	(0.28)	(0.32)	(0.26)	(0.24)	(0.29)
Gold	−0.489*	−0.431*	−0.209	−0.489*	−0.431	−0.209
	(0.20)	(0.21)	(0.23)	(0.24)	(0.27)	(0.24)
Iron	−0.077	−0.254	−0.497	−0.077	−0.254	−0.497
	(0.29)	(0.31)	(0.34)	(0.31)	(0.34)	(0.33)
Lead	1.010	0.698	0.054	1.010	0.698	0.054
	(1.16)	(1.08)	(1.02)	(0.63)	(0.77)	(0.89)
MetMin	−0.385+	−0.521*	−0.585*	−0.385*	−0.521**	−0.585***
	(0.20)	(0.21)	(0.24)	(0.17)	(0.19)	(0.17)
Nickel	−2.552**	−2.744**	−3.439***	−2.552***	−2.744***	−3.439***
	(0.85)	(0.89)	(1.04)	(0.56)	(0.62)	(0.45)
Phosphate	−1.842*	−2.318**	−2.436**	−1.842**	−2.318*	−2.436+
	(0.79)	(0.84)	(0.94)	(0.70)	(1.05)	(1.26)
Platinum	−0.627+	−0.750*	−0.675+	−0.627***	−0.750**	−0.675**
	(0.34)	(0.36)	(0.37)	(0.16)	(0.28)	(0.25)
Potash	0.000	0.000	0.000	0.000	0.000	0.000
	(.)	(.)	(.)	(.)	(.)	(.)
Silver	−1.239	−1.035	−0.891	−1.239	−1.035	−0.891
	(1.14)	(1.15)	(1.17)	(0.97)	(1.08)	(1.17)
Tin	−0.209	−0.361	−0.393	−0.209	−0.361	−0.393
	(1.02)	(1.17)	(1.26)	(0.41)	(0.57)	(0.35)
Zinc	−1.051	−1.011	−0.800	−1.051	−1.011	−0.800
	(0.80)	(0.79)	(0.94)	(0.64)	(0.62)	(0.71)
styr = 1990		0.000	0.000		0.000	0.000
		(.)	(.)		(.)	(.)
styr = 1991		−0.669+	−0.293		−0.669**	−0.293
		(0.37)	(0.39)		(0.23)	(0.19)
styr = 1992		0.249	0.213		0.249	0.213
		(0.37)	(0.39)		(0.45)	(0.58)
styr = 1993		0.087	−0.095		0.087	−0.095
		(0.56)	(0.58)		(0.32)	(0.37)
styr = 1994		0.227	0.262		0.227	0.262
		(0.39)	(0.43)		(0.27)	(0.36)

(continued)

Appendix B

(continued)

	Model 7	Model 82 yFE	Model 9 cyFE	Model 10	Model 11 yFE	Model 12 cyFE
styr = 1995		−0.489	−0.519		−0.489	−0.519
		(0.47)	(0.50)		(0.52)	(0.51)
styr = 1996		1.502*	1.304*		1.502***	1.304***
		(0.59)	(0.61)		(0.15)	(0.18)
styr = 1997		0.564	0.268		0.564	0.268
		(0.50)	(0.53)		(0.48)	(0.48)
styr = 1998		−0.074	−0.118		−0.074	−0.118
		(0.40)	(0.43)		(0.24)	(0.28)
styr = 1999		0.712	0.354		0.712+	0.354
		(0.51)	(0.55)		(0.42)	(0.48)
styr = 2000		0.286	0.291		0.286	0.291
		(0.45)	(0.52)		(0.46)	(0.55)
styr = 2001		0.176	0.112		0.176	0.112
		(0.37)	(0.41)		(0.28)	(0.32)
styr = 2002		0.491	0.207		0.491	0.207
		(0.54)	(0.59)		(0.47)	(0.56)
styr = 2003		0.517	0.330		0.517	0.330
		(0.53)	(0.60)		(0.57)	(0.72)
styr = 2004		0.084	0.359		0.084	0.359
		(0.47)	(0.55)		(0.54)	(0.73)
styr = 2005		0.994*	0.490		0.994*	0.490
		(0.41)	(0.45)		(0.45)	(0.34)
styr = 2006		0.462	0.114		0.462	0.114
		(0.44)	(0.49)		(0.54)	(0.65)
styr = 2007		0.100	0.103		0.100	0.103
		(0.44)	(0.54)		(0.47)	(0.54)
styr = 2008		−0.285	−0.669		−0.285	−0.669
		(0.44)	(0.48)		(0.51)	(0.47)

	Model 7	Model 82 yFE	Model 9 cyFE	Model 10	Model 11 yFE	Model 12 cyFE
styr = 2009		−0.568	−0.558		−0.568	−0.558
		(0.45)	(0.53)		(0.63)	(0.74)
styr = 2010		0.082	−0.174		0.082	−0.174
		(0.55)	(0.64)		(0.43)	(0.69)
styr = 2011		−0.714+	−0.508		−0.714	−0.508
		(0.37)	(0.43)		(0.46)	(0.47)
styr = 2012		−0.389	−0.334		−0.389	−0.334
		(0.33)	(0.38)		(0.36)	(0.31)
styr = 2013		−0.580	−0.721		−0.580	−0.721
		(0.40)	(0.47)		(0.36)	(0.47)
Algeria			0.000			0.000
			(.)			(.)
Angola			−0.034			−0.034
			(1.17)			(0.99)
Botswana			−1.998*			−1.998**
			(0.89)			(0.69)
Burkina Faso			−1.314*			−1.314*
			(0.53)			(0.51)
Burundi			1.705			1.705+
			(1.13)			(0.88)
Cameroon			0.000			0.000
			(.)			(.)
Central African Republic			2.243+			2.243***
			(1.29)			(0.57)
Democratic Republic of Congo			1.397			1.397
			(1.07)			(0.92)
Egypt			0.000			0.000
			(.)			(.)
Eritrea			−0.606			−0.606
			(1.12)			(0.69)
Ethiopia			0.030			0.030
			(0.92)			(0.79)
Gabon			1.413+			1.413***
			(0.77)			(0.34)
Ghana			−0.772			−0.772*
			(0.56)			(0.39)
Guinea			0.100			0.100
			(0.60)			(0.46)

(continued)

Appendix B

(continued)

	Model 7	Model 82 yFE	Model 9 cyFE	Model 10	Model 11 yFE	Model 12 cyFE
Guinea-Bissau		0.000				0.000
		(.)				(.)
Kenya		0.381				0.381
		(0.82)				(0.42)
Lesotho		−1.713				−1.713+
		(1.33)				(0.96)
Liberia		0.094				0.094
		(0.79)				(0.95)
Libya		0.000				0.000
		(.)				(.)
Madagascar		−0.351				−0.351
		(0.81)				(0.60)
Malawi		−0.447				−0.447
		(0.85)				(1.01)
Mali		−1.224				−1.224
		(0.77)				(0.81)
Mauritania		0.513				0.513
		(0.98)				(0.83)
Morocco		−1.586				−1.586**
		(1.19)				(0.53)
Mozambique		0.248				0.248
		(0.71)				(0.94)
Namibia		0.082				0.082
		(0.73)				(0.72)
Niger		1.206				1.206
		(0.98)				(1.09)
Nigeria		0.399				0.399
		(0.63)				(0.46)
Rwanda		0.086				0.086
		(1.26)				(0.77)
Senegal		0.332				0.332
		(0.86)				(0.74)
Sierra Leone		−0.030				−0.030
		(0.84)				(0.95)
Somalia		0.000				0.000
		(.)				(.)
South Africa		0.330				0.330
		(0.66)				(0.63)
Sudan		0.000				0.000
		(.)				(.)

	Model 7	Model 82 yFE	Model 9 cyFE	Model 10	Model 11 yFE	Model 12 cyFE
Swaziland			0.000			0.000
			(.)			(.)
Tanzania			−0.986+			−0.986*
			(0.57)			(0.48)
Togo			0.000			0.000
			(.)			(.)
Uganda			−1.035			−1.035*
			(0.96)			(0.50)
Zambia			−0.281			−0.281
			(0.63)			(0.63)
Zimbabwe			0.000			0.000
			(.)			(.)
Constant	0.901	1.380	2.329	0.901	1.380	2.329
	(0.99)	(1.10)	(1.47)	(1.81)	(1.54)	(2.20)
Pseudo R Sq	.23	.26	.28	.23	.26	.28
Chi-Sq Test	508	569	623	.	.	.
Log-Likelihood	−914.5	−884.0	−840.9	−914.5	−884.0	−840.9
Observations	1996.0	1996.0	1953.0	1996.0	1996.0	1953.0

+ $p < 0.10$, * $p < 0.05$, ** $p < 0.01$, *** $p < 0.001$

Probability of Protest within 20 km – Avg. Tax Rate Placebo

	Model 13 b/se	Model 14 yFE b/se	Model 15 cyFE b/se	Model 16 b/se	Model 17 yFE b/se	Model 18 cyFE b/se
SCAD within 20 km						
Random Log Avg Taxrate	−0.048	−0.033	−0.054	−0.048	−0.033	−0.054
	(0.07)	(0.07)	(0.07)	(0.09)	(0.08)	(0.09)
Population Density (l)	0.669***	0.696***	0.673***	0.669***	0.696***	0.673***
	(0.05)	(0.06)	(0.07)	(0.09)	(0.11)	(0.11)
Infant Mortality Rate	0.003	0.003	−0.004	0.003	0.003	−0.004
	(0.00)	(0.00)	(0.01)	(0.00)	(0.00)	(0.01)

(continued)

(continued)

	Model 13 b/se	Model 14 yFE b/se	Model 15 cyFE b/se	Model 16 b/se	Model 17 yFE b/se	Model 18 cyFE b/se
Distance to Capital (l)	−0.402***	−0.445***	−0.500***	−0.402**	−0.445**	−0.500*
	(0.09)	(0.10)	(0.12)	(0.13)	(0.14)	(0.21)
Road Density	−0.001	−0.002	−0.001	−0.001	−0.002	−0.001
	(0.00)	(0.00)	(0.01)	(0.01)	(0.01)	(0.01)
Country Area	0.000*	0.000*	−0.000	0.000	0.000+	−0.000
	(0.00)	(0.00)	(0.00)	(0.00)	(0.00)	(0.00)
South Africa	0.780*	0.764*		0.780*	0.764*	
	(0.31)	(0.35)		(0.33)	(0.35)	
Polity IV	0.098*	0.121*	0.085	0.098*	0.121*	0.085
	(0.04)	(0.05)	(0.11)	(0.05)	(0.06)	(0.12)
Foreign Owned	−0.062	−0.067	0.102	−0.062	−0.067	0.102
	(0.19)	(0.20)	(0.21)	(0.16)	(0.15)	(0.16)
Coal	0.000	0.000	0.000	0.000	0.000	0.000
	(.)	(.)	(.)	(.)	(.)	(.)
Copper	0.726*	0.508	0.419	0.726**	0.508*	0.419
	(0.34)	(0.36)	(0.40)	(0.24)	(0.23)	(0.33)
Gold	−0.205	−0.190	0.123	−0.205	−0.190	0.123
	(0.25)	(0.27)	(0.30)	(0.19)	(0.21)	(0.20)
Iron	0.626+	0.535	0.331	0.626+	0.535	0.331
	(0.37)	(0.39)	(0.43)	(0.33)	(0.37)	(0.42)
Lead	1.608	1.418	0.953	1.608*	1.418	0.953
	(1.38)	(1.26)	(1.31)	(0.81)	(0.87)	(0.91)
MetMin	0.143	−0.014	−0.153	0.143	−0.014	−0.153
	(0.26)	(0.28)	(0.31)	(0.27)	(0.21)	(0.28)
Nickel	−1.671+	−1.837+	−2.651*	−1.671*	−1.837*	−2.651***
	(0.93)	(0.97)	(1.16)	(0.70)	(0.71)	(0.52)
Phosphate	−0.327	−0.495	−1.242	−0.327	−0.495	−1.242
	(0.75)	(0.79)	(1.03)	(0.68)	(0.63)	(1.27)
Platinum	−0.709+	−0.774+	−0.704	−0.709***	−0.774*	−0.704**
	(0.41)	(0.44)	(0.46)	(0.20)	(0.32)	(0.25)
Potash	0.000	0.000	0.000	0.000	0.000	0.000
	(.)	(.)	(.)	(.)	(.)	(.)
Silver	−0.511	−0.430	−0.456	−0.511	−0.430	−0.456
	(1.25)	(1.32)	(1.40)	(0.79)	(0.86)	(0.93)

	Model 13 b/se	Model 14 yFE b/se	Model 15 cyFE b/se	Model 16 b/se	Model 17 yFE b/se	Model 18 cyFE b/se
Tin	0.000	0.000	0.000	0.000	0.000	0.000
	(.)	(.)	(.)	(.)	(.)	(.)
Zinc	−0.734	−1.036	−0.532	−0.734	−1.036	−0.532
	(1.16)	(1.20)	(1.26)	(1.18)	(1.10)	(1.17)
styr = 1990		0.000	0.000		0.000	0.000
		(.)	(.)		(.)	(.)
styr = 1991		−0.430	−0.099		−0.430+	−0.099
		(0.45)	(0.48)		(0.24)	(0.16)
styr = 1992		0.146	0.277		0.146	0.277
		(0.47)	(0.50)		(0.42)	(0.55)
styr = 1993		0.098	−0.288		0.098	−0.288
		(0.70)	(0.74)		(0.33)	(0.47)
styr = 1994		0.362	0.488		0.362	0.488
		(0.48)	(0.53)		(0.35)	(0.46)
styr = 1995		−0.384	−0.182		−0.384	−0.182
		(0.67)	(0.72)		(0.82)	(0.78)
styr = 1996		1.449+	1.385		1.449**	1.385*
		(0.88)	(0.88)		(0.46)	(0.55)
styr = 1997		0.809	0.495		0.809	0.495
		(0.61)	(0.65)		(0.51)	(0.51)
styr = 1998		−0.485	−0.611		−0.485	−0.611+
		(0.49)	(0.55)		(0.31)	(0.32)
styr = 1999		0.347	0.097		0.347	0.097
		(0.64)	(0.71)		(0.54)	(0.58)
styr = 2000		0.539	0.452		0.539	0.452
		(0.58)	(0.68)		(0.46)	(0.73)
styr = 2001		−0.150	−0.027		−0.150	−0.027
		(0.49)	(0.55)		(0.29)	(0.38)
styr = 2002		−0.060	−0.336		−0.060	−0.336
		(0.75)	(0.85)		(0.57)	(0.72)
styr = 2003		0.919	0.675		0.919	0.675
		(0.64)	(0.73)		(0.62)	(0.82)
styr = 2004		−0.162	−0.446		−0.162	−0.446
		(0.58)	(0.68)		(0.57)	(0.84)
styr = 2005		0.420	0.139		0.420	0.139
		(0.55)	(0.60)		(0.36)	(0.49)
styr = 2006		0.178	−0.120		0.178	−0.120
		(0.57)	(0.66)		(0.48)	(0.56)
styr = 2007		0.249	0.131		0.249	0.131
		(0.54)	(0.69)		(0.60)	(0.82)

(continued)

Appendix B

(continued)

	Model 13 b/se	Model 14 yFE b/se	Model 15 cyFE b/se	Model 16 b/se	Model 17 yFE b/se	Model 18 cyFE b/se
styr = 2008		0.065	−0.428		0.065	−0.428
		(0.54)	(0.60)		(0.63)	(0.33)
styr = 2009		−0.693	−0.706		−0.693	−0.706
		(0.58)	(0.68)		(0.56)	(0.57)
styr = 2010		−0.262	−0.088		−0.262	−0.088
		(0.74)	(0.89)		(0.62)	(1.20)
styr = 2011		−0.602	−0.392		−0.602+	−0.392
		(0.48)	(0.56)		(0.34)	(0.49)
styr = 2012		−0.271	−0.173		−0.271	−0.173
		(0.42)	(0.49)		(0.35)	(0.39)
styr = 2013		−0.601	−0.783		−0.601+	−0.783
		(0.53)	(0.63)		(0.33)	(0.53)
Algeria			0.000			0.000
			(.)			(.)
Angola			1.413			1.413
			(1.40)			(1.32)
Botswana			0.175			0.175
			(0.98)			(0.91)
Burkina Faso			−1.430+			−1.430+
			(0.80)			(0.79)
Burundi			1.793			1.793
			(1.46)			(1.41)
Cameroon			0.000			0.000
			(.)			(.)
Central African Republic			2.927+			2.927***
			(1.52)			(0.87)
Democratic Republic of Congo			2.170			2.170+
			(1.54)			(1.26)
Egypt			0.000			0.000
			(.)			(.)
Eritrea			−0.112			−0.112
			(1.26)			(0.86)
Ethiopia			0.412			0.412
			(1.32)			(0.86)
Gabon			0.357			0.357
			(1.36)			(0.58)

	Model 13 b/se	Model 14 yFE b/se	Model 15 cyFE b/se	Model 16 b/se	Model 17 yFE b/se	Model 18 cyFE b/se
Ghana			−0.758			−0.758
			(0.79)			(0.58)
Guinea			0.643			0.643
			(0.86)			(0.73)
Kenya			−0.092			−0.092
			(1.07)			(0.97)
Lesotho			1.091			1.091
			(1.65)			(0.98)
Liberia			0.532			0.532
			(1.19)			(1.33)
Libya			0.000			0.000
			(.)			(.)
Madagascar			0.272			0.272
			(1.05)			(0.86)
Malawi			−0.125			−0.125
			(1.13)			(1.32)
Mali			−1.071			−1.071
			(1.12)			(1.21)
Mauritania			1.459			1.459
			(1.41)			(1.23)
Morocco			−1.334			−1.334*
			(1.25)			(0.53)
Mozambique			0.948			0.948
			(1.03)			(1.00)
Namibia			0.494			0.494
			(0.96)			(0.90)
Niger			1.360			1.360
			(1.58)			(1.46)
Nigeria			0.680			0.680
			(0.89)			(0.68)
Rwanda			0.000			0.000
			(.)			(.)
Senegal			1.321			1.321
			(1.16)			(1.17)
Sierra Leone			0.370			0.370
			(1.21)			(1.50)
Somalia			0.000			0.000
			(.)			(.)

(continued)

(continued)

	Model 13 b/se	Model 14 yFE b/se	Model 15 cyFE b/se	Model 16 b/se	Model 17 yFE b/se	Model 18 cyFE b/se
South Africa			0.991			0.991
			(0.92)			(0.83)
Sudan			0.000			0.000
			(.)			(.)
Swaziland			0.000			0.000
			(.)			(.)
Tanzania			−0.244			−0.244
			(0.81)			(0.68)
Togo			0.000			0.000
			(.)			(.)
Uganda			0.254			0.254
			(1.17)			(0.59)
Zambia			−0.003			−0.003
			(0.91)			(0.84)
Zimbabwe			0.000			0.000
			(.)			(.)
Constant	0.386	0.734	2.575	0.386	0.734	2.575
	(1.22)	(1.37)	(1.85)	(1.77)	(1.89)	(2.97)
Pseudo R Sq	.24	.27	.3	.24	.27	.3
Chi−Sq Test	329	358	390	.	.	.
Log−Likelihood	−557.3	−542.8	−517.2	−557.3	−542.8	−517.2
Observations	1238.0	1238.0	1214.0	1238.0	1238.0	1214.0

$+ p < 0.10$, $* p < 0.05$, $** p < 0.01$, $*** p < 0.001$

Varying Distance Threshold between Mine and SCAD Event

Decreased Distance of 15 km.

Probability of Protest within 15 km

	Model 19 b/se	Model 20 yFE b/se	Model 21 cyFE b/se	Model 21 b/se	Model 22 yFE b/se	Model 23 cyFE b/se
scad under 15 km						
Railroad within 20 km	1.152***	1.121***	1.156***	1.152***	1.121***	1.156***
	(0.14)	(0.15)	(0.17)	(0.25)	(0.25)	(0.28)

	Model 19 b/se	Model 20 yFE b/se	Model 21 cyFE b/se	Model 21 b/se	Model 22 yFE b/se	Model 23 cyFE b/se
Population Density (l)	0.722***	0.774***	0.814***	0.722***	0.774***	0.814***
	(0.04)	(0.05)	(0.06)	(0.07)	(0.10)	(0.12)
Infant Mortality Rate	0.006*	0.007**	−0.003	0.006+	0.007+	−0.003
	(0.00)	(0.00)	(0.01)	(0.00)	(0.00)	(0.01)
Distance to Capital (l)	−0.287***	−0.294***	−0.211*	−0.287*	−0.294*	−0.211
	(0.06)	(0.07)	(0.09)	(0.12)	(0.11)	(0.15)
Road Density	−0.003	−0.004	−0.002	−0.003	−0.004	−0.002
	(0.00)	(0.00)	(0.00)	(0.01)	(0.01)	(0.01)
Country Area	0.000*	0.000*	−0.000	0.000	0.000+	−0.000**
	(0.00)	(0.00)	(0.00)	(0.00)	(0.00)	(0.00)
Polity IV	0.143***	0.175***	0.128+	0.143*	0.175**	0.128
	(0.04)	(0.04)	(0.08)	(0.06)	(0.07)	(0.12)
South Africa	−0.017	−0.027		−0.017	−0.027	
	(0.24)	(0.28)		(0.31)	(0.35)	
Foreign Owned	0.036	0.058	0.217	0.036	0.058	0.217
	(0.15)	(0.15)	(0.16)	(0.17)	(0.17)	(0.20)
Coal	0.000	0.000	0.000	0.000	0.000	0.000
	(.)	(.)	(.)	(.)	(.)	(.)
Copper	0.602*	0.474+	0.308	0.602*	0.474+	0.308
	(0.26)	(0.28)	(0.32)	(0.28)	(0.27)	(0.29)
Gold	0.012	0.054	0.195	0.012	0.054	0.195
	(0.19)	(0.20)	(0.23)	(0.21)	(0.26)	(0.22)
Iron	0.375	0.318	0.205	0.375	0.318	0.205
	(0.29)	(0.30)	(0.34)	(0.25)	(0.30)	(0.31)
Lead	1.663	1.363	1.149	1.663*	1.363+	1.149
	(1.34)	(1.23)	(1.19)	(0.68)	(0.74)	(0.71)
MetMin	0.128	0.052	−0.057	0.128	0.052	−0.057
	(0.19)	(0.21)	(0.23)	(0.17)	(0.18)	(0.17)
Nickel	−0.883	−0.882	−1.761*	−0.883	−0.882	−1.761**
	(0.64)	(0.65)	(0.81)	(0.72)	(0.66)	(0.65)
Phosphate	−1.128	−1.355+	−2.545*	−1.128+	−1.355+	−2.545
	(0.69)	(0.75)	(1.07)	(0.63)	(0.72)	(2.18)

(continued)

(continued)

	Model 19 b/se	Model 20 yFE b/se	Model 21 cyFE b/se	Model 21 b/se	Model 22 yFE b/se	Model 23 cyFE b/se
Platinum	−0.295	−0.279	−0.304	−0.295	−0.279	−0.304
	(0.34)	(0.36)	(0.37)	(0.20)	(0.31)	(0.30)
Potash	0.000	0.000	0.000	0.000	0.000	0.000
	(.)	(.)	(.)	(.)	(.)	(.)
Silver	−1.051	−0.852	−0.377	−1.051	−0.852	−0.377
	(1.22)	(1.24)	(1.25)	(1.02)	(1.04)	(0.90)
Tin	0.968	0.810	1.095	0.968+	0.810	1.095+
	(0.79)	(0.84)	(0.95)	(0.56)	(0.65)	(0.65)
Zinc	−0.508	−0.562	0.287	−0.508	−0.562	0.287
	(0.75)	(0.76)	(0.88)	(0.59)	(0.68)	(0.80)
styr = 1990		0.000	0.000		0.000	0.000
		(.)	(.)		(.)	(.)
styr = 1991		−0.499	−0.233		−0.499**	−0.233
		(0.35)	(0.37)		(0.17)	(0.20)
styr = 1992		−0.058	0.224		−0.058	0.224
		(0.35)	(0.38)		(0.59)	(0.60)
styr = 1993		−0.244	−0.342		−0.244	−0.342
		(0.52)	(0.54)		(0.29)	(0.40)
styr = 1994		0.107	0.164		0.107	0.164
		(0.37)	(0.41)		(0.33)	(0.40)
styr = 1995		−0.428	−0.383		−0.428	−0.383
		(0.44)	(0.47)		(0.32)	(0.35)
styr = 1996		1.056+	1.169+		1.056**	1.169***
		(0.57)	(0.60)		(0.33)	(0.23)
styr = 1997		−0.294	−0.327		−0.294	−0.327
		(0.47)	(0.51)		(0.44)	(0.55)
styr = 1998		−0.665+	−0.509		−0.665	−0.509
		(0.39)	(0.43)		(0.43)	(0.48)
styr = 1999		0.244	0.195		0.244	0.195
		(0.51)	(0.56)		(0.49)	(0.69)
styr = 2000		−0.206	−0.334		−0.206	−0.334
		(0.47)	(0.57)		(0.46)	(0.66)
styr = 2001		−0.273	−0.073		−0.273	−0.073
		(0.37)	(0.41)		(0.43)	(0.48)
styr = 2002		−0.097	0.012		−0.097	0.012
		(0.54)	(0.59)		(0.56)	(0.73)
styr = 2003		0.495	0.537		0.495	0.537
		(0.51)	(0.60)		(0.68)	(0.88)
styr = 2004		−0.383	0.228		−0.383	0.228
		(0.45)	(0.55)		(0.76)	(1.09)

	Model 19 b/se	Model 20 yFE b/se	Model 21 cyFE b/se	Model 21 b/se	Model 22 yFE b/se	Model 23 cyFE b/se
styr = 2005		0.394 (0.40)	0.338 (0.45)		0.394 (0.31)	0.338 (0.34)
styr = 2006		−0.300 (0.45)	−0.163 (0.51)		−0.300 (0.71)	−0.163 (0.78)
styr = 2007		−0.106 (0.43)	0.155 (0.54)		−0.106 (0.51)	0.155 (0.72)
styr = 2008		−0.654 (0.42)	−1.119* (0.47)		−0.654 (0.84)	−1.119* (0.55)
styr = 2009		−0.626 (0.44)	−0.453 (0.52)		−0.626 (0.52)	−0.453 (0.60)
styr = 2010		−0.244 (0.56)	−0.311 (0.63)		−0.244 (0.43)	−0.311 (0.66)
styr = 2011		−0.989** (0.37)	−0.746+ (0.43)		−0.989* (0.45)	−0.746 (0.54)
styr = 2012		−0.419 (0.32)	−0.208 (0.38)		−0.419 (0.37)	−0.208 (0.39)
styr = 2013		−1.182** (0.40)	−1.028* (0.47)		−1.182* (0.53)	−1.028+ (0.55)
Algeria			0.000 (.)			0.000 (.)
Angola			1.808 (1.15)			1.808 (1.12)
Botswana			−0.901 (0.78)			−0.901 (0.99)
Burkina Faso			−0.750 (0.54)			−0.750 (0.59)
Burundi			2.356* (1.04)			2.356* (1.13)
Cameroon			0.000 (.)			0.000 (.)
Central African Republic			3.773** (1.30)			3.773*** (0.61)
Democratic Republic of Congo			2.509+ (1.28)			2.509* (1.09)

(continued)

(continued)

	Model 19 b/se	Model 20 yFE b/se	Model 21 cyFE b/se	Model 21 b/se	Model 22 yFE b/se	Model 23 cyFE b/se
Egypt			0.000			0.000
			(.)			(.)
Eritrea			0.039			0.039
			(1.05)			(0.84)
Ethiopia			0.529			0.529
			(1.05)			(0.76)
Gabon			0.364			0.364
			(1.17)			(0.49)
Ghana			−1.010+			−1.010*
			(0.56)			(0.46)
Guinea			0.213			0.213
			(0.62)			(0.59)
Guinea−Bissau			0.000			0.000
			(.)			(.)
Kenya			−0.162			−0.162
			(0.76)			(0.70)
Lesotho			−1.138			−1.138
			(1.40)			(1.26)
Liberia			−0.232			−0.232
			(0.81)			(1.10)
Libya			0.000			0.000
			(.)			(.)
Madagascar			−0.765			−0.765
			(0.90)			(0.76)
Malawi			−0.618			−0.618
			(0.79)			(1.08)
Mali			0.319			0.319
			(0.82)			(0.94)
Mauritania			2.262*			2.262**
			(0.98)			(0.81)
Morocco			−2.477+			−2.477***
			(1.31)			(0.73)
Mozambique			0.469			0.469
			(0.73)			(1.00)
Namibia			0.830			0.830
			(0.74)			(0.91)
Niger			3.178**			3.178**
			(1.01)			(1.17)
Nigeria			0.912			0.912
			(0.64)			(0.62)

	Model 19 b/se	Model 20 yFE b/se	Model 21 cyFE b/se	Model 21 b/se	Model 22 yFE b/se	Model 23 cyFE b/se
Rwanda			−1.067			−1.067
			(1.40)			(0.89)
Senegal			2.144**			2.144+
			(0.81)			(1.18)
Sierra Leone			0.596			0.596
			(0.82)			(1.02)
Somalia			0.000			0.000
			(.)			(.)
South Africa			0.523			0.523
			(0.73)			(0.80)
Sudan			0.000			0.000
			(.)			(.)
Swaziland			0.000			0.000
			(.)			(.)
Tanzania			−0.456			−0.456
			(0.60)			(0.54)
Togo			−0.322			−0.322
			(1.33)			(0.48)
Uganda			−2.197+			−2.197**
			(1.25)			(0.67)
Zambia			0.388			0.388
			(0.64)			(0.80)
Zimbabwe			0.000			0.000
			(.)			(.)
Constant	−2.708**	−2.710**	−2.559+	−2.708	−2.710	−2.559
	(0.90)	(1.00)	(1.37)	(1.87)	(1.80)	(2.40)
Pseudo R Sq	.27	.29	.32	.27	.29	.32
Chi-Sq Test	694	740	806	.	.	.
Log-Likelihood	−944.1	−921.0	−873.5	−944.1	−921.0	−87 3.5
Observations	2402.0	2402.0	2356.0	2402.0	2402.0	2356.0
vce	oim	oim	oim	cluster	cluster	cluster

+ p < 0.10, * p < 0.05, ** p < 0.01, * * * p < 0.001

Probability of Protest within 15 km

	Model 24 b/se	Model 25 yFE b/se	Model 26 cyFE b/se	Model 27 b/se	Model 28 yFE b/se	Model 29 cy FE b/se
scad under 15 km						
Soil Productivity	−0.352***	−0.410***	−0.323**	−0.352**	−0.410***	−0.323*
	(0.09)	(0.10)	(0.11)	(0.12)	(0.12)	(0.14)
Percent Cropland (l)	−5.283*	−5.583*	−4.348	−5.283+	−5.583*	−4.348
	(2.27)	(2.38)	(2.77)	(2.81)	(2.54)	(2.92)
Soil Productivity × Percent Cropland (l)	1.137*	1.176*	0.867	1.137+	1.176*	0.867
	(0.53)	(0.56)	(0.64)	(0.59)	(0.58)	(0.67)
Population Density (l)	0.817***	0.888***	0.905***	0.817***	0.888***	0.905***
	(0.05)	(0.05)	(0.06)	(0.09)	(0.14)	(0.15)
Infant Mortality Rate	0.002	0.002	−0.003	0.002	0.002	−0.003
	(0.00)	(0.00)	(0.01)	(0.00)	(0.00)	(0.01)
Distance to Capital (l)	−0.366***	−0.382***	−0.367***	−0.366***	−0.382***	−0.367*
	(0.06)	(0.07)	(0.09)	(0.11)	(0.10)	(0.15)
Road Density	−0.004	−0.005	−0.003	−0.004	−0.005	−0.003
	(0.00)	(0.00)	(0.00)	(0.01)	(0.01)	(0.01)
Country Area	0.000**	0.000***	−0.000	0.000+	0.000**	−0.000*
	(0.00)	(0.00)	(0.00)	(0.00)	(0.00)	(0.00)
South Africa	0.261	0.307		0.261	0.307	
	(0.24)	(0.28)		(0.32)	(0.34)	
Polity IV	0.139***	0.160***	0.109	0.139*	0.160*	0.109
	(0.04)	(0.04)	(0.08)	(0.06)	(0.06)	(0.12)
Foreign Owned	−0.010	0.026	0.174	−0.010	0.026	0.174
	(0.15)	(0.15)	(0.16)	(0.20)	(0.20)	(0.23)
Coal	0.000	0.000	0.000	0.000	0.000	0.000
	(.)	(.)	(.)	(.)	(.)	(.)
Copper	0.697**	0.475+	0.393	0.697*	0.475	0.393
	(0.26)	(0.28)	(0.32)	(0.28)	(0.30)	(0.27)
Gold	−0.277	−0.250	−0.006	−0.277	−0.250	−0.006
	(0.20)	(0.21)	(0.23)	(0.27)	(0.33)	(0.27)

	Model 24 b/se	Model 25 yFE b/se	Model 26 cyFE b/se	Model 27 b/se	Model 28 yFE b/se	Model 29 cy FE b/se
Iron	0.254	0.112	0.044	0.254	0.112	0.044
	(0.29)	(0.31)	(0.34)	(0.27)	(0.33)	(0.34)
Lead	1.746	1.460	1.236	1.746**	1.460*	1.236+
	(1.27)	(1.15)	(1.18)	(0.62)	(0.69)	(0.69)
MetMin	−0.086	−0.209	−0.248	−0.086	−0.209	−0.248
	(0.21)	(0.22)	(0.24)	(0.18)	(0.20)	(0.17)
Nickel	−1.175+	−1.248+	−1.889*	−1.175+	−1.248+	−1.889**
	(0.64)	(0.65)	(0.82)	(0.64)	(0.67)	(0.67)
Phosphate	−1.102	−1.406+	−2.250*	−1.102+	−1.406*	−2.250
	(0.68)	(0.73)	(0.97)	(0.62)	(0.70)	(1.61)
Platinum	−0.602+	−0.653+	−0.584	−0.602**	−0.653+	−0.584+
	(0.34)	(0.36)	(0.37)	(0.21)	(0.37)	(0.33)
Potash	0.000	0.000	0.000	0.000	0.000	0.000
	(.)	(.)	(.)	(.)	(.)	(.)
Silver	−1.252	−1.120	−0.595	−1.252	−1.120	−0.595
	(1.17)	(1.21)	(1.25)	(1.04)	(1.03)	(0.91)
Tin	−0.147	−0.431	0.166	−0.147	−0.431	0.166
	(0.94)	(1.02)	(1.08)	(0.64)	(0.86)	(0.89)
Zinc	−0.741	−0.727	−0.175	−0.741	−0.727	−0.175
	(0.82)	(0.82)	(0.93)	(0.63)	(0.68)	(0.73)
styr = 1990		0.000	0.000		0.000	0.000
		(.)	(.)		(.)	(.)
styr = 1991		−0.544	−0.186		−0.544**	−0.186
		(0.36)	(0.38)		(0.20)	(0.18)
styr = 1992		0.223	0.356		0.223	0.356
		(0.36)	(0.39)		(0.56)	(0.64)
styr = 1993		−0.202	−0.272		−0.202	−0.272
		(0.54)	(0.56)		(0.37)	(0.49)
styr = 1994		0.044	0.142		0.044	0.142
		(0.38)	(0.42)		(0.31)	(0.38)
styr = 1995		−0.340	−0.353		−0.340	−0.353
		(0.45)	(0.47)		(0.36)	(0.36)
styr = 1996		1.414*	1.438*		1.414***	1.438***
		(0.59)	(0.61)		(0.27)	(0.31)
styr = 1997		−0.060	−0.183		−0.060	−0.183
		(0.48)	(0.51)		(0.37)	(0.46)
styr = 1998		−0.575	−0.506		−0.575	−0.506
		(0.39)	(0.44)		(0.45)	(0.47)
styr = 1999		0.238	−0.021		0.238	−0.021
		(0.52)	(0.56)		(0.53)	(0.67)

(continued)

(continued)

	Model 24 b/se	Model 25 yFE b/se	Model 26 cyFE b/se	Model 27 b/se	Model 28 yFE b/se	Model 29 cy FE b/se
styr = 2000		−0.091 (0.47)	−0.297 (0.56)		−0.091 (0.45)	−0.297 (0.61)
styr = 2001		−0.139 (0.37)	0.003 (0.41)		−0.139 (0.36)	0.003 (0.47)
styr = 2002		0.047 (0.56)	0.011 (0.60)		0.047 (0.54)	0.011 (0.73)
styr = 2003		0.490 (0.51)	0.471 (0.59)		0.490 (0.64)	0.471 (0.85)
styr = 2004		0.044 (0.46)	0.459 (0.55)		0.044 (0.64)	0.459 (0.98)
styr = 2005		0.689+ (0.40)	0.427 (0.45)		0.689* (0.32)	0.427 (0.34)
styr = 2006		−0.189 (0.45)	−0.186 (0.50)		−0.189 (0.74)	−0.186 (0.82)
styr = 2007		0.177 (0.43)	0.431 (0.53)		0.177 (0.54)	0.431 (0.71)
styr = 2008		−0.459 (0.42)	−0.921+ (0.47)		−0.459 (0.77)	−0.921+ (0.54)
styr = 2009		−0.710 (0.43)	−0.613 (0.51)		−0.710 (0.57)	−0.613 (0.63)
styr = 2010		−0.051 (0.54)	−0.107 (0.63)		−0.051 (0.47)	−0.107 (0.73)
styr = 2011		−1.100** (0.38)	−0.820+ (0.44)		−1.100* (0.53)	−0.820 (0.64)
styr = 2012		−0.409 (0.33)	−0.221 (0.38)		−0.409 (0.36)	−0.221 (0.39)
styr = 2013		−0.995* (0.40)	−0.947* (0.47)		−0.995* (0.48)	−0.947+ (0.57)
Algeria			0.000 (.)			0.000 (.)
Angola			1.219 (1.13)			1.219 (1.06)
Botswana			−1.149 (0.77)			−1.149 (0.92)
Burkina Faso			−1.505** (0.53)			−1.505** (0.51)
Burundi			1.305 (1.04)			1.305 (1.06)
Cameroon			0.000 (.)			0.000 (.)

	Model 24 b/se	Model 25 yFE b/se	Model 26 cyFE b/se	Model 27 b/se	Model 28 yFE b/se	Model 29 cy FE b/se
Central African Republic			2.950*			2.950***
			(1.30)			(0.55)
Democratic Republic of Congo			2.192+			2.192*
			(1.27)			(0.98)
Egypt			0.000			0.000
			(.)			(.)
Eritrea			−0.966			−0.966
			(1.05)			(0.73)
Ethiopia			−0.467			−0.467
			(0.99)			(0.80)
Gabon			−0.187			−0.187
			(1.18)			(0.41)
Ghana			−1.252*			−1.252**
			(0.57)			(0.48)
Guinea			−0.585			−0.585
			(0.61)			(0.50)
Guinea−Bissau			0.000			0.000
			(.)			(.)
Kenya			−1.030			−1.030
			(0.81)			(0.71)
Lesotho			−1.702			−1.702
			(1.36)			(1.32)
Liberia			−0.660			−0.660
			(0.80)			(1.01)
Libya			0.000			0.000
			(.)			(.)
Madagascar			−1.542+			−1.542*
			(0.91)			(0.65)
Malawi			−1.283			−1.283
			(0.82)			(1.13)
Mali			−0.589			−0.589
			(0.82)			(0.79)
Mauritania			1.152			1.152
			(1.03)			(0.89)
Morocco			−2.402+			−2.402***
			(1.25)			(0.65)

(continued)

(continued)

	Model 24 b/se	Model 25 yFE b/se	Model 26 cyFE b/se	Model 27 b/se	Model 28 yFE b/se	Model 29 cy FE b/se
Mozambique			0.425			0.425
			(0.72)			(0.98)
Namibia			0.743			0.743
			(0.75)			(0.92)
Niger			1.797+			1.797+
			(1.02)			(1.06)
Nigeria			0.382			0.382
			(0.65)			(0.52)
Rwanda			−1.926			−1.926*
			(1.40)			(0.78)
Senegal			1.259			1.259
			(0.81)			(1.13)
Sierra Leone			−0.287			−0.287
			(0.81)			(0.92)
Somalia			0.000			0.000
			(.)			(.)
South Africa			0.592			0.592
			(0.72)			(0.78)
Sudan			0.000			0.000
			(.)			(.)
Swaziland			0.000			0.000
			(.)			(.)
Tanzania			−0.793			−0.793
			(0.60)			(0.53)
Togo			−0.460			−0.460
			(1.33)			(0.49)
Uganda			0.000			0.000
			(.)			(.)
Zambia			0.011			0.011
			(0.63)			(0.77)
Zimbabwe			0.000			0.000
			(.)			(.)
Constant	0.496	0.738	1.570	0.496	0.738	1.570
	(0.98)	(1.10)	(1.49)	(1.64)	(1.52)	(2.20)
Pseudo R Sq	.24	.27	.30	.24	.27	.30
Chi-Sq Test	615	674	734	.	.	.
Log-Likelihood	−950.8	−921.3	−874.5	−950.8	−921.3	−874.5
Observations	2356.0	2356.0	2300.0	2356.0	2356.0	2300.0

+ p < 0.10, * p < 0.05, ** p < 0.01, *** p < 0.001

Probability of Protest within 15 km

	Model 30 b/se	Model 31 yFE b/se	Model 32 cyFE b/se	Model 33 b/se	Model 34 yFE b/se	Model 35 cyFE b/se
scad under 15 km						
Avg Effective Tax Rate (l)	0.459**	0.548***	−0.146	0.459+	0.548*	−0.146
	(0.15)	(0.16)	(0.63)	(0.26)	(0.24)	(0.79)
Population Density (l)	0.769***	0.818***	0.881***	0.769***	0.818***	0.881***
	(0.04)	(0.05)	(0.06)	(0.08)	(0.12)	(0.14)
Infant Mortality Rate	−0.001	−0.001	−0.005	−0.001	−0.001	−0.005
	(0.00)	(0.00)	(0.01)	(0.00)	(0.00)	(0.01)
Distance to Capital (l)	−0.378***	−0.373***	−0.317***	−0.378**	−0.373***	−0.317*
	(0.06)	(0.07)	(0.09)	(0.13)	(0.11)	(0.16)
Road Density	−0.006*	−0.009**	−0.003	−0.006	−0.009	−0.003
	(0.00)	(0.00)	(0.00)	(0.01)	(0.01)	(0.01)
Country Area	0.000	0.000	−0.000	0.000	0.000	−0.000*
	(0.00)	(0.00)	(0.00)	(0.00)	(0.00)	(0.00)
South Africa	0.251	0.134		0.251	0.134	
	(0.24)	(0.27)		(0.30)	(0.33)	
Polity IV	0.174***	0.226***	0.117	0.174*	0.226**	0.117
	(0.04)	(0.04)	(0.07)	(0.07)	(0.08)	(0.12)
Foreign Owned	0.088	0.136	0.233	0.088	0.136	0.233
	(0.15)	(0.15)	(0.16)	(0.20)	(0.18)	(0.21)
Coal	0.000	0.000	0.000	0.000	0.000	0.000
	(.)	(.)	(.)	(.)	(.)	(.)
Copper	0.673**	0.520+	0.385	0.673+	0.520	0.385
	(0.26)	(0.27)	(0.31)	(0.37)	(0.34)	(0.29)
Gold	−0.213	−0.158	0.034	−0.213	−0.158	0.034
	(0.19)	(0.20)	(0.23)	(0.28)	(0.32)	(0.27)
Iron	0.259	0.166	0.070	0.259	0.166	0.070
	(0.29)	(0.30)	(0.34)	(0.31)	(0.34)	(0.36)
Lead	1.611	1.297	1.187	1.611*	1.297+	1.187+
	(1.18)	(1.09)	(1.18)	(0.65)	(0.72)	(0.70)
MetMin	−0.073	−0.159	−0.177	−0.073	−0.159	−0.177
	(0.20)	(0.21)	(0.23)	(0.18)	(0.22)	(0.17)

(continued)

(continued)

	Model 30 b/se	Model 31 yFE b/se	Model 32 cyFE b/se	Model 33 b/se	Model 34 yFE b/se	Model 35 cyFE b/se
Nickel	−1.386*	−1.446*	−1.875*	−1.386**	−1.446**	−1.875**
	(0.65)	(0.66)	(0.80)	(0.53)	(0.52)	(0.64)
Phosphate	−1.312+	−1.607*	−2.387*	−1.312*	−1.607*	−2.387
	(0.68)	(0.73)	(0.97)	(0.60)	(0.73)	(1.64)
Platinum	−0.615+	−0.566	−0.511	−0.615**	−0.566+	−0.511
	(0.33)	(0.35)	(0.37)	(0.21)	(0.34)	(0.32)
Potash	0.000	0.000	0.000	0.000	0.000	0.000
	(.)	(.)	(.)	(.)	(.)	(.)
Silver	−1.272	−1.179	−0.567	−1.272	−1.179	−0.567
	(1.17)	(1.22)	(1.24)	(0.98)	(0.98)	(0.89)
Tin	0.368	0.159	0.634	0.368	0.159	0.634
	(0.74)	(0.79)	(0.91)	(0.48)	(0.56)	(0.59)
Zinc	−0.595	−0.609	0.230	−0.595	−0.609	0.230
	(0.73)	(0.75)	(0.82)	(0.57)	(0.68)	(0.72)
styr = 1990		0.000	0.000		0.000	0.000
		(.)	(.)		(.)	(.)
styr = 1991		−0.558	−0.235		−0.558**	−0.235
		(0.35)	(0.37)		(0.17)	(0.21)
styr = 1992		−0.154	0.169		−0.154	0.169
		(0.35)	(0.38)		(0.62)	(0.64)
styr = 1993		−0.329	−0.352		−0.329	−0.352
		(0.51)	(0.54)		(0.31)	(0.41)
styr = 1994		−0.073	0.233		−0.073	0.233
		(0.38)	(0.41)		(0.29)	(0.40)
styr = 1995		−0.554	−0.374		−0.554	−0.374
		(0.43)	(0.46)		(0.40)	(0.38)
styr = 1996		1.215*	1.276*		1.215***	1.276***
		(0.58)	(0.60)		(0.26)	(0.25)
styr = 1997		−0.310	−0.207		−0.310	−0.207
		(0.48)	(0.51)		(0.47)	(0.47)
styr = 1998		−0.884*	−0.590		−0.884*	−0.590
		(0.39)	(0.43)		(0.45)	(0.47)
styr = 1999		−0.143	−0.092		−0.143	−0.092
		(0.50)	(0.54)		(0.45)	(0.61)
styr = 2000		−0.297	−0.410		−0.297	−0.410
		(0.46)	(0.55)		(0.44)	(0.59)
styr = 2001		−0.517	−0.134		−0.517	−0.134
		(0.37)	(0.41)		(0.40)	(0.45)
styr = 2002		−0.411	−0.243		−0.411	−0.243
		(0.55)	(0.58)		(0.59)	(0.70)

	Model 30 b/se	Model 31 yFE b/se	Model 32 cyFE b/se	Model 33 b/se	Model 34 yFE b/se	Model 35 cyFE b/se
styr = 2003		0.246	0.272		0.246	0.272
		(0.51)	(0.58)		(0.66)	(0.83)
styr = 2004		−0.239	0.357		−0.239	0.357
		(0.45)	(0.54)		(0.60)	(0.92)
styr = 2005		0.260	0.223		0.260	0.223
		(0.40)	(0.45)		(0.36)	(0.34)
styr = 2006		−0.504	−0.335		−0.504	−0.335
		(0.44)	(0.49)		(0.79)	(0.82)
styr = 2007		−0.449	0.284		−0.449	0.284
		(0.44)	(0.52)		(0.56)	(0.69)
styr = 2008		−0.820+	−1.066*		−0.820	−1.066+
		(0.42)	(0.47)		(0.74)	(0.56)
styr = 2009		−0.952*	−0.720		−0.952	−0.720
		(0.43)	(0.50)		(0.64)	(0.65)
styr = 2010		−0.396	−0.166		−0.396	−0.166
		(0.55)	(0.64)		(0.39)	(0.67)
styr = 2011		−1.366***	−0.894*		−1.366**	−0.894
		(0.38)	(0.43)		(0.53)	(0.58)
styr = 2012		−0.681*	−0.319		−0.681+	−0.319
		(0.32)	(0.37)		(0.37)	(0.37)
styr = 2013		−1.256**	−1.083*		−1.256**	−1.083+
		(0.40)	(0.47)		(0.45)	(0.56)
Algeria			0.000			0.000
			(.)			(.)
Angola			1.701			1.701+
			(1.11)			(1.02)
Botswana			−1.311*			−1.311+
			(0.63)			(0.72)
Burkina Faso			−1.428*			−1.428*
			(0.57)			(0.63)
Burundi			1.548			1.548
			(1.66)			(2.22)
Cameroon			0.000			0.000
			(.)			(.)
Central African Republic			3.353*			3.353*
			(1.64)			(1.42)

(continued)

Appendix B

(continued)

	Model 30 b/se	Model 31 yFE b/se	Model 32 cyFE b/se	Model 33 b/se	Model 34 yFE b/se	Model 35 cyFE b/se
Democratic Republic of Congo			2.909			2.909
			(1.79)			(1.80)
Egypt			0.000			0.000
			(.)			(.)
Eritrea			−0.518			−0.518
			(1.20)			(1.05)
Ethiopia			−0.227			−0.227
			(0.97)			(0.57)
Gabon			−0.134			−0.134
			(1.19)			(0.48)
Ghana			−1.367**			−1.367**
			(0.53)			(0.43)
Guinea			−0.161			−0.161
			(0.91)			(1.03)
Guinea−Bissau			0.000			0.000
			(.)			(.)
Kenya			−0.546			−0.546
			(0.78)			(0.77)
Lesotho			−2.077			−2.077*
			(1.30)			(0.93)
Liberia			−0.406			−0.406
			(0.81)			(1.14)
Libya			0.000			0.000
			(.)			(.)
Madagascar			−1.180			−1.180
			(0.90)			(0.73)
Malawi			−1.279+			−1.279
			(0.75)			(1.05)
Mali			−0.095			−0.095
			(0.81)			(0.83)
Mauritania			1.925+			1.925+
			(1.15)			(1.09)
Morocco			−2.896*			−2.896***
			(1.24)			(0.60)
Mozambique			0.694			0.694
			(0.66)			(0.87)
Namibia			0.916			0.916
			(0.56)			(0.58)

	Model 30 b/se	Model 31 yFE b/se	Model 32 cyFE b/se	Model 33 b/se	Model 34 yFE b/se	Model 35 cyFE b/se
Niger			2.372**			2.372***
			(0.87)			(0.58)
Nigeria			0.226			0.226
			(0.53)			(0.36)
Rwanda			−2.220			−2.220**
			(1.37)			(0.81)
Senegal			1.491+			1.491
			(0.88)			(1.28)
Sierra Leone			0.363			0.363
			(1.44)			(1.96)
South Africa			0.543			0.543
			(0.57)			(0.57)
Sudan			0.000			0.000
			(.)			(.)
Swaziland			0.000			0.000
			(.)			(.)
Tanzania			−0.753			−0.753
			(0.59)			(0.51)
Togo			−0.498			−0.498
			(1.36)			(0.66)
Uganda			−2.827*			−2.827***
			(1.22)			(0.63)
Zambia			0.000			0.000
			(.)			(.)
Zimbabwe			0.000			0.000
			(.)			(.)
Constant	−1.994*	−2.228*	0.420	−1.994	−2.228	0.420
	(0.91)	(1.02)	(2.48)	(1.66)	(1.68)	(3.33)
Pseudo R Sq	.25	.27	.30	.25	.27	.30
Chi-Sq Test	635	693	758	.	.	.
Log-Likelihood	−972.4	−943.7	−897.9	−972.4	−943.7	−897.9
Observations	2398.0	2398.0	2356.0	2398.0	2398.0	2356.0

+ p < 0.10, * p < 0.05, ** p < 0.01, * * * p < 0.001

Increased Distance of 25 km.

Probability of Protest within 25 km — Rail

	Model 37 b/se	Model 38 yFE b/se	Model 39 cyFE b/se	Model 40 b/se	Model 41 yFE b/se	Model 42 cyFE b/se
Railroad within 20 km	1.325***	1.291***	1.351***	1.325***	1.291***	1.351***
	(0.13)	(0.13)	(0.15)	(0.20)	(0.21)	(0.22)
Population Density (l)	0.619***	0.675***	0.646***	0.619***	0.675***	0.646***
	(0.04)	(0.04)	(0.05)	(0.09)	(0.11)	(0.11)
Infant Mortality Rate	0.010***	0.011***	0.003	0.010***	0.011***	0.003
	(0.00)	(0.00)	(0.01)	(0.00)	(0.00)	(0.01)
Distance to Capital (l)	−0.382***	−0.400***	−0.423***	−0.382***	−0.400***	−0.423**
	(0.06)	(0.07)	(0.08)	(0.11)	(0.11)	(0.14)
Road Density	−0.007**	−0.009**	−0.011**	−0.007	−0.009	−0.011
	(0.00)	(0.00)	(0.00)	(0.01)	(0.01)	(0.01)
Country Area	0.000	0.000	−0.000	0.000	0.000	−0.000
	(0.00)	(0.00)	(0.00)	(0.00)	(0.00)	(0.00)
Polity IV	0.112***	0.128***	0.132+	0.112+	0.128*	0.132
	(0.03)	(0.04)	(0.07)	(0.06)	(0.06)	(0.11)
South Africa	0.665**	0.732**		0.665+	0.732*	
	(0.22)	(0.25)		(0.35)	(0.33)	
Foreign Owned	−0.013	−0.009	0.178	−0.013	−0.009	0.178+
	(0.14)	(0.14)	(0.15)	(0.12)	(0.14)	(0.10)
Coal	0.000	0.000	0.000	0.000	0.000	0.000
	(.)	(.)	(.)	(.)	(.)	(.)
Copper	0.403+	0.192	0.142	0.403	0.192	0.142
	(0.24)	(0.26)	(0.30)	(0.29)	(0.25)	(0.31)
Gold	−0.010	0.017	0.198	−0.010	0.017	0.198
	(0.18)	(0.19)	(0.22)	(0.22)	(0.24)	(0.23)
Iron	0.513*	0.423	0.209	0.513*	0.423	0.209
	(0.26)	(0.27)	(0.30)	(0.26)	(0.27)	(0.27)
Lead	0.840	0.491	0.202	0.840	0.491	0.202
	(1.29)	(1.22)	(1.11)	(0.63)	(0.65)	(0.65)

	Model 37 b/se	Model 38 yFE b/se	Model 39 cyFE b/se	Model 40 b/se	Model 41 yFE b/se	Model 42 cyFE b/se
MetMin	0.012	−0.112	−0.118	0.012	−0.112	−0.118
	(0.18)	(0.19)	(0.21)	(0.17)	(0.16)	(0.14)
Nickel	−0.214	−0.277	−0.815	−0.214	−0.277	−0.815
	(0.47)	(0.48)	(0.62)	(0.62)	(0.61)	(0.65)
Phosphate	−0.773	−0.898	−1.354+	−0.773	−0.898+	−1.354*
	(0.54)	(0.57)	(0.70)	(0.61)	(0.51)	(0.62)
Platinum	−0.220	−0.264	−0.237	−0.220	−0.264	−0.237
	(0.33)	(0.35)	(0.36)	(0.14)	(0.20)	(0.17)
Potash	0.000	0.000	0.000	0.000	0.000	0.000
	(.)	(.)	(.)	(.)	(.)	(.)
Silver	−0.548	−0.511	−0.167	−0.548	−0.511	−0.167
	(0.93)	(0.94)	(0.93)	(0.69)	(0.79)	(0.82)
Tin	0.409	0.157	−0.187	0.409	0.157	−0.187
	(0.79)	(0.85)	(0.98)	(0.60)	(0.68)	(0.68)
Zinc	−1.013	−1.096	−0.671	−1.013+	−1.096+	−0.671
	(0.75)	(0.74)	(0.86)	(0.59)	(0.58)	(0.58)
styr = 1990		0.000	0.000		0.000	0.000
		(.)	(.)		(.)	(.)
styr = 1991		−0.775*	−0.536		−0.775***	−0.536**
		(0.32)	(0.34)		(0.14)	(0.18)
styr = 1992		−0.090	−0.195		−0.090	−0.195
		(0.33)	(0.35)		(0.36)	(0.44)
styr = 1993		0.176	−0.183		0.176	−0.183
		(0.50)	(0.52)		(0.28)	(0.25)
styr = 1994		−0.009	−0.022		−0.009	−0.022
		(0.34)	(0.37)		(0.32)	(0.37)
styr = 1995		−0.511	−0.702		−0.511+	−0.702**
		(0.40)	(0.44)		(0.29)	(0.27)
styr = 1996		0.366	0.281		0.366+	0.281
		(0.54)	(0.55)		(0.20)	(0.21)
styr = 1997		0.226	−0.043		0.226	−0.043
		(0.45)	(0.48)		(0.61)	(0.68)
styr = 1998		−0.467	−0.542		−0.467+	−0.542+
		(0.35)	(0.38)		(0.24)	(0.29)
styr = 1999		0.626	0.684		0.626+	0.684
		(0.44)	(0.50)		(0.34)	(0.44)
styr = 2000		0.327	0.448		0.327	0.448
		(0.40)	(0.47)		(0.52)	(0.64)
styr = 2001		−0.245	−0.181		−0.245	−0.181
		(0.34)	(0.38)		(0.29)	(0.35)
styr = 2002		−0.165	−0.254		−0.165	−0.254
		(0.50)	(0.55)		(0.53)	(0.67)

(continued)

(continued)

	Model 37 b/se	Model 38 yFE b/se	Model 39 cyFE b/se	Model 40 b/se	Model 41 yFE b/se	Model 42 cyFE b/se
styr = 2003		0.452 (0.46)	0.660 (0.52)		0.452 (0.49)	0.660 (0.72)
styr = 2004		−0.303 (0.41)	0.117 (0.50)		−0.303 (0.56)	0.117 (0.64)
styr = 2005		0.407 (0.38)	0.138 (0.43)		0.407 (0.40)	0.138 (0.40)
styr = 2006		−0.004 (0.41)	−0.163 (0.47)		−0.004 (0.56)	−0.163 (0.64)
styr = 2007		−0.059 (0.39)	−0.068 (0.49)		−0.059 (0.52)	−0.068 (0.66)
styr = 2008		−0.338 (0.39)	−0.884* (0.43)		−0.338 (0.65)	−0.884+ (0.49)
styr = 2009		−0.646+ (0.39)	−0.604 (0.46)		−0.646 (0.57)	−0.604 (0.68)
styr = 2010		−0.973+ (0.54)	−0.965 (0.60)		−0.973* (0.42)	−0.965 (0.62)
styr = 2011		−1.023** (0.34)	−0.840* (0.39)		−1.023** (0.33)	−0.840* (0.33)
styr = 2012		−0.534+ (0.30)	−0.432 (0.35)		−0.534+ (0.29)	−0.432+ (0.26)
styr = 2013		−1.153** (0.36)	−1.231** (0.42)		−1.153** (0.39)	−1.231* (0.52)
Algeria			0.000 (.)			0.000 (.)
Angola			1.869* (0.87)			1.869* (0.90)
Botswana			−1.340+ (0.71)			−1.340+ (0.72)
Burkina Faso			−0.673 (0.48)			−0.673 (0.50)
Burundi			0.000 (.)			0.000 (.)
Cameroon			0.000 (.)			0.000 (.)
Central African Republic			2.554* (1.28)			2.554** (0.81)

	Model 37 b/se	Model 38 yFE b/se	Model 39 cyFE b/se	Model 40 b/se	Model 41 yFE b/se	Model 42 cyFE b/se
Democratic Republic of Congo			1.572			1.572
			(1.01)			(1.04)
Egypt			0.000			0.000
			(.)			(.)
Eritrea			−0.358			−0.358
			(1.05)			(0.78)
Ethiopia			0.170			0.170
			(0.89)			(0.72)
Gabon			1.203			1.203*
			(0.76)			(0.50)
Ghana			−0.102			−0.102
			(0.50)			(0.40)
Guinea			0.408			0.408
			(0.56)			(0.64)
Guinea−Bissau			0.000			0.000
			(.)			(.)
Kenya			2.301*			2.301***
			(0.98)			(0.59)
Lesotho			−1.532			−1.532+
			(1.38)			(0.90)
Liberia			0.152			0.152
			(0.72)			(1.05)
Libya			0.000			0.000
			(.)			(.)
Madagascar			−0.395			−0.395
			(0.77)			(0.70)
Malawi			−0.571			−0.571
			(0.73)			(0.95)
Mali			−0.586			−0.586
			(0.70)			(0.88)
Mauritania			1.642*			1.642+
			(0.78)			(0.88)
Morocco			−1.670			−1.670**
			(1.18)			(0.59)
Mozambique			0.584			0.584
			(0.65)			(1.00)
Namibia			−0.536			−0.536
			(0.67)			(0.76)
Niger			1.797*			1.797+
			(0.90)			(1.07)

(continued)

(continued)

	Model 37 b/se	Model 38 yFE b/se	Model 39 cyFE b/se	Model 40 b/se	Model 41 yFE b/se	Model 42 cyFE b/se
Nigeria			1.520**			1.520**
			(0.59)			(0.57)
Rwanda			1.937			1.937*
			(1.42)			(0.95)
Senegal			1.460*			1.460+
			(0.74)			(0.83)
Sierra Leone			0.411			0.411
			(0.75)			(1.13)
Somalia			0.000			0.000
			(.)			(.)
South Africa			0.818			0.818
			(0.62)			(0.70)
Sudan			0.000			0.000
			(.)			(.)
Swaziland			0.000			0.000
			(.)			(.)
Tanzania			−0.789			−0.789
			(0.52)			(0.53)
Togo			−0.301			−0.301
			(1.29)			(0.42)
Uganda			−0.122			−0.122
			(0.82)			(0.58)
Zambia			0.068			0.068
			(0.59)			(0.74)
Zimbabwe			0.000			0.000
			(.)			(.)
Constant	−0.296	−0.075	1.236	−0.296	−0.075	1.236
	(0.86)	(0.97)	(1.31)	(1.55)	(1.57)	(2.44)
Pseudo R Sq	.27	.29	.32	.27	.29	.32
Chi-Sq Test	811	877	944	.	.	.
Log-Likelihood	−1122.0	−1089.0	−1021.4	−1122.0	−1089.0	−1021.4
Observations	2402.0	2402.0	2343.0	2402.0	2402.0	2343.0
vce	oim	oim	oim	cluster	cluster	cluster

$+ p < 0.10, * < 0.05, ** p < 0.01, *** p < 0.001$

Probability of Protest within 25 km − Soil and Cropland

	Model 43 b/se	Model 44 yFE b/se	Model 45 cyFE b/se	Model 46 b/se	Model 47 yFE b/se	Model 48 cyFE b/se
	Model 42 b/se	Model 43 b/se	Model 44 b/se	Model 45 b/se	Model 46 b/se	Model 47 b/se
Soil Productivity	−0.289***	−0.351***	−0.325***	−0.289*	−0.351**	−0.325*
	(0.08)	(0.08)	(0.10)	(0.12)	(0.12)	(0.14)
Percent Cropland (l)	−5.398**	−6.450**	−9.027***	−5.398+	−6.450*	−9.027**
	(2.03)	(2.16)	(2.62)	(2.91)	(2.68)	(2.93)
Soil Productivity × Percent Cropland (l)	1.432**	1.666**	2.097***	1.432*	1.666*	2.097**
	(0.48)	(0.51)	(0.60)	(0.67)	(0.68)	(0.74)
Population Density (l)	0.702***	0.770***	0.738***	0.702***	0.770***	0.738***
	(0.04)	(0.04)	(0.05)	(0.11)	(0.14)	(0.14)
Infant Mortality Rate	0.005**	0.006**	−0.001	0.005	0.006*	−0.001
	(0.00)	(0.00)	(0.01)	(0.00)	(0.00)	(0.01)
Distance to Capital (l)	−0.442***	−0.461***	−0.571***	−0.442***	−0.461***	−0.571***
	(0.06)	(0.07)	(0.09)	(0.12)	(0.12)	(0.16)
Road Density	−0.008**	−0.010***	−0.013**	−0.008	−0.010+	−0.013+
	(0.00)	(0.00)	(0.00)	(0.01)	(0.01)	(0.01)
Country Area	0.000*	0.000**	−0.000	0.000	0.000+	−0.000*
	(0.00)	(0.00)	(0.00)	(0.00)	(0.00)	(0.00)
South Africa	0.895***	0.985***		0.895*	0.985**	
	(0.22)	(0.25)		(0.35)	(0.35)	
Polity IV	0.109***	0.119***	0.119+	0.109+	0.119*	0.119
	(0.03)	(0.04)	(0.07)	(0.06)	(0.06)	(0.11)
Foreign Owned	−0.086	−0.066	0.098	−0.086	−0.066	0.098
	(0.14)	(0.14)	(0.15)	(0.11)	(0.11)	(0.11)
Coal	0.000	0.000	0.000	0.000	0.000	0.000
	(.)	(.)	(.)	(.)	(.)	(.)
Copper	0.566*	0.285	0.279	0.566*	0.285	0.279
	(0.24)	(0.26)	(0.29)	(0.29)	(0.29)	(0.25)

(continued)

Appendix B

(continued)

	Model 43 b/se	Model 44 yFE b/se	Model 45 cyFE b/se	Model 46 b/se	Model 47 yFE b/se	Model 48 cyFE b/se
Gold	−0.239	−0.222	0.032	−0.239	−0.222	0.032
	(0.18)	(0.19)	(0.22)	(0.32)	(0.39)	(0.36)
Iron	0.452+	0.257	0.144	0.452	0.257	0.144
	(0.26)	(0.27)	(0.30)	(0.35)	(0.40)	(0.37)
Lead	1.037	0.684	0.229	1.037	0.684	0.229
	(1.20)	(1.13)	(1.10)	(0.64)	(0.73)	(0.77)
MetMin	−0.082	−0.249	−0.242	−0.082	−0.249	−0.242
	(0.19)	(0.20)	(0.22)	(0.20)	(0.26)	(0.17)
Nickel	−0.471	−0.606	−1.016	−0.471	−0.606	−1.016
	(0.47)	(0.49)	(0.62)	(0.60)	(0.65)	(0.69)
Phosphate	−1.109*	−1.277*	−1.394+	−1.109*	−1.277*	−1.394*
	(0.56)	(0.60)	(0.74)	(0.57)	(0.56)	(0.59)
Platinum	−0.473	−0.563	−0.483	−0.473*	−0.563+	−0.483
	(0.33)	(0.35)	(0.36)	(0.19)	(0.33)	(0.31)
Potash	0.000	0.000	0.000	0.000	0.000	0.000
	(.)	(.)	(.)	(.)	(.)	(.)
Silver	−0.768	−0.739	−0.316	−0.768	−0.739	−0.316
	(0.88)	(0.95)	(0.96)	(0.68)	(0.83)	(0.86)
Tin	−1.140	−1.616	−1.964	−1.140+	−1.616+	−1.964+
	(0.95)	(1.05)	(1.32)	(0.68)	(0.91)	(1.03)
Zinc	−1.215	−1.286	−0.753	−1.215+	−1.286*	−0.753
	(0.80)	(0.79)	(0.91)	(0.64)	(0.62)	(0.62)
styr = 1990		0.000	0.000		0.000	0.000
		(.)	(.)		(.)	(.)
styr = 1991		−0.776*	−0.432		−0.776***	−0.432**
		(0.32)	(0.34)		(0.21)	(0.15)
styr = 1992		0.274	−0.024		0.274	−0.024
		(0.33)	(0.36)		(0.35)	(0.52)
styr = 1993		0.201	−0.030		0.201	−0.030
		(0.50)	(0.53)		(0.32)	(0.30)
styr = 1994		−0.026	0.030		−0.026	0.030
		(0.34)	(0.38)		(0.28)	(0.33)
styr = 1995		−0.420	−0.544		−0.420	−0.544
		(0.40)	(0.43)		(0.40)	(0.36)
styr = 1996		0.660	0.435		0.660**	0.435+
		(0.58)	(0.58)		(0.25)	(0.24)
styr = 1997		0.576	0.203		0.576	0.203
		(0.45)	(0.48)		(0.57)	(0.59)
styr = 1998		−0.451	−0.641+		−0.451	−0.641*
		(0.35)	(0.38)		(0.28)	(0.26)
styr = 1999		0.628	0.369		0.628	0.369
		(0.45)	(0.50)		(0.40)	(0.47)

	Model 43 b/se	Model 44 yFE b/se	Model 45 cyFE b/se	Model 46 b/se	Model 47 yFE b/se	Model 48 cyFE b/se
styr = 2000		0.307	0.280		0.307	0.280
		(0.40)	(0.46)		(0.47)	(0.53)
styr = 2001		−0.150	−0.192		−0.150	−0.192
		(0.34)	(0.38)		(0.28)	(0.33)
styr = 2002		−0.138	−0.417		−0.138	−0.417
		(0.51)	(0.55)		(0.48)	(0.60)
styr = 2003		0.407	0.403		0.407	0.403
		(0.45)	(0.52)		(0.49)	(0.71)
styr = 2004		0.120	0.208		0.120	0.208
		(0.41)	(0.49)		(0.42)	(0.52)
styr = 2005		0.679+	0.155		0.679	0.155
		(0.38)	(0.42)		(0.43)	(0.37)
styr = 2006		0.004	−0.320		0.004	−0.320
		(0.40)	(0.45)		(0.55)	(0.66)
styr = 2007		0.081	0.061		0.081	0.061
		(0.38)	(0.49)		(0.57)	(0.67)
styr = 2008		−0.144	−0.679		−0.144	−0.679
		(0.39)	(0.43)		(0.58)	(0.47)
styr = 2009		−0.734+	−0.888*		−0.734	−0.888
		(0.38)	(0.45)		(0.71)	(0.78)
styr = 2010		−0.819	−0.818		−0.819+	−0.818
		(0.53)	(0.60)		(0.47)	(0.65)
styr = 2011		−1.142***	−0.957*		−1.142**	−0.957*
		(0.34)	(0.39)		(0.36)	(0.41)
styr = 2012		−0.620*	−0.561		−0.620*	−0.561*
		(0.30)	(0.35)		(0.25)	(0.26)
styr = 2013		−0.991**	−1.232**		−0.991*	−1.232*
		(0.36)	(0.42)		(0.39)	(0.57)
Algeria		0.000			0.000	
		(.)			(.)	
Angola		1.563+			1.563+	
		(0.87)			(0.93)	
Botswana		−1.661*			−1.661*	
		(0.69)			(0.72)	
Burkina Faso		−1.440**			−1.440**	
		(0.47)			(0.48)	
Burundi		0.000			0.000	
		(.)			(.)	
Cameroon		0.000			0.000	
		(.)			(.)	

(continued)

(continued)

	Model 43 b/se	Model 44 yFE b/se	Model 45 cyFE b/se	Model 46 b/se	Model 47 yFE b/se	Model 48 cyFE b/se
Central African Republic			1.764			1.764*
			(1.27)			(0.71)
Democratic Republic of Congo			1.984+			1.984+
			(1.03)			(1.03)
Egypt			0.000			0.000
			(.)			(.)
Eritrea			−1.578			−1.578*
			(1.02)			(0.70)
Ethiopia			−0.766			−0.766
			(0.90)			(0.73)
Gabon			0.422			0.422
			(0.73)			(0.37)
Ghana			−0.603			−0.603
			(0.50)			(0.42)
Guinea			−0.307			−0.307
			(0.54)			(0.60)
Guinea−Bissau			0.000			0.000
			(.)			(.)
Kenya			1.555			1.555***
			(0.96)			(0.44)
Lesotho			−2.576+			−2.576**
			(1.33)			(0.85)
Liberia			−0.292			−0.292
			(0.70)			(1.00)
Libya			0.000			0.000
			(.)			(.)
Madagascar			−0.964			−0.964
			(0.76)			(0.68)
Malawi			−1.231			−1.231
			(0.76)			(1.00)
Mali			−1.178+			−1.178
			(0.70)			(0.89)
Mauritania			0.785			0.785
			(0.81)			(0.96)
Morocco			−2.598*			−2.598***
			(1.18)			(0.70)
Mozambique			0.772			0.772
			(0.63)			(1.06)

	Model 43 b/se	Model 44 yFE b/se	Model 45 cyFE b/se	Model 46 b/se	Model 47 yFE b/se	Model 48 cyFE b/se
Namibia			−0.614			−0.614
			(0.68)			(0.78)
Niger			0.554			0.554
			(0.91)			(1.06)
Nigeria			0.911			0.911+
			(0.61)			(0.52)
Rwanda			1.677			1.677*
			(1.69)			(0.72)
Senegal			0.374			0.374
			(0.73)			(0.72)
Sierra Leone			−0.436			−0.436
			(0.74)			(1.10)
Somalia			0.000			0.000
			(.)			(.)
South Africa			0.885			0.885
			(0.62)			(0.66)
Sudan			0.000			0.000
			(.)			(.)
Swaziland			0.000			0.000
			(.)			(.)
Tanzania			−0.989+			−0.989*
			(0.52)			(0.50)
Togo			−0.421			−0.421
			(1.28)			(0.46)
Uganda			−0.875			−0.875+
			(0.84)			(0.51)
Zambia			−0.367			−0.367
			(0.57)			(0.68)
Zimbabwe			0.000			0.000
			(.)			(.)
Constant	2.430**	2.848**	6.057***	2.430	2.848+	6.057**
	(0.92)	(1.04)	(1.41)	(1.59)	(1.52)	(2.28)
Pseudo R Sq	.23	.26	.29	.23	.26	.29
Chi-Sq Test	692	778	847	.	.	.
Log-Likelihood	−1149.8	−1106.7	−1038.0	−1149.8	−1106.7	−1038.0
Observations	2356.0	2356.0	2297.0	2356.0	2356.0	2297.0

+ p < 0.10, * p < 0.05, ** p < 0.01, *** p < 0.001

Probability of Protest within 25 km – Government Take

	Model 49 b/se	Model 50 yFE b/se	Model 51 cyFE b/se	Model 52 b/se	Model 53 yFE b/se	Model 54 cyFE b/se
Avg Effective Tax Rate (l)	0.485***	0.548***	0.325	0.485*	0.553*	0.325
	(0.13)	(0.16)	(0.57)	(0.24)	(0.23)	(0.68)
Population Density (l)	0.666***	0.818***	0.713***	0.666***	0.717***	0.713***
	(0.04)	(0.05)	(0.05)	(0.10)	(0.12)	(0.13)
Infant Mortality Rate	0.002	−0.001	0.001	0.002	0.002	0.001
	(0.00)	(0.00)	(0.01)	(0.00)	(0.00)	(0.01)
Distance to Capital (l)	−0.486***	−0.373***	−0.560***	−0.486***	−0.496***	−0.560***
	(0.06)	(0.07)	(0.08)	(0.10)	(0.11)	(0.14)
Road Density	−0.010***	−0.009**	−0.010**	−0.010	−0.012+	−0.010
	(0.00)	(0.00)	(0.00)	(0.01)	(0.01)	(0.01)
Country Area	0.000	0.000	−0.000	0.000	0.000	−0.000
	(0.00)	(0.00)	(0.00)	(0.00)	(0.00)	(0.00)
South Africa	0.948***	0.134		0.948**	0.924**	
	(0.21)	(0.27)		(0.34)	(0.33)	
Polity IV	0.143***	0.226***	0.125+	0.143*	0.174*	0.125
	(0.03)	(0.04)	(0.07)	(0.07)	(0.07)	(0.11)
Foreign Owned	0.023	0.136	0.170	0.023	0.047	0.170+
	(0.13)	(0.15)	(0.15)	(0.09)	(0.09)	(0.10)
Coal	0.000	0.000	0.000	0.000	0.000	0.000
	(.)	(.)	(.)	(.)	(.)	(.)
Copper	0.436+	0.520+	0.215	0.436	0.225	0.215
	(0.23)	(0.27)	(0.28)	(0.34)	(0.30)	(0.26)
Gold	−0.298+	−0.158	0.029	−0.298	−0.234	0.029
	(0.17)	(0.20)	(0.21)	(0.28)	(0.32)	(0.30)
Iron	0.344	0.166	0.091	0.344	0.228	0.091
	(0.25)	(0.30)	(0.29)	(0.31)	(0.33)	(0.34)
Lead	0.819	1.297	0.156	0.819	0.471	0.156
	(1.12)	(1.09)	(1.09)	(0.64)	(0.73)	(0.74)

	Model 49 b/se	Model 50 yFE b/se	Model 51 cyFE b/se	Model 52 b/se	Model 53 yFE b/se	Model 54 cyFE b/se
MetMin	−0.210	−0.159	−0.262	−0.210	−0.344+	−0.262+
	(0.18)	(0.21)	(0.21)	(0.17)	(0.20)	(0.15)
Nickel	−0.692	−1.446*	−1.025+	−0.692	−0.765	−1.025
	(0.49)	(0.66)	(0.62)	(0.53)	(0.54)	(0.66)
Phosphate	−1.012+	−1.607*	−1.450*	−1.012+	−1.235*	−1.450**
	(0.53)	(0.73)	(0.67)	(0.57)	(0.52)	(0.47)
Platinum	−0.619+	−0.566	−0.518	−0.619***	−0.628*	−0.518*
	(0.32)	(0.35)	(0.35)	(0.18)	(0.25)	(0.24)
Potash	0.000	0.000	0.000	0.000	0.000	0.000
	(.)	(.)	(.)	(.)	(.)	(.)
Silver	−0.940	−1.179	−0.389	−0.940	−0.910	−0.389
	(0.88)	(1.22)	(0.95)	(0.71)	(0.88)	(0.93)
Tin	−0.280	0.159	−0.622	−0.280	−0.554	−0.622
	(0.73)	(0.79)	(0.92)	(0.46)	(0.53)	(0.49)
Zinc	−1.134	−0.609	−0.687	−1.134*	−1.169*	−0.687
	(0.72)	(0.75)	(0.80)	(0.55)	(0.57)	(0.50)
styr = 1990		0.000	0.000		0.000	0.000
		(.)	(.)		(.)	(.)
styr = 1991		−0.558	−0.526		−0.868***	−0.526**
		(0.35)	(0.34)		(0.17)	(0.19)
styr = 1992		−0.154	−0.265		−0.153	−0.265
		(0.35)	(0.34)		(0.39)	(0.51)
styr = 1993		−0.329	−0.222		0.033	−0.222
		(0.51)	(0.52)		(0.31)	(0.29)
styr = 1994		−0.073	0.089		−0.126	0.089
		(0.38)	(0.37)		(0.31)	(0.36)
styr = 1995		−0.554	−0.673		−0.629	−0.673+
		(0.43)	(0.42)		(0.39)	(0.35)
styr = 1996		1.215*	0.439		0.589*	0.439*
		(0.58)	(0.56)		(0.23)	(0.19)
styr = 1997		−0.310	0.183		0.429	0.183
		(0.48)	(0.48)		(0.70)	(0.65)
styr = 1998		−0.884*	−0.631+		−0.644*	−0.631*
		(0.39)	(0.37)		(0.26)	(0.27)
styr = 1999		−0.143	0.207		0.279	0.207
		(0.50)	(0.48)		(0.26)	(0.38)
styr = 2000		−0.297	0.174		0.190	0.174
		(0.46)	(0.46)		(0.52)	(0.54)
styr = 2001		−0.517	−0.252		−0.463	−0.252
		(0.37)	(0.37)		(0.28)	(0.30)

(continued)

(continued)

	Model 49 b/se	Model 50 yFE b/se	Model 51 cyFE b/se	Model 52 b/se	Model 53 yFE b/se	Model 54 cyFE b/se
styr = 2002		−0.411 (0.55)	−0.566 (0.54)		−0.401 (0.51)	−0.566 (0.61)
styr = 2003		0.246 (0.51)	0.292 (0.51)		0.224 (0.50)	0.292 (0.70)
styr = 2004		−0.239 (0.45)	0.249 (0.48)		−0.107 (0.45)	0.249 (0.52)
styr = 2005		0.260 (0.40)	−0.050 (0.41)		0.283 (0.44)	−0.050 (0.37)
styr = 2006		−0.504 (0.44)	−0.393 (0.45)		−0.246 (0.61)	−0.393 (0.67)
styr = 2007		−0.449 (0.44)	0.050 (0.48)		−0.392 (0.56)	0.050 (0.66)
styr = 2008		−0.820+ (0.42)	−0.808+ (0.42)		−0.490 (0.54)	−0.808 (0.49)
styr = 2009		−0.952* (0.43)	−0.926* (0.45)		−0.972 (0.74)	−0.926 (0.78)
styr = 2010		−0.396 (0.55)	−0.802 (0.60)		−1.040** (0.37)	−0.802 (0.63)
styr = 2011		−1.366*** (0.38)	−0.986* (0.39)		−1.378*** (0.39)	−0.986** (0.38)
styr = 2012		−0.681* (0.32)	−0.597+ (0.34)		−0.806** (0.28)	−0.597* (0.25)
styr = 2013		−1.256** (0.40)	−1.309** (0.41)		−1.197*** (0.36)	−1.309* (0.58)
Algeria			0.000 (.)			0.000 (.)
Angola			1.479+ (0.84)			1.479+ (0.79)
Botswana			−1.574** (0.55)			−1.574*** (0.45)
Burkina Faso			−1.644** (0.51)			−1.644** (0.52)
Burundi			0.000 (.)			0.000 (.)
Cameroon			0.000 (.)			0.000 (.)
Central African Republic			1.415 (1.55)			1.415 (1.40)

	Model 49 b/se	Model 50 yFE b/se	Model 51 cyFE b/se	Model 52 b/se	Model 53 yFE b/se	Model 54 cyFE b/se
Democratic Republic of Congo			1.367			1.367
			(1.47)			(1.61)
Egypt			0.000			0.000
			(.)			(.)
Eritrea			−1.398			−1.398+
			(1.16)			(0.79)
Ethiopia			−0.522			−0.522
			(0.84)			(0.46)
Gabon			0.610			0.610
			(0.76)			(0.44)
Ghana			−0.610			−0.610
			(0.46)			(0.39)
Guinea			−0.489			−0.489
			(0.82)			(0.97)
Guinea−Bissau			0.000			0.000
			(.)			(.)
Kenya			1.509			1.509**
			(0.95)			(0.51)
Lesotho			−2.336+			−2.336***
			(1.27)			(0.65)
Liberia			−0.366			−0.366
			(0.72)			(1.00)
Libya			0.000			0.000
			(.)			(.)
Madagascar			−0.911			−0.911
			(0.76)			(0.67)
Malawi			−1.321+			−1.321
			(0.69)			(0.92)
Mali			−1.199+			−1.199
			(0.69)			(0.78)
Mauritania			1.062			1.062
			(0.92)			(1.05)
Morocco			−2.479*			−2.479***
			(1.14)			(0.45)
Mozambique			0.830			0.830
			(0.58)			(0.94)
Namibia			−0.064			−0.064
			(0.52)			(0.59)

(continued)

(continued)

	Model 49 b/se	Model 50 yFE b/se	Model 51 cyFE b/se	Model 52 b/se	Model 53 yFE b/se	Model 54 cyFE b/se
Niger			1.228			1.228*
			(0.78)			(0.52)
Nigeria			0.728			0.728*
			(0.50)			(0.32)
Rwanda			0.497			0.497
			(1.46)			(0.81)
Senegal			0.475			0.475
			(0.80)			(0.89)
Sierra Leone			−0.800			−0.800
			(1.32)			(1.81)
South Africa			0.991*			0.991+
			(0.47)			(0.51)
Sudan			0.000			0.000
			(.)			(.)
Swaziland			0.000			0.000
			(.)			(.)
Tanzania			−1.153*			−1.153**
			(0.50)			(0.45)
Togo			−0.635			−0.635
			(1.31)			(0.56)
Uganda			−0.986			−0.986+
			(0.78)			(0.55)
Zambia			0.000			0.000
			(.)			(.)
Zimbabwe			0.000			0.000
			(.)			(.)
Constant	0.594	−2.228*	3.098	0.594	0.707	3.098
	(0.85)	(1.02)	(2.24)	(1.29)	(1.35)	(3.04)
Pseudo R Sq	.23	.27	.29	.23	.27	.29
Chi-Sq Test	707	693	857	.	.	.
Log-Likelihood	−1172.6	−943.7	−1065.0	−1172.6	−1131.1	−1065.0
Observations	2398.0	2398.0	2343.0	2398.0	2398.0	2343.0

+ p < 0.10, * p < 0.05, ** p < 0.01, *** p < 0.001

Appendix C

ROBUSTNESS TESTS ON REPRESSION LIKELIHOOD (CH. 10)

The following pages provide the following robustness checks: bivariate analysis and placebo tests for key independent variables. Six variations of each of these tests are provided to include clustered errors, year fixed effects, and country fixed effects.

TABLE C.1: *Bivariate regression on repression*

	Model 19 b/se	Model 20 b/se	Model 21 b/se	Model 22 b/se
Repressed Election	−0.465+			
	(0.24)			
Polity IV		−0.173***		
		(0.04)		
Commodity Price (l)			0.180***	
			(0.05)	
Years Current Leader in Office (l)				0.015
				(0.09)
Constant	−0.598***	0.433	−1.798***	−0.815***
	(0.10)	(0.26)	(0.30)	(0.15)
Pseudo R Sq	.006	.03	.01	.00
Chi-Sq Test	4	23	12	0
Log-Likelihood	−337.5	−407.9	−418.0	−424.2
Observations	533.0	673.0	684.0	684.0

+ p < 0.10, * p < 0.05, ** p < 0.01, *** p < 0.001

Appendix C

Placebo Tests

Probability of Repression (of Protest within 20 km) – Election Placebo

	Model 1 b/se	Model 2 cFE b/se	Model 3 cyFE b/se	Model 4 b/se	Model 5 cFE b/se	Model 6 cyFE b/se
Repressed Random election = 0	0.000	0.000	0.000	0.000	0.000	0.000
	(.)	(.)	(.)	(.)	(.)	(.)
Random election = 1	0.428	1.197	1.617	0.428	1.197	1.617
	(0.82)	(1.02)	(1.37)	(0.62)	(0.98)	(1.31)
Polity IV	0.106	0.045	0.020	0.106	0.045	0.020
	(0.06)	(0.12)	(0.20)	(0.08)	(0.20)	(0.29)
Random election = 0 × Polity IV	0.000	0.000	0.000	0.000	0.000	0.000
	(.)	(.)	(.)	(.)	(.)	(.)
Random election = 1 × Polity IV	−0.057	−0.186	−0.233	−0.057	−0.186	−0.233
	(0.11)	(0.14)	(0.19)	(0.08)	(0.12)	(0.17)
Commodity Price (l)	0.592+	1.089*	0.885	0.592+	1.089*	0.885
	(0.32)	(0.46)	(1.07)	(0.34)	(0.48)	(0.89)
Road Density	0.022***	0.031**	0.021+	0.022*	0.031	0.021
	(0.01)	(0.01)	(0.01)	(0.01)	(0.02)	(0.02)
Distance to Capital (l)	−0.055	0.060	0.206	−0.055	0.060	0.206
	(0.09)	(0.13)	(0.18)	(0.18)	(0.26)	(0.20)
Population Density (l)	−0.060	0.043	0.128	−0.060	0.043	0.128
	(0.07)	(0.08)	(0.11)	(0.09)	(0.08)	(0.09)
etype = 1	0.000	0.000	0.000	0.000	0.000	0.000
	(.)	(.)	(.)	(.)	(.)	(.)
etype = 2	−0.338	−0.922*	−2.026**	−0.338	−0.922	−2.026*
	(0.37)	(0.45)	(0.74)	(0.50)	(0.66)	(0.81)
etype = 3	−0.948+	−1.773**	−1.366	−0.948+	−1.773*	−1.366*
	(0.49)	(0.67)	(0.98)	(0.52)	(0.71)	(0.68)
etype = 4	0.412	0.427	−0.224	0.412	0.427	−0.224
	(0.32)	(0.38)	(0.62)	(0.49)	(0.80)	(0.90)

	Model 1 b/se	Model 2 cFE b/se	Model 3 cyFE b/se	Model 4 b/se	Model 5 cFE b/se	Model 6 cyFE b/se
etype = 6	−2.808***	−3.661***	−3.838***	−2.808***	−3.661**	−3.838**
	(0.67)	(0.91)	(1.11)	(0.68)	(1.28)	(1.48)
etype = 8	−1.410*	−0.267	−0.287	−1.410	−0.267	−0.287
	(0.62)	(0.76)	(1.06)	(1.12)	(1.66)	(1.77)
etype = 9	−1.578***	−1.881***	−2.530***	−1.578***	−1.881**	−2.530**
	(0.35)	(0.40)	(0.61)	(0.39)	(0.66)	(0.96)
etype = 10	0.000	0.000	0.000	0.000	0.000	0.000
	(.)	(.)	(.)	(.)	(.)	(.)
Cumulative SCAD to Date	−0.002***	−0.003***	0.004*	−0.002***	−0.003***	0.004+
	(0.00)	(0.00)	(0.00)	(0.00)	(0.00)	(0.00)
Foreign Owned	0.826**	0.928**	0.842*	0.826***	0.928***	0.842**
	(0.26)	(0.31)	(0.38)	(0.23)	(0.16)	(0.26)
Coal and Mineral Rents	−0.006	−0.018	−0.118*	−0.006	−0.018	−0.118+
	(0.03)	(0.04)	(0.06)	(0.03)	(0.07)	(0.07)
Coal	0.000	0.000	0.000	0.000	0.000	0.000
	(.)	(.)	(.)	(.)	(.)	(.)
Copper	−1.501	−3.074	−3.168	−1.501	−3.074	−3.168
	(1.43)	(2.02)	(4.65)	(1.60)	(2.21)	(3.82)
Gold	0.445	−0.968	−0.348	0.445	−0.968	−0.348
	(0.87)	(1.20)	(2.75)	(0.96)	(1.21)	(2.29)
Iron	0.769	1.000	0.485	0.769+	1.000+	0.485
	(0.52)	(0.62)	(0.76)	(0.40)	(0.58)	(1.02)
Lead	0.000	0.000	0.000	0.000	0.000	0.000
	(.)	(.)	(.)	(.)	(.)	(.)
MetMin	1.095**	0.975*	0.708	1.095**	0.975*	0.708
	(0.39)	(0.46)	(0.60)	(0.35)	(0.43)	(0.43)
Nickel	0.000	0.000	0.000	0.000	0.000	0.000
	(.)	(.)	(.)	(.)	(.)	(.)
Phosphate	0.522	0.828	2.516	0.522	0.828	2.516
	(1.26)	(1.39)	(1.57)	(1.17)	(1.11)	(1.54)
Platinum	0.765	−0.798	−0.342	0.765	−0.798	−0.342
	(1.05)	(1.38)	(3.07)	(1.08)	(1.45)	(2.44)
Silver	0.000	0.000	0.000	0.000	0.000	0.000
	(.)	(.)	(.)	(.)	(.)	(.)

(continued)

Appendix C

(continued)

	Model 1 b/se	Model 2 cFE b/se	Model 3 cyFE b/se	Model 4 b/se	Model 5 cFE b/se	Model 6 cyFE b/se
Tin	−2.047	−2.459	−2.318	−2.047	−2.459	−2.318
	(2.14)	(2.80)	(5.93)	(2.82)	(2.93)	(4.59)
Zinc	1.222	−1.535	−2.312	1.222	−1.535	−2.312
	(1.63)	(2.34)	(4.52)	(2.20)	(2.25)	(3.64)
Algeria		0.000	0.000		0.000	0.000
		(.)	(.)		(.)	(.)
Angola		−0.025	1.369		−0.025	1.369
		(1.49)	(1.63)		(0.71)	(1.07)
Botswana		0.000	0.000		0.000	0.000
		(.)	(.)		(.)	(.)
Burkina Faso		−1.822*	−0.342		−1.822***	−0.342
		(0.80)	(1.39)		(0.51)	(1.49)
Burundi		−2.925*	−4.765**		−2.925***	−4.765***
		(1.36)	(1.81)		(0.80)	(1.19)
Central African Republic		0.000	0.000		0.000	0.000
		(.)	(.)		(.)	(.)
Democratic Republic of Congo		−4.507**	−7.260***		−4.507***	−7.260***
		(1.42)	(1.76)		(1.04)	(1.29)
Eritrea		0.000	0.000		0.000	0.000
		(.)	(.)		(.)	(.)
Ethiopia		1.519	−0.486		1.519	−0.486
		(1.33)	(1.80)		(1.22)	(1.37)
Gabon		−0.933	−3.354+		−0.933	−3.354*
		(1.47)	(1.85)		(0.97)	(1.39)
Ghana		0.706	2.067		0.706	2.067
		(0.85)	(1.35)		(0.64)	(1.76)
Guinea		−0.054	3.225*		−0.054	3.225+
		(1.09)	(1.58)		(0.64)	(1.66)
Kenya		0.043	−0.699		0.043	−0.699
		(0.94)	(1.38)		(0.44)	(1.01)
Lesotho		0.000	0.000		0.000	0.000
		(.)	(.)		(.)	(.)
Liberia		−1.157	−2.173		−1.157	−2.173
		(0.96)	(1.44)		(0.81)	(1.46)
Madagascar		0.000	0.000		0.000	0.000
		(.)	(.)		(.)	(.)

	Model 1 b/se	Model 2 cFE b/se	Model 3 cyFE b/se	Model 4 b/se	Model 5 cFE b/se	Model 6 cyFE b/se
Malawi		−0.181	1.539		−0.181	1.539
		(1.13)	(1.50)		(0.96)	(1.50)
Mali		−0.214	−1.833		−0.214	−1.833
		(1.05)	(1.90)		(0.82)	(1.60)
Mauritania		0.983	3.598+		0.983	3.598
		(1.64)	(2.13)		(1.70)	(2.30)
Morocco		0.000	0.000		0.000	0.000
		(.)	(.)		(.)	(.)
Mozambique		−1.878+	0.676		−1.878*	0.676
		(1.07)	(1.70)		(0.88)	(2.08)
Namibia		0.498	3.017+		0.498	3.017
		(1.23)	(1.73)		(1.86)	(2.39)
Niger		2.501+	0.523		2.501	0.523
		(1.48)	(2.60)		(1.88)	(2.72)
Nigeria		−1.034	−3.350+		−1.034*	−3.350+
		(0.92)	(1.75)		(0.46)	(1.73)
Rwanda		0.000	0.000		0.000	0.000
		(.)	(.)		(.)	(.)
Senegal		−1.210	−2.615+		−1.210	−2.615
		(1.07)	(1.58)		(0.96)	(2.04)
Sierra Leone		−1.505	−0.778		−1.505*	−0.778
		(0.92)	(1.36)		(0.70)	(1.63)
Somalia		0.000	0.000		0.000	0.000
		(.)	(.)		(.)	(.)
South Africa		−0.316	−4.399*		−0.316	−4.399*
		(0.83)	(1.82)		(0.84)	(2.14)
Swaziland		0.000	0.000		0.000	0.000
		(.)	(.)		(.)	(.)
Tanzania		−0.419	2.354+		−0.419	2.354
		(0.99)	(1.39)		(0.76)	(1.70)
Togo		0.000	0.000		0.000	0.000
		(.)	(.)		(.)	(.)
Uganda		−3.088*	0.144		−3.088***	0.144
		(1.48)	(2.32)		(0.72)	(1.97)
Zambia		-0.587	0.175		-0.587	0.175
		(1.10)	(1.56)		(0.99)	(1.73)
Zimbabwe		0.000	0.000		0.000	0.000
		(.)	(.)		(.)	(.)

(continued)

(continued)

	Model 1 b/se	Model 2 cFE b/se	Model 3 cyFE b/se	Model 4 b/se	Model 5 cFE b/se	Model 6 cyFE b/se
styr = 1990			0.000 (.)			0.000 (.)
styr = 1991			−1.098 (0.74)			−1.098* (0.50)
styr = 1992			−7.250*** (1.51)			−7.250*** (1.77)
styr = 1993			−4.203** (1.31)			−4.203** (1.62)
styr = 1994			−1.667 (1.17)			−1.667 (1.05)
styr = 1995			−6.595*** (1.78)			−6.595** (2.47)
styr = 1996			−5.174** (1.57)			−5.174** (1.98)
styr = 1997			−4.194** (1.44)			−4.194* (1.81)
styr = 1998			−6.274*** (1.70)			−6.274* (3.02)
styr = 1999			−7.609*** (1.73)			−7.609** (2.43)
styr = 2000			−7.898*** (1.75)			−7.898*** (1.94)
styr = 2001			−5.380*** (1.62)			−5.380* (2.37)
styr = 2002			−6.565*** (1.90)			−6.565** (2.44)
styr = 2003			0.000 (.)			0.000 (.)
styr = 2004			0.000 (.)			0.000 (.)
styr = 2005			−3.156* (1.60)			−3.156 (1.97)
styr = 2006			−3.713* (1.83)			−3.713+ (1.95)
styr = 2007			−2.776 (2.05)			−2.776 (2.20)
styr = 2008			−3.574+ (1.83)			−3.574+ (2.12)
styr = 2009			−7.907*** (1.95)			−7.907* (3.39)

	Model 1 b/se	Model 2 cFE b/se	Model 3 cyFE b/se	Model 4 b/se	Model 5 cFE b/se	Model 6 cyFE b/se
styr = 2010			-2.040			-2.040
			(2.79)			(4.91)
styr = 2011			-8.018***			-8.018***
			(2.09)			(1.98)
styr = 2012			-6.365**			-6.365**
			(1.99)			(2.08)
styr = 2013			-7.804***			-7.804**
			(2.02)			(2.63)
Constant	-5.483***	-8.786***	-3.671	-5.483*	-8.786*	-3.671
	(1.65)	(2.55)	(4.91)	(2.19)	(3.78)	(4.19)
Pseudo R Sq	.26	.35	.5	.26	.35	.5
Chi-Sq Test	212	283	387	674	(.)	(.)
Log-Likelihood	-304.9	-256.5	-193.6	-304.9	-256.5	-193.6
Observations	655.0	633.0	606.0	655.0	633.0	606.0

$+ \ p < 0.10, * \ p < 0.05, ** \ p < 0.01, *** \ p < 0.001$

Probability of Repression (of Protest within 20 km) – Commodity Year Price Placebo

	Model 7 b/se	Model 8 cFE b/se	Model 9 cyFE b/se	Model 10 b/se	Model 11 cFE b/se	Model 12 cyFE b/se
Repressed						
Election = 0	0.000	0.000	0.000	0.000	0.000	0.000
	(.)	(.)	(.)	(.)	(.)	(.)
Election = 1	0.017	-0.182	245.090+	0.017	-0.182	245.090*
	(1.35)	(2.32)	(144.25)	(1.42)	(2.87)	(117.33)
Polity IV	0.125	-0.135	2.726	0.125	-0.135	2.726
	(0.10)	(0.28)	(1.70)	(0.15)	(0.28)	(3.70)
Election = 0 × Polity IV	0.000	0.000	0.000	0.000	0.000	0.000
	(.)	(.)	(.)	(.)	(.)	(.)
Election = 1 × Polity IV	-0.054	0.073	-45.558+	-0.054	0.073	-45.558*
	(0.19)	(0.30)	(26.14)	(0.19)	(0.35)	(20.71)

(continued)

(continued)

	Model 7 b/se	Model 8 cFE b/se	Model 9 cyFE b/se	Model 10 b/se	Model 11 cFE b/se	Model 12 cyFE b/se
Log Random Com- myearprice	0.050	0.185	0.295	0.050	0.185	0.295
	(0.19)	(0.29)	(0.57)	(0.14)	(0.22)	(0.78)
Road Density	0.026**	0.034+	0.374**	0.026	0.034	0.374***
	(0.01)	(0.02)	(0.13)	(0.02)	(0.05)	(0.11)
Distance to Capital (l)	−0.059	0.247	3.360*	−0.059	0.247	3.360+
	(0.14)	(0.26)	(1.35)	(0.18)	(0.34)	(1.78)
Population Density (l)	−0.199+	−0.084	1.169+	−0.199+	−0.084	1.169
	(0.11)	(0.18)	(0.64)	(0.12)	(0.11)	(0.99)
etype = 1	0.000	0.000	0.000	0.000	0.000	0.000
	(.)	(.)	(.)	(.)	(.)	(.)
etype = 2	−0.521	−2.973*	−3.074	−0.521	−2.973+	−3.074
	(0.62)	(1.17)	(4.76)	(0.77)	(1.71)	(27.79)
etype = 3	−0.740	−4.585**	−20.347*	−0.740	−4.585***	−20.347*
	(0.78)	(1.51)	(9.34)	(0.82)	(1.25)	(9.88)
etype = 4	0.502	−0.556	12.602*	0.502	−0.556	12.602
	(0.59)	(0.96)	(5.86)	(0.61)	(1.17)	(24.78)
etype = 6	0.000	0.000	0.000	0.000	0.000	0.000
	(.)	(.)	(.)	(.)	(.)	(.)
etype = 8	0.000	0.000	0.000	0.000	0.000	0.000
	(.)	(.)	(.)	(.)	(.)	(.)
etype = 9	−1.841**	−2.294**	8.092*	−1.841**	−2.294*	8.092
	(0.60)	(0.72)	(3.66)	(0.70)	(1.10)	(7.22)
etype = 10	0.000	0.000	0.000	0.000	0.000	0.000
	(.)	(.)	(.)	(.)	(.)	(.)
Cumulative SCAD to Date	−0.003**	−0.002	0.184*	−0.003***	−0.002	0.184***
	(0.00)	(0.00)	(0.07)	(0.00)	(0.00)	(0.04)
Foreign Owned	1.196*	1.233+	−0.455	1.196**	1.233*	−0.455
	(0.48)	(0.64)	(1.49)	(0.42)	(0.62)	(0.76)
Coal and Mineral Rents	0.099+	0.251**	−15.479*	0.099*	0.251***	−15.479***

	Model 7 b/se	Model 8 cFE b/se	Model 9 cyFE b/se	Model 10 b/se	Model 11 cFE b/se	Model 12 cyFE b/se
	(0.05)	(0.09)	(7.64)	(0.05)	(0.07)	(4.55)
Coal	0.000	0.000	0.000	0.000	0.000	0.000
	(.)	(.)	(.)	(.)	(.)	(.)
Copper	0.315	1.129	−7.862	0.315	1.129	−7.862+
	(0.79)	(1.32)	(5.39)	(0.62)	(1.43)	(4.56)
Gold	1.472*	0.522	−0.639	1.472+	0.522	−0.639
	(0.58)	(0.85)	(2.30)	(0.82)	(1.18)	(1.52)
Iron	0.124	−0.790	−9.624*	0.124	−0.790	−9.624+
	(0.85)	(1.46)	(4.55)	(0.77)	(2.62)	(5.71)
Lead	0.000	0.000	0.000	0.000	0.000	0.000
	(.)	(.)	(.)	(.)	(.)	(.)
MetMin	0.703	−0.562	−6.352	0.703	−0.562	−6.352
	(0.62)	(0.90)	(4.52)	(0.73)	(1.18)	(4.27)
Phosphate	0.000	0.000	0.000	0.000	0.000	0.000
	(.)	(.)	(.)	(.)	(.)	(.)
Platinum	2.252*	1.737	4.499	2.252**	1.737*	4.499
	(1.09)	(1.31)	(8.38)	(0.74)	(0.81)	(13.16)
Silver	0.000	0.000	0.000	0.000	0.000	0.000
	(.)	(.)	(.)	(.)	(.)	(.)
Tin	0.000	0.000	0.000	0.000	0.000	0.000
	(.)	(.)	(.)	(.)	(.)	(.)
Angola		0.000	0.000		0.000	0.000
		(.)	(.)		(.)	(.)
Botswana		0.000	0.000		0.000	0.000
		(.)	(.)		(.)	(.)
Burkina Faso		−0.640	−263.940*		−0.640	−263.940**
		(2.51)	(131.12)		(1.95)	(96.05)
Democratic Republic of Congo		0.000	0.000		0.000	0.000
		(.)	(.)		(.)	(.)
Eritrea		0.000	0.000		0.000	0.000
		(.)	(.)		(.)	(.)
Ethiopia		2.408	−24.185		2.408+	−24.185
		(2.33)	(8580.06)		(1.37)	(32.56)
Gabon		1.245	−113.708		1.245	−113.708
		(2.84)	(72.46)		(3.54)	(72.33)
Ghana		3.496	−23.729*		3.496*	−23.729
		(2.58)	(11.32)		(1.66)	(27.01)

(continued)

(continued)

	Model 7 b/se	Model 8 cFE b/se	Model 9 cyFE b/se	Model 10 b/se	Model 11 cFE b/se	Model 12 cyFE b/se
Guinea	0.000	0.000			0.000	0.000
	(.)	(.)			(.)	(.)
Kenya	0.000	0.000			0.000	0.000
	(.)	(.)			(.)	(.)
Lesotho	0.000	0.000			0.000	0.000
	(.)	(.)			(.)	(.)
Liberia	−2.151	54.602+			−2.151	54.602***
	(2.28)	(29.09)			(1.62)	(15.77)
Madagascar	0.000	0.000			0.000	0.000
	(.)	(.)			(.)	(.)
Malawi	0.968	65.145			0.968	65.145
	(2.52)	(.)			(1.68)	(.)
Mali	0.000	0.000			0.000	0.000
	(.)	(.)			(.)	(.)
Mauritania	0.000	0.000			0.000	0.000
	(.)	(.)			(.)	(.)
Mozambique	0.000	0.000			0.000	0.000
	(.)	(.)			(.)	(.)
Namibia	5.298+	24.713*			5.298	24.713
	(2.93)	(12.61)			(4.65)	(32.43)
Niger	2.614	60.526			2.614	60.526
	(2.33)	(.)			(2.19)	(.)
Nigeria	−1.944	−60.985			−1.944	−60.985+
	(2.48)	(2581.43)			(1.79)	(34.45)
Rwanda	0.000	0.000			0.000	0.000
	(.)	(.)			(.)	(.)
Senegal	−0.758	−129.099*			−0.758	−129.099+
	(2.65)	(63.34)			(1.86)	(67.00)
Sierra Leone	−0.507	−12.586			−0.507	−12.586
	(2.58)	(8.33)			(2.12)	(19.87)
Somalia	0.000	0.000			0.000	0.000
	(.)	(.)			(.)	(.)
South Africa	−0.451	−151.839**			−0.451	−151.839**
	(2.38)	(57.57)			(2.01)	(50.85)
Swaziland	0.000	0.000			0.000	0.000
	(.)	(.)			(.)	(.)
Tanzania	2.329	0.000			2.329	0.000
	(2.46)	(.)			(2.00)	(.)

	Model 7 b/se	Model 8 cFE b/se	Model 9 cyFE b/se	Model 10 b/se	Model 11 cFE b/se	Model 12 cyFE b/se
Uganda		0.387	0.000		0.387	0.000
		(2.68)	(.)		(1.68)	(.)
Zambia		−0.908	107.667+		−0.908	107.667***
		(2.86)	(56.02)		(1.88)	(31.10)
Zimbabwe		0.999	−9.490		0.999	−9.490
		(2.06)	(6.76)		(1.21)	(12.99)
styr = 1990			0.000			0.000
			(.)			(.)
styr = 1991			−33.588**			−33.588**
			(12.78)			(10.29)
styr = 1992			0.000			0.000
			(.)			(.)
styr = 1993			−84.065*			−84.065***
			(32.94)			(21.89)
styr = 1994			79.861			79.861
			(65.19)			(50.74)
styr = 1995			−128.320*			−128.320***
			(52.33)			(29.80)
styr = 1996			−156.678			−156.678
			(.)			(.)
styr = 1997			−179.266*			−179.266**
			(73.49)			(57.21)
styr = 1998			−173.583*			−173.583***
			(69.83)			(50.50)
styr = 1999			−148.230			−148.230**
			(7156.66)			(47.80)
styr = 2000			−170.699*			−170.699***
			(68.40)			(45.01)
styr = 2001			−190.891*			−190.891***
			(76.79)			(46.82)
styr = 2002			−234.697			−234.697
			(.)			(.)
styr = 2003			0.000			0.000
			(.)			(.)
styr = 2004			0.000			0.000
			(.)			(.)
styr = 2005			−157.473*			−157.473***
			(62.48)			(45.11)
styr = 2006			101.212			101.212*
			(69.38)			(50.09)

(continued)

	Model 7 b/se	Model 8 cFE b/se	Model 9 cyFE b/se	Model 10 b/se	Model 11 cFE b/se	Model 12 cyFE b/se
styr = 2007			−161.405			−161.405***
			(4438.26)			(40.12)
styr = 2008			−54.750*			−54.750***
			(22.85)			(12.85)
styr = 2009			0.000			0.000
			(.)			(.)
Constant	−3.312	−6.649	81.071+	−3.312	−6.649	81.071**
	(3.04)	(5.42)	(44.85)	(2.48)	(6.20)	(25.50)
Pseudo R Sq	.27	.36	.6	.27	.36	.6
Chi-Sq Test	73	96	160	290	(.)	(.)
Log-Likelihood	−105.6	−73.9	−27.6	−105.6	−73.9	−27.6
Observations	214.0	181.0	156.0	214.0	181.0	156.0

+ p < 0.10, * p < 0.05, ** p < 0.01, *** p < 0.001

Probability of Repression (of Protest within 20 km) – Leader Years Placebo

	Model 13 b/se	Model 14 c FE b/se	Model 15 cy FE b/se	Model 16 b/se	Model 17 c FE b/se	Model 18 cy FE b/se
Log Random leader years in office	0.087	−0.312	1.879	0.087	−0.312	1.879
	(0.50)	(0.78)	(1.90)	(0.42)	(0.60)	(2.03)
Polity IV	0.172	−0.624	2.277	0.172	−0.624	2.277
	(0.71)	(1.06)	(2.53)	(0.68)	(0.79)	(2.13)
Log Random leaderyearsin-office × Polity IV	−0.009	0.037	−0.233	−0.009	0.037	−0.233
	(0.07)	(0.10)	(0.25)	(0.07)	(0.08)	(0.24)
Commodity Price (l)	0.898+	1.709+	8.403*	0.898+	1.709*	8.403
	(0.51)	(0.91)	(3.77)	(0.46)	(0.74)	(5.63)
Road Density	0.025**	0.037*	0.145**	0.025	0.037	0.145***
	(0.01)	(0.02)	(0.05)	(0.02)	(0.04)	(0.04)
Distance to Capital (l)	−0.090	−0.009	0.737+	−0.090	−0.009	0.737+
	(0.13)	(0.22)	(0.42)	(0.17)	(0.33)	(0.38)

	Model 13 b/se	Model 14 c FE b/se	Model 15 cy FE b/se	Model 16 b/se	Model 17 c FE b/se	Model 18 cy FE b/se
Population Density (l)	−0.154	−0.102	0.343	−0.154	−0.102	0.343*
	(0.11)	(0.15)	(0.30)	(0.12)	(0.07)	(0.16)
etype = 1	0.000	0.000	0.000	0.000	0.000	0.000
	(.)	(.)	(.)	(.)	(.)	(.)
etype = 2	−0.377	−2.223*	−4.362*	−0.377	−2.223*	−4.362
	(0.53)	(0.88)	(2.11)	(0.53)	(1.09)	(3.57)
etype = 3	−0.175	−3.161*	−9.185*	−0.175	−3.161***	−9.185
	(0.70)	(1.26)	(4.03)	(0.68)	(0.90)	(6.67)
etype = 4	0.741	0.237	3.403*	0.741	0.237	3.403
	(0.49)	(0.62)	(1.73)	(0.58)	(1.09)	(3.09)
etype = 6	0.000	0.000	0.000	0.000	0.000	0.000
	(.)	(.)	(.)	(.)	(.)	(.)
etype = 8	−0.733	−0.293	−24.686	−0.733	−0.293	−24.686***
	(0.92)	(1.34)	(1204.96)	(1.03)	(2.31)	(7.17)
etype = 9	−1.305*	−1.592**	−0.263	−1.305*	−1.592+	−0.263
	(0.52)	(0.62)	(1.23)	(0.53)	(0.89)	(1.72)
etype = 10	0.000	0.000	0.000	0.000	0.000	0.000
	(.)	(.)	(.)	(.)	(.)	(.)
Cumulative SCAD to Date	−0.003***	−0.003**	0.010*	−0.003***	−0.003***	0.010***
	(0.00)	(0.00)	(0.00)	(0.00)	(0.00)	(0.00)
Foreign Owned	0.752+	0.984*	1.186	0.752+	0.984**	1.186+
	(0.39)	(0.50)	(0.90)	(0.39)	(0.31)	(0.67)
Coal and Mineral Rents	−0.017	0.043	0.207	−0.017	0.043	0.207
	(0.05)	(0.09)	(0.22)	(0.06)	(0.14)	(0.32)
Coal	0.000	0.000	0.000	0.000	0.000	0.000
	(.)	(.)	(.)	(.)	(.)	(.)
Copper	−2.966	−5.772	−36.667*	−2.966	−5.772+	−36.667
	(2.21)	(3.96)	(16.57)	(2.05)	(3.46)	(23.86)
Gold	−0.700	−2.582	−17.360*	−0.700	−2.582	−17.360
	(1.36)	(2.25)	(8.79)	(1.35)	(1.64)	(12.80)
Iron	0.150	0.188	−5.886*	0.150	0.188	−5.886**
	(0.76)	(1.18)	(2.33)	(0.69)	(1.41)	(2.08)
Lead	0.000	0.000	0.000	0.000	0.000	0.000
	(.)	(.)	(.)	(.)	(.)	(.)

(continued)

(continued)

	Model 13 b/se	Model 14 c FE b/se	Model 15 cy FE b/se	Model 16 b/se	Model 17 c FE b/se	Model 18 cy FE b/se
MetMin	0.583	−0.240	−2.421	0.583	−0.240	−2.421
	(0.58)	(0.79)	(1.54)	(0.66)	(1.08)	(1.61)
Phosphate	0.182	1.322	3.655	0.182	1.322	3.655
	(1.43)	(1.58)	(2.92)	(1.33)	(1.05)	(2.25)
Platinum	0.196	−1.936	−17.855+	0.196	−1.936	−17.855
	(1.66)	(2.63)	(9.33)	(1.44)	(1.98)	(13.63)
Silver	0.000	0.000	0.000	0.000	0.000	0.000
	(.)	(.)	(.)	(.)	(.)	(.)
Tin	0.000	0.000	0.000	0.000	0.000	0.000
	(.)	(.)	(.)	(.)	(.)	(.)
Angola		0.000	0.000		0.000	0.000
		(.)	(.)		(.)	(.)
Botswana		0.000	0.000		0.000	0.000
		(.)	(.)		(.)	(.)
Burkina Faso		−4.677*	−13.677**		−4.677*	−13.677*
		(2.04)	(4.37)		(1.87)	(5.82)
Burundi		0.000	0.000		0.000	0.000
		(.)	(.)		(.)	(.)
Central African Republic		0.000	0.000		0.000	0.000
		(.)	(.)		(.)	(.)
Democratic Republic of Congo		−3.785+	−19.555***		−3.785*	−19.555**
		(2.14)	(5.37)		(1.68)	(6.66)
Eritrea		0.000	0.000		0.000	0.000
		(.)	(.)		(.)	(.)
Ethiopia		−0.657	−4.010		−0.657	−4.010
		(2.37)	(3.77)		(1.39)	(3.93)
Gabon		−1.684	0.859		−1.684	0.859
		(2.74)	(5.00)		(1.90)	(7.80)
Ghana		1.550	−4.983		1.550	−4.983
		(2.28)	(4.56)		(1.77)	(4.09)
Guinea		−1.347	−7.386+		−1.347	−7.386*
		(2.46)	(4.21)		(2.18)	(3.75)
Kenya		0.000	0.000		0.000	0.000
		(.)	(.)		(.)	(.)
Lesotho		0.000	0.000		0.000	0.000
		(.)	(.)		(.)	(.)

	Model 13 b/se	Model 14 c FE b/se	Model 15 cy FE b/se	Model 16 b/se	Model 17 c FE b/se	Model 18 cy FE b/se
Liberia	−2.466	−4.736			−2.466	−4.736
	(2.07)	(4.09)			(1.62)	(6.98)
Madagascar	0.000	0.000			0.000	0.000
	(.)	(.)			(.)	(.)
Malawi	0.641	3.290			0.641	3.290
	(2.24)	(4.64)			(1.16)	(4.34)
Mali	−0.503	3.702			−0.503	3.702
	(2.64)	(.)			(1.88)	(.)
Mauritania	0.000	0.000			0.000	0.000
	(.)	(.)			(.)	(.)
Morocco	0.000	0.000			0.000	0.000
	(.)	(.)			(.)	(.)
Mozambique	−1.989	0.000			−1.989	0.000
	(2.29)	(.)			(1.48)	(.)
Namibia	3.481	13.340*			3.481	13.340**
	(2.62)	(5.73)			(2.97)	(4.28)
Niger	2.643	3.445			2.643	3.445
	(2.69)	(5.93)			(3.00)	(7.63)
Nigeria	−3.865	−13.567*			−3.865+	−13.567*
	(2.48)	(5.63)			(2.02)	(5.38)
Rwanda	0.000	0.000			0.000	0.000
	(.)	(.)			(.)	(.)
Senegal	−2.185	−8.034+			−2.185	−8.034
	(2.22)	(4.54)			(1.41)	(5.05)
Sierra Leone	−2.225	−5.656			−2.225	−5.656
	(2.34)	(4.70)			(1.80)	(4.74)
Somalia	0.000	0.000			0.000	0.000
	(.)	(.)			(.)	(.)
South Africa	−0.627	−18.843**			−0.627	−18.843**
	(2.06)	(6.06)			(1.79)	(6.26)
Swaziland	0.000	0.000			0.000	0.000
	(.)	(.)			(.)	(.)
Tanzania	0.766	0.000			0.766	0.000
	(2.19)	(.)			(0.98)	(.)
Uganda	−1.478	0.000			−1.478	0.000
	(2.66)	(.)			(1.66)	(.)
Zambia	−0.122	−2.885			−0.122	−2.885
	(2.36)	(4.63)			(2.05)	(4.30)

(continued)

(continued)

	Model 13 b/se	Model 14 c FE b/se	Model 15 cy FE b/se	Model 16 b/se	Model 17 c FE b/se	Model 18 cy FE b/se
Zimbabwe		−0.911 (1.94)	−7.700* (3.50)		−0.911 (1.25)	−7.700** (2.70)
styr = 1990			0.000 (.)			0.000 (.)
styr = 1991			−5.884** (2.14)			−5.884*** (0.96)
styr = 1992			0.000 (.)			0.000 (.)
styr = 1993			−11.633** (4.22)			−11.633*** (2.60)
styr = 1994			−9.005** (3.38)			−9.005*** (1.75)
styr = 1995			−8.834* (3.99)			−8.834** (2.78)
styr = 1996			−14.956** (4.95)			−14.956*** (3.45)
styr = 1997			−18.194** (5.86)			−18.194*** (3.89)
styr = 1998			−14.563** (4.69)			−14.563** (5.45)
styr = 1999			−13.957** (5.31)			−13.957** (4.74)
styr = 2000			−14.937** (4.87)			−14.937*** (3.74)
styr = 2001			−17.543** (5.97)			−17.543* (7.35)
styr = 2002			−14.379 (16.03)			−14.379*** (3.11)
styr = 2003			0.000 (.)			0.000 (.)
styr = 2004			0.000 (.)			0.000 (.)
styr = 2005			−13.808** (4.95)			−13.808** (4.38)
styr = 2006			−14.653* (5.75)			−14.653*** (4.05)
styr = 2007			−11.736* (4.69)			−11.736* (5.86)
styr = 2008			−21.371** (6.70)			−21.371*** (4.53)

	Model 13 b/se	Model 14 c FE b/se	Model 15 cy FE b/se	Model 16 b/se	Model 17 c FE b/se	Model 18 cy FE b/se
styr = 2009			0.000 (.)			0.000 (.)
styr = 2010			9.852 (1204.97)			9.852 (6.85)
styr = 2011			0.000 (.)			0.000 (.)
styr = 2012			−26.243*** (7.67)			−26.243*** (6.70)
styr = 2013			−22.962*** (6.75)			−22.962*** (5.28)
Constant	−6.332 (5.65)	−4.213 (9.84)	−55.239* (27.37)	−6.332 (4.17)	−4.213 (7.20)	−55.239 (40.68)
Pseudo R Sq	.27	.34	.53	.27	.34	.53
Chi-Sq Test	93	143	183	339	.	.
Log-Likelihood	−138.8	−104.8	−55.6	−138.8	−104.8	−55.6
Observations	284.0	270.0	218.0	284.0	270.0	218.0

+ p < 0.10, * p < 0.05, ** p < 0.01, *** p < 0.001

Bibliography

Acemoglu, Daron. 2005. "Politics and Economics in Weak and Strong States." *Journal of Monetary Economics* 52(7):1199–1226.

Acemoglu, Daron, and James A. Robinson. 2001. "A Theory of Political Transitions." *American Economic Review* pp. 938–963.

Aflatooni, Afra, and Michael Patrick Allen. 1991. "Government Sanctions and Collective Political Protest in Periphery and Semiperiphery States: A Time-Series Analysis." *Journal of Political and Military Sociology* 19(1):29.

African Development Bank. 2012. Mozambique 2012. Technical report.

African Natural Resources Center. n.d. African Development Bank.

Alexander, Jocelyn. 1997. "The Local State in Post-War Mozambique: Political Practice and Ideas about Authority." *Africa* 67(01):1–26.

Amengual, Matthew. 2018. "Buying Stability: The Distributive Outcomes of Private Politics in the Bolivian Mining Industry." *World Development* 104:31–45.

Aravat, Anwar. 2012. EITI Program Director World Bank, Lusaka. Lusaka, Zambia. Private Interview.

Arce, Moises. 2014. *Resource Extraction and Protest in Peru.* University of Pittsburgh Press.

Arce, Moisés, and Rebecca E. Miller. 2016. "Mineral Wealth and Protest in Sub-Saharan Africa." *African Studies Review* 59:83–105.

Arellano-Yanguas, Javier. 2011. "Local Politics, Conflict and Development in Peruvian Mining Regions." Thesis.

Asal, Victor et al. "Political Exclusion, Oil, and Ethnic Armed Conflict." *Journal of Conflict Resolution* 60.8 (2016): 1343–1367.

Ashley, P. M., and B. G. Lottermoser. 1999. "Arsenic Contamination at the Mole River Mine, Northern New South Wales." *Australian Journal of Earth Sciences* 46(6):861–874.

Augustinus, Clarissa. 2003. "Key Issues for Africa and Globally." *Nairobi, Kenya: United Nations Human Settlements Program (UN-Habitat)* http://citeseerx.ist.psu.edu/viewdoc/download?doi=10.1.1.199.1625&rep=rep1&type=pdf

Baron, David. 2001. "Private Politics, Corporate Social Responsibility, and Integrated Strategy." *Journal of Economics and Management Strategy* 10(1): 7–45.

Basedau, Matthias, and Jan Henryk Pierskalla. 2014. "How Ethnicity Conditions the Effect of Oil and Gas on Civil Conflict: A Spatial Analysis of Africa from 1990 to 2010." *Political Geography* 38:1–11.

Bates, Robert H. 2005. *Markets and States in Tropical Africa: The Political Basis of Agricultural Policies: With a New Preface*. University of California Press.

Bates, Robert H. 2015. *When Things Fell Apart*. Cambridge University Press.

Batley, Richard and Claire Mcloughlin. 2010. "Engagement with Non-State Service Providers in Fragile States: Reconciling State-Building and Service Delivery." *Development Policy Review* 28(2):131–154.

Bazzi, Samuel and Christopher Blattman. 2014. "Economic Shocks and Conflict: Evidence from Commodity Prices." *American Economic Journal: Macroeconomics* 6(4):1–38.

Bebbington, Anthony. 2010. "Extractive Industries and Stunted States: Conflict, Responsibility and Institutional Change in the Andes." *Corporate Social Responsibility: Discourses, Practices and Perspectives:* 97–116.

Bebbington, Anthony, Denise Humphreys, Jeffrey Bury, Jeannet Lingan, Juan Pablo Muñoz, and Martin Scurrah. 2008. "Mining and Social Movements: Struggles Over Livelihood and Rural Territorial Development in the Andes." *World Development* 36(12):2888–2905.

Bebbington, Anthony, Leonith Hinojosa, Denise Humphreys Bebbington, Maria Luisa Burneo, and Ximena Warnaars. 2008. "Contention and Ambiguity: Mining and the Possibilities of Development." *Development and Change* 39(6):887–914.

Bennett, Juliette. 2002. "Multinational Corporations, Social Responsibility and Conflict." *Journal of International Affairs* 55(2):55–80.

Bensch, Gunther, Jörg Peters, and Linda Schraml. 2010. Energy Use and Socio-Economic Conditions in Mozambique: Evidence from GTZ Electrification Project Regions. Technical report rwi Materialien.

Berdal, Mats R., and David M. Malone. 2000. *Greed and Grievance: Economic Agendas in Civil Wars*. Lynne Rienner Publishers.

Besley, Timothy, and Torsten Persson. 2010. "State Capacity, Conflict, and Development." *Econometrica* 78(1):1–34.

Bhasin, Tavishi, and Jennifer Gandhi. 2013. "Timing and Targeting of State Repression in Authoritarian Elections." *Electoral Studies* 32(4):620–631.

Bienen, Henry and Nicolas van de Walle. 1989. "Time and Power in Africa." 83(1):19–34. www.jstor.org.proxyiub.uits.iu.edu/stable/1956432

Birchard, Ralph. 1940. "Copper in the Katanga Region of the Belgian Congo." *Economic Geography* 16(4):429–436.

Boone, Catherine. 1998. "State Building in the African Countryside: Structure and Politics at the Grassroots." *Journal of Development Studies* 34(4): 1–31.

Boone, Catherine. 2003. *Political Topographies of the African State: Territorial Authority and Institutional Choice*. Cambridge University Press.

Borzel, Tanja A., Adrienne Heritier, Nicole Kranz, and Christian Thauer. 2011. "Racing to the Top? Regulatory Competition among Firms in Areas of Limited Statehood." In *Governance without a State*, ed. Thomas Risse. Columbia University Press.

Brass, Jennifer N. 2016. *Allies or Adversaries: NGOs and the State in Africa.* Cambridge University Press.

Bratton, Michael. 1989. "The Politics of Government-NGO Relations in Africa." *World Development* 17(4):569–587.

Bratton, Michael and Eldred Masunungure. 2007. "Popular Reactions to State Repression: Operation Murambatsvina in Zimbabwe." *African Affairs* 106(422):21–45.

Bratton, Michael and Nicolas van de Walle. 1994. "Neopatrimonial Regimes and Political Transitions in Africa." *World Politics* 46(4):453–489.

Brousseau, Eric and M. H. Farès. 2000*a*. "Incomplete Contracts and Governance Structures: Are Incomplete Contract Theory and New Institutional Economics Substitutes or Complements." *Institutions, Contracts and Organizations: Perspectives from New institutional Economics*, pp. 399–421.

Brousseau, Eric and Mhand Fares. 2000*b*. *Institutions, Contracts and Organizations: Perspectives from New Institutions Economics.* Edward Elgar Publishing.

Bruce, John W. and Anna Knox. 2009. "Structures and Stratagems: Making Decentralization of Authority over Land in Africa Cost-Effective." *World Development* 37(8):1360–1369.

Brunnschweiler, Christa N. 2008. "Cursing the Blessings? Natural Resource Abundance, Institutions, and Economic Growth." *World Development* 36(3):399–419.

Buhaug, Halvard, and Jan Ketil Rød. 2006. "Local Determinants of African Civil Wars, 1970–2001." *Political Geography* 25(3):315–335.

Buhaug, Halvard, Kristian Skrede Gleditsch, Helge Holtermann, Gudrun Øtby, and Andreas Forø Tollefsen. 2011. "It's the Local Economy, Stupid! Geographic Wealth Dispersion and Conflict Outbreak Location." *Journal of Conflict Resolution* 55(5):814–840.

Buhaug, Halvard, and Scott Gates. 2002. "The Geography of Civil War." *Journal of Peace Research* 39(4):417–433.

Burkey, Stan et al. 1993. *People First: A Guide to Self-Reliant Participatory Rural Development.* Zed Books Ltd.

Bury, Jeffrey. 2005. "Mining Mountains: Neoliberalism, Land Tenure, Livelihoods, and the New Peruvian Mining Industry in Cajamarca." *Environment and Planning A* 37(2):221–239. http://journals.sagepub.com/doi/10.1068/a371

Bury, Jeffrey Todd. 2007. "Livelihoods, Mining and Peasant Protests in the Peruvian Andes." *Journal of Latin American Geography* 1(1):1–19.

Campbell, Keith. 2012. "Vale's Mozambican Coal Operation Starts Exports But Encounters Protest." *Mining Weekly* www.miningweekly.com/article/brazilian-groups-mozambican-coal-operation-starts-exports-but-encounters-protest-2012-01-20

Carey, Sabine C. 2010. "The Use of Repression as a Response to Domestic Dissent." *Political Studies* 58(1):167–186. http://journals.sagepub.com /doi/10.1111/j.1467-9248.2008.00771.x

Carter Center. 2012. Les Investissements Miniers en Republique Democratique du Congo: Developpement ou Appauvrissement des Communautes Locales? Rapport d'impact des investissements miniers érangès sur les droits humains Cas des investissements Chemical of Africa (Chemaf) et Ruashi Mining au Katanga. Technical report.

Castro, Alfonso Peter, and Erik Nielsen. 2001. "Indigenous People and Comanagement: Implications for Conflict Management." *Environmental Science & Policy* 4(4):229–239.

Cederman, Lars-Erik, Nils B. Weidmann, and Kristian Skrede Gleditsch. 2011. "Horizontal Inequalities and Ethnonationalist Civil War: A Global Comparison." *American Political Science Review* 105(03):478–495.

Center for International Earth Science Information Network – CIESIN – Columbia University and Information Technology Outreach Services – ITOS – University of Georgia and NASA Socioeconomic Data and Applications Center (SEDAC). 2013. "Global Roads Open Access Data Set, Ersion 1 (gROADSv1)." http://dx.doi.org/10.7927/H4VD6WCT

Centre for Research on Multinational Corporations (SOMO) and Action against Impunity for Human Rights (ACIDH). 2011. Unheard Voices: Mining Activities in the Katanga Province and the Impact on Local Communities. Technical report.

Cernea, Michael M. 2010. "Risks, Safeguards and Reconstruction: A Model for Population Displacement and Resettlement." In Michael M., Risks and *Reconstruction: Experiences of Resettlers and Refugees*. Banca Mondialã, Washington.

Chairman Private Interview. 2012. Chairman, Konkola North Township. Konkola North Zambia. Private Interview.

Christensen, Darin, Alexandra Hartman and Cyrus Samii. n.d. "Property Rights, Investment, and Land Grabs: An Institutional Natural Experiment in Liberia."

Clark, John. 1997. "Petro-Politics in Congo." *Journal of Democracy* 8(3):62–76.

Coelho, João Paulo Borges. 1998. "State Resettlement Policies in Postcolonial Rural Mozambique: the Impact of the Communal Village Programme on Tete province, 1977–1982." *Journal of Southern African Studies* 24(1): 61–91.

Collier, Paul, and Anke Hoeffler. 2005. "Resource Rents, Governance, and Conflict." *Journal of Conflict Resolution* 49.4: 625–633.

Consultec Consultoria Associados, Diagonal Urbana and ERM Brasil Ltda. 2006. Estudo de impacto ambiental – EIA complexo industrial de Moatize Rio Doce Mozambique. Technical report.

Cornwall, Andrea. 2003. "Whose Voices? Whose Choices? Reflections on Gender and Participatory Development." *World Development* 31(8):1325–1342.

Daló, Ernesto. 2006. "Regulatory Capture: A Review." *Oxford Review of Economic Policy* 22(2):203–225. www.jstor.org.proxyiub.uits.iu.edu/stable /23606888

Dashwood, Hevina S. 2007. "Canadian Mining Companies and Corporate Social Responsibility: Weighing the Impact of Global Norms." *Canadian Journal of Political Science / Revue canadienne de science politique* 40(1):129–156.

Dashwood, Hevina S. 2012. *The Rise of Global Corporate Social Responsibility: Mining and the Spread of Global Norms.* Cambridge University Press.

Davenport, Christian. 1995. "Multi-Dimensional Threat Perception and State Repression: An Inquiry into Why States Apply Negative Sanctions." *American Journal of Political Science* 39(3):683.

Davenport, Christian. 2007. "State Repression and Political Order." *Annual Review of Political Science* 10:1–23.

Davenport, Christian, and David A. Armstrong. 2004. "Democracy and the Violation of Human Rights: A Statistical Analysis from 1976 to 1996." *American Journal of Political Science.* 48(3):538–554.

Davies Private Interview. 2012. Carrie Davies, Executive Director, Association of Commerce and Industry. Beira, Mozambique. Private interview.

Davis, David R., and Michael D. Ward. 1990. "They Dance Alone: Deaths and the Disappeared in Contemporary Chile." *Journal of Conflict Resolution* 34(3):449–475.

Davis, Rachel, and Daniel M. Franks. 2014. Costs of Company-Community Conflict in the Extractive Sector. Technical report Harvard Kennedy School.

De Goede, Meike. 2008. Private and Public Security in Post-War Democratic Republic of Congo. In *The Private Security Sector in Africa*, ed. Sabelo Gumetze. p. 35.

De Soysa, Indra, and Eric Neumayer. 2007. "Resource Wealth and the Risk of Civil War Onset: Results from a New Dataset of Natural Resource Rents, 1970–1999." *Conflict Management and Peace Science* 24(3):201–218.

Deaton, Angus. 1999. "Commodity Prices and Growth in Africa." *Journal of Economic Perspectives* 13(3):23–40.

Dickovick, J. Tyler, and Rachel Beatty Riedl. 2010. Comparative Assessment of Decentralization in Africa: Final Report and Summary of Findings. Technical report. USAID.

Dietz, Kristina, and Bettina Engels. 2017. "Contested Extractivism: Actors and Strategies in Conflicts over Mining." *DIE ERDE–Journal of the Geographical Society of Berlin* 148(2–3):111–120.

Downey, Liam, Eric Bonds, and Katherine Clark. 2010. "Natural Resource Extraction, Armed Violence, and Environmental Degradation." *Organization & environment* 23(4):417–445.

Doyle, Cathal, and Preeti Patel. 2008. "Civil Society Organisations and Global Health Initiatives: Problems of Legitimacy." *Social Science and Medicine* 66(9):1928–1938.

Dube, Oeindrila, and Juan F. Vargas. 2013. "Commodity Price Shocks and Civil Conflict: Evidence from Colombia." *The Review of Economic Studies* 80:1384–1421.

Dudka, Stanislaw, and Domy C. Adriano. 1997. "Environmental Impacts of Metal Ore Mining and Processing: a Review." *Journal of Environmental Quality* 26(3):590–602.

Dweidary, Haya, Séverine Koen, Emma Loebelson, and Anna Snyder. 2012. Foreign Direct Investment in the Context of the Extractive Industries: Improving Prospects for Statebuilding. Democratic Republic of Congo. Technical report UNDP, Center for International Conflict Resolution, and Columbia SIPA.

Elbadawi, Ibrahim, and Nicholas Sambanis. 2002. "How Much War Will We See?: Explaining the Prevalence of Civil War." *Journal of Conflict Resolution* 46(3):307–334.

Electoral Commission of Zambia. 2011. Technical report.

Engels, Bettina, and Kristina Dietz. 2017. *Contested Extractivism, Society and the State: Struggles over Mining and Land.* Springer.

Englebert, Pierre. 2002. *State Legitimacy and Development in Africa.* Lynne Rienner Publishers.

Environmentally and Socially Sustainable Development Africa Region. 2008. Congo, Democratic Republic of – Growth with Governance in the Mineral Sector. Technical report. World Bank.

Extractive Industry Transparency Initiative Report, Zambia. 2009. Technical report.

Fearon, James. 2005. "Primary Commodity Exports and Civil War." *Journal of Conflict Resolution* 49:483–507.

Fearon, James D. 1995. "Rationalist Explanations for War." *International Organization* 49:379–379.

Fearon, James D., and David D. Laitin. 2003. "Ethnicity, Insurgency, and Civil War." *The American Political Science Review* 97(1).

Ferejohn, John and Debra Satz. 1995. "Unification, Universalism, and Rational Choice Theory." *Critical Review* 9(1–2):71–84.

Ferguson, James. 2005. "Seeing Like an Oil Company: Space, Security, and Global Capital in Neoliberal Africa." *American Anthropologist* 107(3):377–382.

Franks, D. M., R. Davis, A. J. Bebbington, S. H. Ali, D. Kemp, and M. Scurrah. 2014. "Conflict Translates Environmental and Social Risk into Business Costs." *Proceedings of the National Academy of Sciences* 111(21):7576–7581.

Frynas, Jędrzej George. 2001. "Corporate and State Responses to Anti-Oil Protests in the Niger Delta." *African Affairs* 100(398):27–54.

Frynas, Jedrzej George. 2005. "The False Developmental Promise of Corporate Social Responsibility: Evidence from Multinational Oil Companies." *International Affairs* 81(3):581–598.

Global Value Chains: Investment and Trade for Development. 2007.

Global Witness (Organization). 2006. "Digging in Corruption: Fraud, Abuse and Exploitation in Katanga's Copper and Cobalt Mines: A Report by Global Witness, July 2006." www.globalwitness.org/en/archive/digging-corruption/

Goemans, H. E., K. S. Gleditsch, and G. Chiozza. 2009. "Introducing Archigos: A Dataset of Political Leaders." *Journal of Peace Research* 46(2): 269–283.

Golder Associates. 2009. Resettlement Action Plan Benga Mine Project Rio Tinto. Technical report.

Golder Associates, Impacto: Projectos e Estudos Ambientals and Riversdale Min-
    ing. 2009. Environmental Impact Assessment (EIA) Riversdale Benga Coal
    Project. Technical report.
Goldsmith, Arthur A. 2001. "Foreign Aid and Statehood in Africa." *Interna-
    tional Organization* 55(01):123–148.
Government of DRC. 2010. Extractive Industry Transparency Initiative Report,
    DRC. Technical report.
Griffin, Jennifer J., and John F. Mahon. 1997. "The Corporate Social Perfor-
    mance and Corporate Financial Performance Debate Twenty-Five Years of
    Incomparable Research." *Business & Society* 36(1):5–31.
Gunningham, Neil, Robert A. Kagan, and Dorothy Thornton. 2004. "Social
    License and Environmental Protection: Why Businesses Go beyond Compli-
    ance." *Law & Social Inquiry* 29(2):307–341.
Haber, Stephen, and Victor Menaldo. 2011. "Do Natural Resources Fuel Author-
    itarianism? A Reappraisal of the Resource Curse." *American Political Science
    Review* 105(01):1–26.
Hafner-Burton, Emilie M., Susan D. Hyde, and Ryan S. Jablonski. 2014. "When
    Do Governments Resort to Election Violence?" *British Journal of Political
    Science* 44:149–179.
Hallberg, Johan Dittrich. 2012. "PRIO Conflict Site 1989–2008: A Geo-
    Referenced Dataset on Armed Conflict." *Conflict Management and Peace
    Science* 29(2):219–232.
Hart, Stuart L. 1995. "A Natural-Resource-Based View of the Firm." *Academy
    of Management Review* 20(4):986–1014.
Haslam, Paul Alexander and Nasser Ary Tanimoune. 2016. "The Deter-
    minants of Social Conflict in the Latin American Mining Sector: New
    Evidence with Quantitative Data." *World Development* 78:401–419.
    http://linkinghub.elsevier.com/retrieve/pii/S0305750X15002429
Hatcher, Jessica. 2013, February 8. "The White Stuff: Mining Giant Rio Tinto
    Unearths Unrest in Madagascar." *Time.* http://world.time.com/2013/02/08/
    the-white-stuff-mining-giant-rio-tinto-unearths-unrest-in-madagascar/
Henderson, Conway W. 1991. "Conditions Affecting the Use of Political Repres-
    sion." *Journal of Conflict Resolution* 35(1):120–142.
Hendrix, Idean, Cullen S. Hendrix, Jesse Hamner, Christina Case, Christopher
    Linebarger, Emily Stull and Jennifer Williams. 2012. "Social Conflict in Africa:
    A New Database." *International Interactions* 38(4):503–511.
Henisz, Witold J., Sinziana Dorobantu, and Lite J. Nartey. 2014. "Spinning
    Gold: The Financial Returns to Stakeholder Engagement: Financial Returns to
    Stakeholder Engagement." *Strategic Management Journal* 35(12):1727–1748.
Herbst, Jeffrey. 2000. *States and Power in Africa: Comparative Lessons in
    Authority and Control.* Princeton University Press.
Héritier, Adrienne, and Dirk Lehmkuhl. 2008. "The Shadow of Hierarchy and
    New Modes of Governance." *Journal of Public Policy* 28.
Hilling, David. 1969. "The Evolution of the Major Ports of West Africa." *The
    Geographical Journal* 135(3):365–378.
Hilson, Gavin. 2002. "An Overview of Land Use Conflicts in Mining Communi-
    ties." *Land Use Policy* 19(1):65–73.

Hönke, Jana. 2009. *Transnational Pockets of Territoriality: Governing the Security of Extraction in Katanga (DRC).* Leipziger Univ.-Verlag.

Human Rights Watch. 2013. "What Is a House without Food? Mozambique's Coal Mining Boom and Resettlements." www.hrw.org/report/2013/05/23/what-house-without-food/mozambiques-coal-mining-boom-and-resettlements

Humphreys, Macartan. 2005. "Natural Resources, Conflict, and Conflict Resolution Uncovering the Mechanisms." *Journal of Conflict Resolution* 49(4):508–537.

Intellica. 2014. Fifth EITI-M Report 2012. Technical report.

International Finance Corporation, World Bank Group. 2002. Handbook for Preparing a Resettlement Action Plan. Technical report.

International Finance Corporation, World Bank Group. 2012. Performance Standards on Environmental and Social Sustainability. Technical report.

Interview, Anonymous Private. 2012*a*. Rio Tinto Employee. Tete, Mozambique. Private interview.

Interview, Mambwe Private. 2012*b*. Chisunka Mambwe. Development Planning Officer, Chalilabombwe. Chalilabombwe, Zambia. Private interview.

Johnson, Omotunde E. G. 1972. "Economic Analysis, the Legal Framework and Land Tenure Systems." *The Journal of Law & Economics* 15(1): 259–276.

Joireman, S. F. 2008. "The Mystery of Capital Formation in Sub-Saharan Africa: Women, Property Rights and Customary Law." *World Development* 36(7):1233–1246.

Jones Luong, Pauline. 2014. *The Politics of Non-State Social Welfare in the Global South.* Cornell University Press.

Jones Luong, Pauline, and Erika Weinthal. 2010. *Oil Is Not a Curse: Ownership Structure and Institutions in Soviet Successor States.* Cambridge University Press.

Kabemba, Claude, and Camilo Nhancale. 2012. "Coal versus Communities in Mozambique: Exposing Poor Practices by Vale and Rio Tinto." *Southern Africa Resources Watch.*

Kapelus, Paul. 2002. "Mining, Corporate Social Responsibility and the Community: The Case of Rio Tinto, Richards Bay Minerals and the Mbonambi." *Journal of Business Ethics* 39:275–296.

Kasara, Kimuli. 2007. "Tax Me If You Can: Ethnic Geography, Democracy, and the Taxation of Agriculture in Africa." *The American Political Science Review* 101(1):159–172.

Khanna, Madhu. 2001. "Non-Mandatory Approaches to Environmental Protection." *Journal of Economic Surveys* 15(3):291–324.

Khanna, Madhu, and William Rose Q. Anton. 2002. "Corporate Environmental Management: Regulatory and Market-Based Incentives." *Land Economics* 78(4):539–558.

Koubi, Vally, Gabriele Spilker, Tobias Böhmelt, and Thomas Bernauer. 2014. "Do Natural Resources Matter for Interstate and Intrastate Armed Conflict?" *Journal of Peace Research* 51(2):227–243.

KPMJ. 2013. Zambia Country Mining Guide. Technical report.

Larmer, Miles. 2006. "The Hour Has Come at the Pit?: The Mineworkers' Union of Zambia and the Movement for Multi-Party Democracy, 1982–1991." *Journal of Southern African Studies* 32(2):293–312.

Le Billon, Philippe. 2001*a*. "Angola's Political Economy of War: The Role of Oil and Diamonds, 1975–2000." *African Affairs* 100(398):55–80.

Le Billon, Philippe. 2001*b*. "The Political Ecology of War: Natural Resources and Armed Conflicts." *Political Geography* 20(5):561–584.

Leipziger, Deborah. 2015. *The Corporate Responsibility Code Book.* Greenleaf Publishing.

Levi, Margaret. 1989. *Of Rule and Revenue.* Vol. 13. University of California Press.

Lichbach, Mark I. 1994. "Rethinking Rationality and Rebellion: Theories of Collective Action and Problems of Collective Dissent." *Rationality and Society* 6(1):8–39.

Lohmann, Susanne. 1994. "The Dynamics of Informational Cascades: The Monday Demonstrations in Leipzig, East Germany, 1989–91." *World Politics* 47:42–101.

Ltd., Hart Nurse, and Baker Tilly Meralis. 2012. EITI Reconciliation Report Zambia 2010. Technical report.

Lujala, Paivi. 2009. "Deadly Combat over Natural Resources: Gems, Petroleum, Drugs, and the Severity of Armed Civil Conflict." *Journal of Conflict Resolution* 53(1):50–71.

Lungu, John, and Chomba Mulenga. 2005. *Corporate Social Responsibility Practices in the Extractive Industry in Zambia.* Vol. 2005. Mission Press.

Mamdani, Mahmood. 1996. *Citizen and Subject: Contemporary Africa and the Legacy of Late Colonialism.* Princeton University Press.

Mann, Michael. 1984. "The Autonomous Power of the State: Its Origins, Mechanisms and Results." *European Journal of Sociology* 25(02):185–213.

Mansour, Mario and others. 2014. "A Tax Revenue Dataset for Sub-Saharan Africa: 1980-2010." Foundation pour les etudes et recherches sur le developpement international (FERDI).

Marshall, Monty, Tedd Roberg Gurr, and Keith Jaggers. 2014. "Polity IV Project." www.systemicpeace.org/inscrdata.html.

Marwell, Gerald, and Pamela Oliver. 1993. *The Critical Mass in Collective Action.* Cambridge University Press.

Mayntz, Renate, and Fritz W. Scharpf. 1995. "Der Ansatz des akteurzentrierten Institutionalismus." *Gesellschaftliche Selbstregelung und politische Steuerung* 23:39–72.

Maystadt, Jean-François, Giacomo De Luca, Petros G. Sekeris, and John Ulimwengu. 2014. "Mineral Resources and Conflicts in DRC: A Case of Ecological Fallacy?" *Oxford Economic Papers* 66(3):721–749.

Mcloughlin, Claire. 2011. "Factors Affecting State-Non-Governmental Organization Relations in Service Provision: Key Themes from the Literature." *Public Administration and Development* 31(4):240–251.

McWilliams, Abagail, and Donald Siegel. 2000. "Corporate Social Responsibility and Financial Performance: Correlation or Misspecification?" *Strategic Management Journal* 21(5):603–609.

Menaldo, Victor. 2016. *The Institutions Curse.* Cambridge University Press.

Metorex Limited. 2009. Metorex Limited Annual Report. Technical report.

Metorex Limited. 2010. Metorex Limited Annual Report. Technical report.

Min, Brian. 2009. Distributing Power: Public Service Provision to the Poor in India. In *American Political Science Association Conference, Toronto.*

MinAxis Pty Ltd. 2010. A Confidential and Independent Report on the Mozambique Coal Industry. Technical report.

Ministry of Finance. Government of Mozambique. 2011. Mozambique Budget 2011. Technical report.

Mobbs, Philip M. 2012. The Mineral Industry of Zambia. Technical report.

Mohan, Giles and Kristian Stokke. 2000. "Participatory Development and Empowerment: the Dangers of Localism." *Third World Quarterly* 21(2):247–268.

Morgan, George A. and Staff. 2000. "The Mineral Industry of Africa 1990."

Morrison, Kevin M. 2009. "Oil, Nontax Revenue, and the Redistributional Foundations of Regime Stability." *International Organization* pp. 107–138.

Mosca, João, and Tomás Selemane. 2011. "El Dorado Tete: Os mega projects de mineracao." Centro de Integridade Pública.

Moser, Christine. 2008. "Poverty Reduction, Patronage, or Vote Buying? The Allocation of Public Goods and the 2001 Election in Madagascar." *Economic Development and Cultural Change* 57(1):137–162.

Mozambique: 14 People Arrested in Moatize Protests. 2012. http://allafrica .com/stories/201201130340.html. Accessed: Nov. 2013.

Mozambique: Tete Govt Changes Resettlement Strategy. 2012. http://allafrica .com/stories/201202030484.html. Accessed: 14 Nov. 2013.

Mozambique: Vale Renovates 576 Houses in Cateme. 2013. http://allafrica .com/stories/201306181236.html. Accessed: 14 Nov. 2013.

Muller, Edward N. 1985. "Income Inequality, Regime Repressiveness, and Political Violence." *American Sociological Review* 50(1):47–61.

Mushota Private Interview. 2012. Webby Mushota. Safety Officer, Mining Union of Zambia. Kitwe, Zambia. Private Interview.

Mwale Private Interview. 2012. Margaret Mwale, Community Development Officer, Chibuluma Mines. Kalulushi, Zambia. Private interview.

Ndola Lime Continues Operating. 2011. http://allafrica.com/stories/201106140 637.html. Accessed: Nov. 2013.

Negi, Rohit. 2011. "The Micropolitics of Mining and Development in Zambia: Insights from the Northwestern Province." *African Studies Quarterly* 12(2):27–44.

Nelson, Nici, Susan Wright et al. 1995. *Power and Participatory Development: Theory and Practice.* ITDG Publishing.

Ngoy-Kangoy, Hubert Kabungulu. 2008. "The Political Role of the Ethnic Factor around Elections in the Democratic Republic of the Congo." *African Journal on Conflict Resolution* 7(2):219–238.

Njovu, Alex. 2012. "MUZ Happy with Mining Companies? Work." Accessed: Nov. 2013.

O'Donnell, Guillermo. 1993. "On the State, Democratization and Some Conceptual Problems: A Latin American View with Glances at Some Postcommunist Countries." *World Development* 21(8):1355–1369.

OECD. 2002. An Empirical Analysis of Environmental Impact of Foeign Direct Investment in the Mining Sector in Sub Saharan Africa.

Oil Gas and Mining Policy Division Africa Region. 2013. PAD on a Proposed Grant in the Amount of SDR 33.1 million (US$50 million Equivalent) to the Democratic Republic of Congo for a Growth with Governance in the Mineral Sector Tachnical Assistance Project. Technical report. World Bank.

Okwi, Paul O., Godfrey Ndeng'e, Patti Kristjanson, Mike Arunga, An Notenbaert, Abisalom Omolo, Norbert Henninger, Todd Benson, Patrick Kariuki, and John Owuor. 2007. "Spatial Determinants of Poverty in Rural Kenya." *Proceedings of the National Academy of Sciences* 104(43):16769–16774.

Olson, Mancur. 1993. "Dictatorship, Democracy, and Development." *American Political Science Review* 87(3):567–576.

Olson, Mancur. 2009. *The Logic of Collective Action*. Harvard University Press.

Orlitzky, Marc, Frank L. Schmidt, and Sara L. Rynes. 2003. "Corporate Social and Financial Performance: A Meta-analysis." *Organization Studies* 24(3):403–441.

Ostrom, Elinor. 2014. "Collective Action and the Evolution of Social Norms." *Journal of Natural Resources Policy Research* 6(4):235–252.

Peru Anti-Mining Protest Sees Deadly Clashes. 2015-9-29. *BBC News.* www.bbc.com/news/world-latin-america-34389803

Pierskalla, Jan Henryk. 2010. "Protest, Deterrence, and Escalation: The Strategic Calculus of Government Repression." *Journal of Conflict Resolution* 54(1):117–145.

Pitcher, M. Anne. 1996. "Recreating Colonialism or Reconstructing the State? Privatisation and Politics in Mozambique." *Journal of Southern African Studies* 22(1):49–74.

Program, SSATP Africa Transport Policy. 2006. RMI Matrix: Policy Refform Status by Country. Technical report.

Raleigh, Clionadh, Andrew Linke, Håvard Hegre, and Joakim Karlsen. 2010. "Introducing ACLED: An Armed Conflict Location and Event Dataset." *Journal of Peace Research* 47(5):651–660.

Rasler, Karen. 1996. "Concessions, Repression, and Political Protest in the Iranian Revolution." *American Sociological Review* pp. 132–152.

Reed, Kristin. 2009. *Crude Existence: Environment and the Politics of Oil in Northern Angola*. Vol. 12 University of California Press.

Regan, Patrick M., and Errol A Henderson. 2002. "Democracy, Threats and Political Repression in Developing Countries: Are Democracies Internally Less Violent?" *Third World Quarterly* 23(1):119–136.

Reno, William. 1997. "African Weak States and Commercial Alliances." 96(383):165–186. http://afraf.oxfordjournals.org/content/96/383/165.short

Resenfeld, David. 2012. "The Coal Mining Sector in Mozambique: A Simple Mode of Predicting Government Revenue." Conference Paper. Vol. 19. 2012.

Ribot, Jesse C. 2002*a*. *Democratic Decentralization of Natural Resources: Institutionalizing Popular Participation.* World Resources Institute. OCLC: ocm51212248.

Ribot, Jesse C. 2002*b*. "Local Actors, Powers and Accountability in African Decentralizations: A Review of Issues." *International Development Research Centre of Canada Assessment of Social Policy Reforms Initiative* 25 (2001): 104.

Rio Tinto Threatens to Exit Madagascar after CEO Is Trapped by Protesters. 2013-01-11. *The Telegraph.*

Robinson, James, Ragnar Torvik and Tierry Verdier. 2006. "Political Foundations of the Resource Curse." *Journal of Development Economics* 79:447–468.

Rodriquez, Lucia. 2012. Worldvision Consultant. Tete, Mozambique. Private Interview.

Ross, Michael. 2001*a*. *Timber Booms and Institutional Breakdown in Southeast Asia.* Cambridge University Press.

Ross, Michael. 2006. "A Closer Look at Oil, Diamonds, and Civil War." *Annu. Rev. Polit. Sci.* 9:265–300.

Ross, Michael L. 2001*b*. "Does Oil Hinder Democracy?" *World Politics* 53(03):325–361.

Ross, Michael L. 2004*a*. "What Do We Know About Natural Resources and Civil War?" *Journal of Peace Research* 41(3):337–356.

Ross, Michael L. 2004*b*. "How Do Natural Resources Influence Civil War? Evidence from Thirteen Cases." *International Organization* 58.1 (2004): 35–67.

Salehyan, Idean and Christopher Linebarger. 2015. "Elections and Social Conflict in Africa, 1990–2009." *Studies in Comparative International Development* 50(1):23–49.

Salemene, Thomas. 2013. "Mozambique Political Process Bulletin." Centro de Integridade Publica

Sarkar, Sunrita, Alastair Gow-Smith, Tunde Morakinyo, Roberto Frau, and Matthew Kuniholm. 2010. Mining Community Development Agreements – Practical Experiences and Field Studies. Technical report Environmental Resources Management.

Scharpf, Fritz W. 1997. "Economic Integration, Democracy and the Welfare State." *Journal of European Public Policy* 4(1):18–36.

Schodde, Richard. n.d. "Global Discovery Trends 1950–2009: What Where and Who Found Them." www.minexconsulting.com/publications/Global Discovery Trends 1950-2009 PDAC March 2010.pdf

Scott, Colin. 2004. *Regulation in the Age of Governance: the Rise of the Post Regulatory State.* Edward Elgar Publishing.

Scott, James. 1987. *Weapons of the Weak: Everyday Forms of Peasant Resistance.* Yale University Press.

Scott, James C. 2009. *The Art of Not Being Governed: An Anarchist History of Upland Southeast Asia.* Yale University Press.

Shah, Meera Kaul. 1998. *The Myth of Community: Gender Issues in Participatory Development.* ITGD Publishing.

Sikamo Private Interview. 2012. Jackson Sikamo, Environmental and Metallur-gical Plant Manager, Chibuluma Mines. Kalulushi, Zambia. Private interview.

Smith, Benjamin. 2004. "Oil Wealth and Regime Survival in the Devel-oping World, 1960–1999." *American Journal of Political Science* 48(2): 232–246.

Smith, Benjamin. 2017. "Resource Wealth as Rent Leverage: Rethinking the Oil-Stability Nexus." *Conflict Management and Peace Science.* 34.6:597–617.

SNL Financial (formerly IntierraRMG). 2014. "Raw Materials Database."

Snyder, Richard. 2006. "Does Lootable Wealth Breed Disorder? A Political Economy of Extraction Framework." *Comparative Political Studies* 39(8): 943–968.

Snyder, Richard, and Ravi Bhavnani. 2005. "Diamonds, Blood, and Taxes A Revenue-Centered Framework for Explaining Political Order." *Journal of Conflict Resolution* 49(4):563–597.

Soifer, Hillel. 2012. "Measuring State Capacity in Contemporary Latin America." *Revista de Ciencia Política* 32(3):585–598. www.scielo.cl/pdf/revcipol/v32n3/art04.pdf

Soysa, Indra De, and Eric Neumayer. 2007. "Resource Wealth and the Risk of Civil War Onset: Results from a New Dataset of Natural Resource Rents, 1970–1999." *Conflict Management and Peace Science* 24:201–218.

SRK Consulting. 2010. A Competent Person's Report and Valuation Report on the Mineral Assets of Metorex (PTY) LTD in the Democratic Repub-lic of Congo and the Republic of Zambia. Prepared for Jinchuan Group International Resources Co. Ltd. Technical report.

Steinberg, Jessica. 2018. "Protecting the Capital? On African Geographies of Protest Escalation and Repression." *Political Geography* 62:12–22. www.sciencedirect.com/science/article/pii/S0962629817300057

Sullivan, Christopher M. 2015. "Undermining Resistance: Mobilization, Repres-sion, and the Enforcement of Political Order." doi:10.1177/0022002714567951.

Svendlund Private Interview. 2012. Nick Svendlund, Managing Director, Mesa Group Zambia. Lusaka, Zambia. Private Interview.

Thauer, Christian R. 2014. *The Managerial Sources of Corporate Social Responsibility: The Spread of Global Standards.* Cambridge University Press.

Tilly, Charles, and Sidney Tarrow. 2006. *Contentious Politics.* Oxford University Press.

Tinto, Rio. 2012. Rio Tinto 2012 Annual Report.

Transnational Corporations, Extractive Industries and Development. 2007.

Umpala Private Interview. 2012. Emmanual Umpala, Action Against Impunity for Human Rights (ACIDH). Lubumbashi, DRC. Private Interview.

UNCTAD, ed. 2015. *Reforming international investment governance.* Number 2015 *in* "World investment report" New York: United Nations.

Unctad Secretariat. 1993. "Transnational Corporations and Integrated Inter-national Production." *Foreign Trade Review* 28(1):91–112. http://journals.sagepub.com/doi/10.1177/0015732515930106

United Nations Environment Programme. Accessed: Dec. 2013. Global Resource Information Database. Technical report.

van de Walle, Nicolas. 2001. *African Economies and the Politics of Permanent Crisis, 1979–1999.* Cambridge University Press.

Vale. 2009. Sustainability Report. Technical report.

Vale. 2011. Sustainability Report. Technical report.

Vale. 2012. Delivering value through capital efficiency: Annual Report 2012.

Vale: Another quality addition to mining in Zambia. 2012. Accessed: Nov. 2013.

Valentino, Benjamin A. 2013. *Final Solutions: Mass Killing and Genocide in the 20th Century.* Cornell University Press.

Vernon, Raymond. 1971. "Sovereignty at Bay: The Multinational Spread of US Enterprises." *Thunderbird International Business Review* 13(4):1–3.

Waldman, David A., Donald S. Siegel, and Mansour Javidan. 2006. "Components of CEO Transformational Leadership and Corporate Social Responsibility." *Journal of Management Studies* 43(8):1703–1725.

Wantchekon, L., and P. Stanig. 2015. "The Curse of Good Soil? Land Fertility, Roads, and Rural Poverty in Africa." Unpublished manuscript.

Watts, Michael. 2004. "Resource Curse? Governmentality, Oil and Power in the Niger Delta, Nigeria." *Geopolitics* 9:50–80.

Weeks, Jessica L. 2008. "Autocratic Audience Costs: Regime Type and Signaling Resolve." 62(1):35–64. www.jstor.org.proxyiub.uits.iu.edu/stable/40071874

Weidmann, Nils B., and Michael D. Ward. 2010. "Predicting Conflict in Space and Time." *Journal of Conflict Resolution* 54(6):883–901.

Weinstein, Jeremy M. 2005. "Resources and the Information Problem in Rebel Recruitment." *Journal of Conflict Resolution* 49(4):598–624.

Weiss, Herbert F. 2007. "Voting for Change in the DRC." *Journal of Democracy* 18(2):138–151.

Williamson, Oliver. 1985. *The Economic Institutions of Capitalism: Firms, Markets, Relational Contracting.* Free Press.

Wolf, Klaus Dieter, Nicole Deitelhoff, and Stefan Engert. 2007. "Corporate Security Responsibility." *Cooperation and Conflict* 42(3):294–320.

World Bank. 2007. Democratic Republic of the Congo Poverty and Social Impact Analysis Mine Sector Reform. Technical report.

World Bank. 2009. *Africa's Infrastructure: A Time for Transformation.* The World Bank.

World Bank Group. 2009. Environmental Impact Assessment (EIA) and Safeguard Policies. Technical report.

World Bank International Development Agency. 2013. PAD for Mining and Gas Technical Assistance Project. Technical report. World Bank.

World Development Indicators | Data. n.d. Technical report. World Bank. http://data.worldbank.org/data-catalog/world-development-indicators

Yager, Thomas R., Omayra Bermudez-Lugo, Philip M. Mobbs, Harold R. Newman, Mowafa Taib, Glenn J. Wallace and David R. Wilburn. 2012. The Minerals Industries of Africa 2010. Technical report. https://minerals.usgs.gov/minerals/pubs/country/2010/myb3-sum-2010-africa.pdf

Yager, Thomas R., Omayra Bermudez-Lugo, Philip M. Mobbs, Harold R. Newman, Mowafa Taib, Glenn J. Wallace, and David R. Wilburn. 2013. The Mineral Industries of Africa 2013. Technical report USGS.

Yepes, Tito, Justin Pierce, and Vivian Foster. 2009. Making Sense of Africa's Infrastructure Endowment: A Benchmarking Approach. Policy Research Working Paper 4912 World Bank.

Zambia Chamber of Mines. n.d. http://mines.org.zm/. Accessed: Nov. 2013.

ZEMA Orders Mopani Mine to Shut Down Part of Its Operation after Complaints from Butondo Community. 2006. www.lusakatimes.com/2012/03/06/zema-orders-mopani-shut-part-operation-complaints-butondo-community. Accessed: Nov. 2013.

Zhuwakinyu, Martin. 2001. "First new copperbelt mine in 30 years." www.miningweekly.com/article/first-new-copperbelt-mine-in-30-years-2001-06-15. Accessed: Nov. 2013.

Index

actors, *see also* government; local populations; extractive firms, 4, 11, 12, 17, 18, 21, 22, 27, 35, 37, 62, 69, 176
actors' beliefs, *see* beliefs
Africa, *see also* DRC; Mozambique; Zambia
  natural resources, 1, 4–6, 89, 103–119
  political/economic development, 3, 25, 37, 44–48, 131, 162
Agence National de Renseignement (ANR), 87, 108
agriculture, *see also* livelihoods; soil productivity, 3, 42, 71, 95, 99, 105, 138
Angola, 18, 156
ANR (Agence National de Renseignement), 87, 108
Armed Forces of the Democratic Republic of the Congo (FARDC), 108
artisanal mining, 26, 49, 105, 117, 119, 131, 135

Bagamoyo, 94
beliefs, actors', *see also* governance outcomes; social conflict, 113–115, 117, 123, 125
  governance outcomes, 21, 31, 51, 60, 70, 112, 125, 179, 183
  governance outcomes and, 76–78

Benga, *see also* Rio Tinto, 90, 92, 94, 95, 98, 183
built housing, 1, 90–91, 94, 96, 110

CAMI (Le Cadastre Minier), 107
Capanga, 92, 94
Cateme, 90–92, 94, 96, 101
CDA (Community Development Agreements), 187–188
CHEMAF, 116, 124
Chibuluma Mine, *see also* Metorex, 104, 109, 112–120, 124
Chililabombwe, 110
Chipanga, 94
coal mines, *see* coal mining concessions
coal mining concessions, *see also* Mozambique, Rio Tinto, Vale
  governance outcomes, 90–98, 101, 123
  social conflict, 90–93
coal production, 1, 6, 89
cobalt mining, 4, 103, 104, 116, 118
Cold War, 25, 162
collective action, *see also* local populations; social conflict
  cost of, 58, 61, 71–73, 97, 133
  social conflict, 50, 101, 121
Community Development Agreements, *see* CDA
community liaisons, 40, 52, 62, 94, 110, 187

277